Through
Western
Eyes

Eastern Orthodoxy: A Reformed Perspective

Robert Letham

Through Western Eyes

Eastern Orthodoxy: A Reformed Perspective

Robert Letham

MENTOR

Dr. Robert Letham is Lecturer in Systematic and Historical Theology at Wales Evangelical School of Theology. He has been in pastoral ministry for 25 years - and at Emmanuel Orthodox Presbyterian Church, Wilmington, Delaware since 1989. He has taught at London Bible College and is Adjunct Professor of Systematic Theology at Westminster Theological Seminary, Philadelphia and visiting Professor of Theology at Reformed Theological Seminary, Washington/Baltimore.

ISBN 1-84550-247-7
ISBN 978-1-84550-247-8

© Robert Letham

10 9 8 7 6 5 4 3 2 1

Published in 2007
in the
Mentor Imprint
by
Christian Focus Publications, Ltd.,
Geanies House, Fearn, Ross-shire,
IV20 1TW, Great Britain.

www.christianfocus.com

Cover design by Danie Van Straaten

Printed and bound by
CPD, Wales

Contents

Abbreviations

ANF	*The Ante-Nicene Fathers*, ed . A. Roberts and J. Donaldson, rev. A.C. Coxe (reprint, Grand Rapids: Eerdmans, 1969-73)
BDEC	Parry, K. et.al. *The Blackwell Dictionary of Eastern Christianity*, (Oxford: Blackwell, 2001)
BQ	*Baptist Quarterly*
CD	Karl Barth, *Church Dogmatics*, ed. G.W. Bromiley and T.F. Torrance (Edinburgh: T.&T. Clark, 1956-77)
CO	John Calvin, *Opera quae supersunt omnia*, ed. Guilielmus Baum, Eduardus Cunitz, and Eduardus Reiss, 59 vols. Corpus Reformatorum, vols. 29-87 (Brunswick, 1863-1900)
JTS	*Journal of Theological Studies*
LN	Johannes P. Louw and Eugene A. Nida, *A Greek-English Lexicon of the New Testament based on Semantic Domains* (New York: United Bible Societies, 1988)
LS	Henry George Liddell and Robert Scott, *A Greek English Lexicon*, rev. Henry Stuart Jones, 9th edition (Oxford: Clarendon Press, 1940)
LXX	Septuagint
NPNF[1]	*A Select Library of the Nicene and Post-Nicene Fathers of the Christian Church* [First Series] ed. P. Schaff (reprint, Grand Rapids: Eerdmans, 1978-79)
NPNF[2]	*A Select Library of the Nicene and Post-Nicene Fathers of the Christian Church* [Second Series] ed. P. Schaff and H. Wace (reprint, Grand Rapids: Eerdmans, 1979)
OCP	*Orientalia Christiana Periodica*
OS	*Joannis Calvini Opera Selecta*, ed. P. Barth and W. Niesel, 5 vols. (Munich: Chr. Kaiser, 1926-52)
PG	J.P. Migne, et. al. ed., *Patrologia Graeca* (Paris, 1857-66)
PL	J.P. Migne, et. al. ed., *Patrologia Latina* (Paris, 1878-90)
RechScRel	*Recherches de Science Religieuse*
SBET	*Scottish Bulletin of Evangelical Theology*
Service Book	*Service Book of the Holy Orthodox-Catholic Apostolic Church*, comp. and trans. Isabel Florence Hapgood, 3rd ed. (Brooklyn, New York: Syrian Antiochene Orthodox Archdiocese of New York and All North America, 1956)
SJT	*Scottish Journal of Theology*
StPatr	*Studia Patristica*
StVladThQ	*St Vladimir's Theological Quarterly*
ST	Thomas Aquinas, *Summa Theologica*
TB	*Tyndale Bulletin*
VE	*Vox Evangelica*

Citations from the English Bible, unless otherwise indicated, are from *The Holy Bible: English Standard Version* (Wheaton, Illinois: Crossway Bibles, 2001).

A Chronology of Persons and Events

AD

30	Death and resurrection of Jesus, Pentecost
c36	Conversion of Paul
44	James beheaded
49	Council of Jerusalem (Acts 15)
52	Thomas takes the gospel to India
64	Persecution at Rome spearheaded by Emperor Nero
64-67	Martyrdom of Peter and Paul
70	Destruction of Jerusalem
95-100	Death of the apostle John
130-140	Birth of Irenaeus
c150	Birth of Clement of Alexandria
c170	Muratorian canon listing New Testament books
185	Birth of Origen
c200	Death of Irenaeus, birth of Cyprian
215	Death of Clement of Alexandria
240	Mani founds Manichaeism
c242	Death of Ammonius Saccas
249-251	Persecution under Emperor Decius
254	Origen dies in prison
258	Death of Cyprian
270	Death of Plotinus
295	Birth of Athanasius
303-305	Persecution under Emperor Diocletian
312	Conversion of Constantine, and his accession as Roman Emperor
313	Edict of Milan, legalizing Christianity
318	Outbreak of the Arian controversy in Alexandria

324	Constantine establishes a new capital, calling it Constantinople
325	Nicaea I, called by Constantine, condemns Arius
328	Athanasius becomes Bishop of Alexandria
336	Death of Arius
355–360	Athanasius writes his *Letters to Serapion on the Holy Spirit*
362	Council of Alexandria prepares the way for the resolution of the trinitarian crisis
370	Basil writes *On the Holy Spirit*
370–389	The writings of the Cappadocians (Basil, Gregory of Nyssa, Gregory of Nazianzus) resolve the trinitarian controversy
373	Death of Athanasius
379	Death of Basil
381	Constantinople I, called by Emperor Theodosius I, condemns Eunomius pronounces on the Trinity
382	Emperor Theodosius I makes Christianity the official religion
386	Chrysostom (349–407) writes *On the Priesthood*
387	Augustine (354–430) baptized by Ambrose in Milan
391	Deaths of Apollinaris and Gregory of Nazianzus
394	Death of Gregory of Nyssa
396	Chrysostom becomes Bishop of Constantinople
407	Chrysostom dies in exile
415–420	Augustine publishes *On the Trinity*
418	Council of Carthage condemns Pelagius
428	Outbreak of the Nestorian controversy; Cyril (378–444) attacks Nestorius
430	Death of Augustine
431	Council of Ephesus condemns Nestorius
444	Cyril of Alexandria dies
449	The 'Robber Council' of Ephesus backs Eutyches
451	Council of Chalcedon, called by Emperor Marcian, condemns Eutyches
476	End of the Roman Empire; thereafter the Empire is based at Constantinople
484–518	Temporary schism between Constantinople and Rome
c500–550	Dionysius the Areopagite, whose mystical theology is seminal
527–565	Justinian I is Emperor
532–536	Leontius of Jerusalem contributes to the Christological debate
551	Edict of Justinian
553	Constantinople II, called by Justinian I, condemns Origenists and monophysitism, refines Chalcedon
580–662	Maximus the Confessor, who opposes the monothelites
597	Augustine of Canterbury sets foot in England, sent by Pope Gregory the Great
610–641	Emperor Heraclius I
634	Synod of Jerusalem proclaims that Christ has two wills
635–845	Nestorian mission to China at its height
636	Ecthesis, issued by Bishop Sergius of Constantinople, adopts monoenergism

638–645	Muslim invasions
649	Dyothelite Council called by Pope Martin I at the Lateran Palace
650–662	Monothelite reaction; deaths of Martin I and Maximus the Confessor
680–1	Constantinople III, called by Emperor Constantine IV, condemns monotheletism
692	Quinisext Council
673–735	The Venerable Bede, notable for Biblical commentaries and a history of England
c675–749	John of Damascus; in mid-eighth century writes against iconoclasts
726	Outbreak of the iconoclast controversy: John of Damascus defends icons
740	Emperor Constantine IV defends iconoclasm
750	Abbasid dynasty (until 945): center of Islam switches from Damascus to near Baghdad
754	John of Damascus condemned by the iconoclast Council of Hiereia
780	Empress Irene suspends persecution of iconodules
787	Nicaea II, called by Empress Irene, condemns iconoclasm
795	Crisis over Emperor Constantine VI's divorce and remarriage
800	Charlemagne crowned Roman Emperor in Rome by Pope Leo III
815	New attack on icons instigated by Emperor Leo V the Armenian
826	Death of Theodore of Studion (b759)
843	The Triumph of Orthodoxy, as Empress Theodosia ends persecution of iconodules
858–67,	Photius is Patriarch of Constantinople; writes 880–86 against the *filioque* clause
c988	Conversion of Russia to Orthodoxy
1050–84	German reforms of the Papacy
1054	Mutual anathemas between the Bishops of Rome and Constantinople
1093–1109	Anselm Archbishop of Canterbury
1204	The Crusaders ransack Constantinople and stay until 1261
1222–3	Tatar (Mongol) invasion of Russia; the church is granted freedom and exemption from taxation
1225–74	Thomas Aquinas
1274	Council of Lyons; agreement on the *filioque* accepted in the West, rejected in the East
1296	Birth of Gregory Palamas (1296-1359)
1322	Birth of Nicholas Cabasilas (d ?)
1439	Council of Florence; the East, desperate for Western military support, rejects its declarations
1453	Fall of Constantinople and the end of the Byzantine Empire
1517	Martin Luther nails his 95 Theses to the door of the Castle Church in Wittemberg
1536	John Calvin (1509-64) publishes the first edition of his *Institute of the Christian Religion*

1623-38	Cyril Lucar Bishop of Constantinople
1643	The Westminster Assembly is convened by Parliament
1721	Peter the Great regulates the Russian Church, making it a department of state
1792	Birth of Makary Glucharev (1792-1849)
1797	Birth of Innokenty Venyaminov (1797-1879), missionary to the Far East and Alaska
1850-1917	Revival of Russian religious, theological and philosophical thought; together with rapid missionary expansion to the east
1917	Bolshevik revolution, ensuing persecution and emigration of church leaders and theologians to the West
1965	Anathemas of 1054 withdrawn

Preface

The doorbell rings. Outside there stands a complete stranger. It is obvious he is from Australia – the hat, with pieces of cork dangling on string to ward off the flies, is a giveaway, and so too is the tanned complexion. First impressions are confirmed by the nasal drawl. Apparently, he is a distant cousin. How can this be? He seems so different and alien from one's comfortable surroundings in the English Home Counties. He is a stranger. But you let him in, you sit and talk, and gradually – bit by bit – there are fleeting points of recognition; facial expressions, the shape of the nose, the physical build. After a while it seems credible that there is, after all, a real flesh and blood connection there – despite the differences.

This experience is not too dissimilar to impressions of Eastern Christianity common among Western Protestants. The culture of the Eastern Church is alien to their experience. I remember many years ago listening on the BBC to a broadcast service from a Russian Orthodox cathedral. The liturgy – with the magnificent music – was impressive but strange, and after some time we switched off. A while later we returned to the

broadcast and, as far as I could determine, it seemed no different
to when we had heard it earlier. Yet the more we familiarize
ourselves with the Eastern Church the more we recognize, for
all the differences, the family resemblances. The family has been
parted for a very long time. But chances have arisen to meet
again and get to know one another.

In recent years, Eastern Orthodoxy has emerged vividly on
the radar of Western Christians. Hitherto, it was largely ignored.
Theologians of the stature of B.B. Warfield (1851–1921) hardly
refer to the Eastern Church or its theologians, and show little
direct knowledge of it. This has been due to the long-term
historical disruption caused by differences in language, outlook
and theology and eventually by the depredations of Islam. East
and West went their separate ways. As a result, their respective
theologies appear at times to inhabit parallel universes.

According to Timothy Ware Kallistos '... western Christians,
whether Free Churchmen, Anglicans, or Roman Catholics,
have a common background in the past. All alike (although they
may not always care to admit it) have been profoundly influenced by the same events: by the Papal centralization and the
Scholasticism of the Middle Ages, by the Renaissance, by the
Reformation and Counter-Reformation. But behind members
of the Orthodox Church – Greeks, Russians, and the rest – there
lies a very different background. They have known no Middle
Ages (in the Western sense) and have undergone no Reformations
or Counter-Reformations; they have only been affected in
an oblique way by the cultural and religious upheaval which
transformed western Europe in the sixteenth and seventeenth
centuries. Christians in the west, both Roman and Reformed,
generally start by asking the same questions, although they may
disagree about the answers. In Orthodoxy, however, it is not
only the answers that are different – the questions themselves
are not the same as in the west.'[1] Ware goes on to observe that
'Protestantism was hatched from the egg that Rome had laid'.[2]

---

[1] T. Ware, *The Orthodox Church* (London: Penguin Books, 1969), 9.

However, this ignorance is changing. The Bolshevik Revolution in Russia drove leading Russian theologians into exile in the West, especially Paris. Latterly, many found their way to the United States. This enforced exposure to the Western intellectual scene brought significant interaction. Eastern Orthodoxy is increasingly popular in the Anglo-Saxon world. It conveys a sense of mystery, of continuity with the past, of dignified worship at a time when evangelical Protestantism is increasingly cheapened and trivialized.

This book examines the history and theology of Orthodoxy from a Reformed Protestant perspective. I will argue that there are clear and significant areas of agreement, a common allegiance to the triune God, to the person of Christ, to the authority of Scripture and the truth of the gospel. At the same time, there are many areas of disagreement, where it seems that Orthodoxy and Protestantism are at odds. However, there are also misunderstandings on both sides, where proponents of either position are not normally dealing accurately with what the other holds to be true. I hope that, in drawing attention to the agreements and misunderstandings, readers may come to a better understanding of exactly where the real differences lie. My aim has been to learn from Orthodoxy, on the assumption that the most important thing is to grow in our knowledge of Christ. I have sought to represent the Orthodox as accurately as I can. Where I may have failed, I beg indulgence and ask for kind correction.

As for terminology, Anastasios Kallis points out that *Orthodox Church* is the most common term in use today; *Orthodox Catholic Church* expresses the ecclesiastical reality in Orthodox eyes; the phrase *Eastern Orthodox Church* underlines the cultural and geographical aspects, since the bulk of Orthodoxy is located to the east of the Latin Church; the term *Eastern Church* goes back to the division of the Roman Empire in AD 395, and so has long historical use, but is rather outdated, since neither the Eastern nor the Western Church is an ecclesial unity; *Greek Orthodox*

---

[2] Ibid., 10.

Church stresses the common bond of all Orthodox churches, since the Greek cultural tradition influenced the development of the theological structure and spirituality of Orthodoxy more than any other; while the phrase *Catholic Church* which was preferred by the older Councils and the Church Fathers stresses its historical continuity, and is now paired with *Orthodox* to denote its division from Rome. In turn, we may add that *Oriental Orthodox Churches* refers to those churches that were unable to accept the Definition of Chalcedon and so were separated from the *Eastern Orthodox Church* – among these were the Nestorians and the Coptic Church.

I want to thank Malcolm MacLean and Willie MacKenzie of Christian Focus Publications for their interest in this project at respective stages in its production. The staff of the Montgomery Library, Westminster Theological Seminary, Philadelphia have, as usual, been very helpful. I have also been grateful for the facilities of the Library of Congress. I wish to thank Presbyterian & Reformed Publishing Company for permission to use some sections of chapters in my book *The Holy Trinity: In Scripture, History, Theology, and Worship* (2004), on the Arian controversy, the Council of Constantinople (AD 381), and the Filioque controversy. These occur in chapters one, nine, and ten here and are noted where appropriate. In particular, I am greatly indebted – beyond what I can say – to Dr. Gary Jenkins, Van Gorden Professor of History at Eastern University, Pennsylvania for his immense help, way beyond the call of duty, in reading the manuscript and making many invaluable suggestions and corrections. His own commitment to, and knowledge of, the Orthodox faith, and of the Presbyterianism with which he was previously connected, has provided much needed input. Any inaccuracies or other inadequacies in what I have written cannot under any circumstances be laid at his door; responsibility rests with me alone.

The reader should be warned in advance, in Kallis' words, that 'Orthodoxy as a living organism expressed in liturgy cannot be studied solely on the basis of accepted scholarly criteria and analyses, for in its essence it is a multifaceted life in which there is participation in an existential process that calls more for feeling and sensibility than for rationality. Examining special issues by means of objective academic criteria can give a knowledge of facts but not a knowledge of the essence itself, a knowledge best attained through the liturgical life of Orthodoxy.' And 'Many misunderstandings and prejudices concerning the Orthodox Church thus go back to a wrong approach as students try to form, merely with the help of sources and scholarship, a picture of Orthodoxy, which is not really doctrine but a way of life, with its own system-related criteria and thought forms.'[3] In this, I express my appreciation for the welcome and help received at the Syrian-Antiochene Church of Saint Athanasius, Claymont, Delaware and its priest, Father James Dougherty, and for the helpful comments of Father Mina of the Egyptian Coptic Church (one of the *Oriental Orthodox Churches*), Newark, Delaware.

My own interest in Orthodoxy goes back many years, stemming in particular from my reading of the Greek Fathers, especially Athanasius, Gregory of Nazianzus, and Cyril of Alexandria. In an earlier book on the trinity I refer positively to the contribution of John Calvin and John Owen; Owen himself had in his library volumes of Gregory Palamas, while Calvin referred frequently to Chrysostom and Gregory of Nazianzus (not always in context it is true). It is my hope that, like them, we may learn with discrimination from those from whom we may in some ways differ, 'until we all attain to the unity of the faith and of the knowledge of the Son of God' (Eph. 4:13).

Pentecost

June 2006

---

[3] Anastasios Kallis, 'Orthodox Church,' in *The Encyclopedia of Christianity* (Grand Rapids: Eerdmans, 2003), 3:866-8.

Part One:

The Church
of the
Ecumenical
Councils

1

From Jerusalem to Constantinople

The most appropriate place to begin a discussion of Eastern Orthodoxy is with worship and the liturgy, for this is the heart of the Eastern Church. The entrance to the world of the Orthodox is precisely here, for theology is integrally bound up with piety and worship in a way that is not so in the Western Church. However, since this book is written expressly for Reformed Christians, for whom doctrine and belief is of first importance, we begin with the major theological foundations of the Orthodox Church. This means starting with the seven ecumenical councils, for insofar as Orthodoxy has a doctrinal basis it is with their declarations. This will demonstrate right at the start what the Reformed and Orthodox Churches have in common. It will place their significant differences in the light of the even more important agreements.

From Pentecost to Constantine
The New Testament records the spread of the church in the first decades after Pentecost. The focus in Acts is on the ministry of Peter and Paul. The church began in Jerusalem, expanded

to Samaria, before eventually the Gentiles were brought into the fold. Churches were established in Syria, Asia Minor, Macedonia, Achaia and Rome. Paul states his plan to take the gospel to Spain in the far west and, according to early tradition, succeeded in this aim before his martyrdom in AD 65.

However, the New Testament is not exhaustive. There is a tradition that the apostle Thomas took the Christian faith to India by AD 52 and, since the apostles were all evangelists, it is reasonable to suppose they were each instrumental in reaching many areas not mentioned in the Bible. Even on the day of Pentecost, converts were made from all over the known world (Acts 2:5-12). We may assume that many of them returned home and established churches in their native lands; later, a leading official from Ethiopia is featured (Acts 8:26-40).

Nevertheless, the centre of gravity of early Christianity lay within the bounds of the Roman Empire. Politically the major force in the world of the day, its clear lines of communication aided the church's growth and co-ordination. Moreover, two common languages bound it together – Latin, used in politics and administration, and Greek, the language of everyday commerce, rather like English today. The church was soon shaped by the Latin- and Greek-speaking areas where its dominant strength lay – Latin in the west, Greek in the east. Elsewhere, in Palestine, Jewish Christianity withered in the second century with the Empire's brutal suppression of the Jews, following the war of AD 66-70 and the Bar Kochba revolt of AD 135. The remnant of Jewish Christianity left after these disturbances relapsed into the Ebionite heresy, in which Jesus was regarded as merely human. Other branches of the church existed and in some cases flourished, whether Syriac, Ethiopic, or Armenian. However, their distance from the hub of first- and second-century life rendered their influence on wider ecclesiastical and theological developments minimal.[1] So it transpired that the major ecclesiastical centres in

---

[1] S. Neill, *Christian Missions* (London: Penguin, 1964) 13–30; F.F. Bruce, *The Spreading Flame: The Rise and Progress of Christianity from Its First Beginnings Until the Conversion of the English* (London: Paternoster Press, 1958) 13–158; M. Green,

the first centuries were Jerusalem – for largely historical reasons – Antioch, Alexandria and Rome. Following his conversion in 312 and accession as Emperor, Constantine's issuance of the Edict of Milan in the following year legalized the church's status. Soon afterwards, in 324, he proclaimed a new capital city for the Empire, not surprisingly named after himself – Constantinople in the Greek east. It is with the Greek part of the church that we are concerned in this book, although not exclusively so for the Eastern Church includes far more than the Greeks today, and extended beyond the Greek world then, for the Syriac and Armenian Churches were as much part of the East as the Greeks. Notwithstanding, the Greeks or the Greek-speakers were the driving force in the early centuries. At the same time, we note well Ware's caution that the whole of Europe was part of Orthodoxy.[2] There was then no schism, no serious division. The church was one, its languages many.

Most notable in the East before 313 was the attempt by theologians at Alexandria to place Christian theology in the context of the surrounding Hellenistic culture. In particular, the philosophy of Neoplatonism developed at Alexandria by Ammonius Saccas (d. c242) and Plotinus (204/5–270) impacted Christian philosopher-theologians like Clement of Alexandria (c150–215) and Origen (185–254), who sought to relate the Christian faith to this dominant philosophy. Origen was most influential, a mixture of teacher of the Catholic faith and daring speculative thinker who bordered on, and sometimes crossed, the lines of what was acceptable Christian teaching.[3]

During this period, the Church was an illegal institution. At first it was protected by the imperial power (witness the

Evangelism in the Early Church (Grand Rapids: Eerdmans, 1970); R.M. Grant, *From Augustus to Constantine: The Rise and Triumph of Christianity in the Roman World* (San Francisco: Harper and Row, 1970).

[2] T. Ware, *The Orthodox Church* (London: Penguin Books, 1969),10–2.

[3] See H. Crouzel, *Origen* (A. Worrall; Edinburgh: T.&T. Clark, 1989); J. R. Lyman, *Christology and Cosmology: Models of Divine Activity in Origen, Eusebius, and Athanasius* (Oxford: Clarendon, 1993); P. Widdicombe, *The Fatherhood of God from Origen to Athanasius* (Oxford: Clarendon, 1994).

record in Acts) since it was perceived to be a Jewish sect, but the Jewish War of 66–70 put an end to that. Its international nature, undercutting the largely territorial character of religion in the Graeco-Roman world, made it peculiarly vulnerable to accusations that it was angering the various national deities by drawing away adherents. National religions were accepted by Rome and afforded civil protection, for the authorities believed it important that the various national deities be placated so as to ensure peace and stability throughout the Empire. Once Christianity was seen to be international, it was a threat. It faced sporadic, mainly localized, occasionally severe, outbreaks of persecution. On a number of occasions hostility was more wide-spread, instigated by particular Emperors. This was particularly the case from the third century, during the reigns of Decius (249–51), who required all Roman citizens to offer libations and sacrifices to the imperial deities, and Diocletian (284–305), who also tried to impose uniform religious cohesion in the Empire.

The age of the ecumenical councils

The conversion of Constantine and his protection of the church ushered in the era of the ecumenical councils. From this time on, the peace of the Church and the peace of the Empire were interlocked, especially in the minds of successive Emperors. This was even more so when, in 382, Emperor Theodosius I made Christianity the official religion of the Empire. It was, then, the establishment of Christianity as, first, a legal religion and then the official religion that made possible gatherings of bishops from throughout the Empire in general councils. Before Constantine, this was not possible; such episcopal councils were, of necessity, on a smaller scale. The ecumenical councils, so called since their decrees have found acceptance by the whole church both in the East and West,[4] were each called by Emperors

---

[4] The Roman Catholic Church calls some of its own councils 'ecumenical' insofar as bishops owning allegiance to the Bishop of Rome attended from throughout the world, they were under the jurisdiction of the Pope or his representatives, and their decrees received Papal endorsement. However, these councils can hardly be

to resolve divisions that threatened the Church's unity and so posed a problem for the harmony and well-being of the body politic. Such problems were not caused by merely casual differences. The issues at stake, in each case, reached right to the heart of the faith and affected the question of salvation. These councils were important since they adjudicated questions vital to the gospel. As Percival comments, it was not necessary that these councils be large, nor representative of the whole world, nor even that they be summoned with the *intention* of being ecumenical. What makes them ecumenical is that their decisions are universally accepted afterwards. The councils did not look upon themselves as introducing anything new but rather as reaffirming the faith once for all delivered to the saints.[5]

In another sense, these councils are significant since Orthodoxy is the church of the seven ecumenical councils. Insofar as the Orthodox Church has a doctrinal standard, these councils provide it. They placed Christian doctrine on its foundations – the trinity and the incarnation – excluding false ways of viewing the faith. They were not speculative – they simply placed 'a fence around the mystery'.[6]

Nicaea I 325

This, the first ecumenical council, was summoned by the Emperor Constantine as a result of the furore caused by the Alexandrian presbyter, Arius.[7] His claim, which had spread rapidly, was that the Son of God was created. Concerned to maintain God's

---

termed ecumenical if they exclude at least half the church and, besides, not all the universally accepted ecumenical councils were under Papal oversight.

[5] H. R. Percival, *The Seven Ecumenical Councils of the Undivided Church: Their Canons and Dogmatic Decrees* (A Select Library of Nicene and Post-Nicene Fathers of the Christian Church: second series; Edinburgh: T.&T. Clark, 1997 reprint), xi–xii.

[6] Ware, *Orthodox Church*, 25–8.

[7] See J. Kelly, *Early Christian Doctrines* (London: Adam & Charles Black, 1968), 223–51. Sections of this chapter are adapted from parts of my book *The Holy Trinity: In Scripture, History, Theology, and Worship* (Phillipsburg, New Jersey: Presbyterian & Reformed, 2004), and used with permission.

unity, he argued that God is solitary, the Father unique. In turn, the Son had an origin, *ex nihilo* (out of nothing). He was created, existing by the will of God. Before he was created he did not exist. The logic here is that since everything created came into being out of non-existence, and the Word of God is a creature, so the Word of God also came into being out of non-existence. Thus God was not always Father, for before he created the Son he was solitary. What happened was that, when he wanted to create, God made a person (Word, Spirit, Son) and so created through an intermediary, for it is not possible for him to have direct contact with the world. It followed from this that the Word has a changeable nature and remains good by freewill only so long as he chooses. The *ousiai* (substances or beings) of the Father, the Son, and the Spirit are divided and differ from one another. The Father is the Son's origin, and the Son's God.

Gregg and Groh have argued that paramount for Arius is his view of salvation rather than his ideas about God or cosmology. There is some truth to this. According to this argument, it was necessary that the pre-existent Christ be a creature to secure the closest possible link with his fellow-creatures who were to be saved. Thus he had free moral choice, advanced in virtue and obedience, and became a perfected creature, always in subordinate dependence on God. The text, John 10:30, where Jesus says 'I and the Father are one', was taken to mean a unity in harmonious agreement of will, not identity of being. Thus for Arius will is primary rather than being. The Son was an underworker, an assistant to the Father, operating under orders.[8] From his opponents' perspective, the main problem was that Arius' attempt to identify the Son with human beings severed his connection with God. In particular, they were concerned with his idea that the Son came into existence from non-existence. This clearly taught that the Son was a creature.

---

[8] R. C. Gregg, *Early Arianism – a Way of Salvation* (Philadelphia: Fortress Press, 1981), 1–129.

The eruption of the controversy led to Constantine's summons of a church council. He based its procedure on the Roman Senate. The Emperor had no vote in the Senate; neither did he in the Council.[9] He simply confirmed the decisions of the bishops, enabling the Church to maintain its doctrinal autonomy, since he considered the bishops' decisions to be in accord with the will of God. Unfortunately, there are no official minutes extant, so we have no idea how many bishops actually attended the council, nor can we be exactly sure of the course of debate.[10]

At first, an attempt to resolve the crisis was made using purely Biblical language. Athanasius provides a glimpse of what happened. Originally, the statement was proposed to the Council that the Son came 'from God'. By this it was intended to say that he was not from some other source, nor was he a creature. However, those who sympathized with Arius agreed to the phrase, since in their eyes all creatures came forth from God. Athanasius records them nodding and winking at each other knowingly. Consequently, the Council was forced to look for a word that excluded all possibility of an Arian interpretation.[11] Biblical language could not resolve the issue, for the conflict was over the meaning of Biblical language in the first place. This reminds us that to understand this or that we have to consider it in a context other than its own, for meaning cannot be derived by the repetition of that about which meaning is sought. A dictionary is an obvious example of a tool that explains meanings of words in terms of other words and phrases.

Eventually a Syro-Palestinian creed was used to resolve the problem. The following is the Creed of Nicaea:

We believe in one God Father Almighty maker of all things, seen and unseen:

---

[9] Note the similarity with the United States Constitution, where the President and Vice-President have no vote in the legislature, although the latter presides over the Senate.

[10] L. D. Davis, *The First Seven Ecumenical Councils (325–787)* (College-ville, Minnesota: The Liturgical Press, 1990), 57–9.

[11] Athanasius, *On the Decrees of the Synod of Nicaea*, 19–21.

And in one Lord Jesus Christ the Son of God, begotten as only-begotten of the Father, that is of the substance (*ousia*) of the Father, God of God, Light of Light, true God of true God, begotten not made, consubstantial with the Father, through whom all things came into existence, both things in heaven and things on earth; who for us men and for our salvation came down and was incarnate and became man, suffered and rose again the third day, ascended into the heavens, is coming to judge the living and the dead:

And in the Holy Spirit.

But those who say, 'there was a time when he did not exist', and 'before being begotten he did not exist,' and that he came into being from non-existence, or who allege that the Son of God is of another *hypostasis* or *ousia*, or who is alterable or changeable, these the Catholic and Apostolic Church condemns.

The Council hit on a number of phrases that explicitly denied Arian teaching. The phrase 'from the substance of the Father' asserted that the Son is not a creature or an intermediary but is generated from the Father's very being. 'Begotten, not made' affirmed that the Son was not begotten by the Father's will and so is not a creature. The expression 'of one substance (homoousios) with the Father' was the key.

However, some of these terms were ambiguous then and for half a century thereafter. Confusion would reign. For example, the words *hypostasis* and *ousia* were used interchangeably in Greek and by the Greek Fathers. For many, they were synonyms. Their eventual meanings (person/substance or being) were *not* what anyone understood by them for most of the fourth century and it is anachronistic to project these meanings back to an earlier time when they simply do not apply. There was not at this time a single word for what God is as three that could command wide, let alone universal, agreement. Thus at the time of Nicaea (1) *hypostasis/ousia* could be synonyms and used to describe either what God is as three or what he is as one, (2) *hypostasis* could refer to the three and *ousia* be either ignored or rejected, (3) *hypostasis* could be used for 'distinct existence' and *ousia* for 'nature',

(4) or uncertainty could prevail. Sometimes single writers move from one meaning to the other. A few (Hanson cites Arius and Asterius[12]) do clearly distinguish them. Hanson sums up when he says that even for those who distinguish the terms the concept 'of what each person of the Trinity is in his existence and proper form distinct from the others had not yet been distinguished from the concept of what all of them were as full and equal (or even as partial and unequal) members of the Godhead'.[13] Not only was there no commonly agreed term for the three but the concept itself had barely appeared on the theological radar.

As for *homoousios* (of the same substance), this term had been used by the gnostics, never to mean equality or identity.[14] Even worse, it was associated with Paul of Samosata and cited in his condemnation by the Council of Antioch in 268. Athanasius, who championed the term later, was forced to recognize this unpalatable fact and tried to extricate himself by saying that Paul used the word in a different sense than Nicaea. The problem for us is that it is impossible to know how Paul used it![15] Whatever the case, it did not have a happy history before Nicaea! Moreover, it does not seem to have acquired a steady and recognized meaning. It hardly means 'shared being',[16] let alone 'identity of being'. Hanson suggests it is inserted because Arius disliked it, but people like Eusebius of Caeasarea – who had been favourable to Arius – signed Nicaea, so we can be reasonably sure it was not intended to teach the numerical identity of the Father and the Son.[17] In fact, it may not have been intended to say very much other than to unite all opposed to Arius, by denying that the Son came from a source other than God.[18]

---

[12] R. Hanson, *The Search for the Christian Doctrine of God: The Arian Controversy 318–381* (Edinburgh: T.&T. Clark, 1988), 187.

[13] Ibid., 190.

[14] Ibid., 190–1.

[15] Ibid., 195; C. Stead, *Divine Substance* (Oxford: Clarendon, 1977), 216–17.

[16] G. Prestige, *God in Patristic Thought* (London: SPCK, 1952), 209–11.

[17] Hanson, *Search*, 202.

[18] Stead, *Divine Substance*, 233–42; R. Person, *The Mode of Decision Making at the Early Ecumenical Councils: An Inquiry Into the Function of Scripture and Tradition at*

The council also issued anathemas attacking the Arians' catch-phrases 'there was when he was not', and 'before being born he was not', and twenty canons on administrative and disciplinary matters.[19]

Constantinople I 381

The aftermath of Nicaea I was messy. It did not resolve the controversy – if anything it made it worse. Problems rumbled on and grew more intense and difficult as the years passed. Eventually the clouds lifted. This was due to two closely related factors.

First, Athanasius (c295–373) recognized that what is of prime importance is not the precise terms used to refer to the trinity but the meaning intended by those terms. He had the breadth of mind to recognize that what matters is right belief and intention even if words and phrases are not precisely what he might want. This he brought out very effectively at the Council of Alexandria (362), allowing that *ousia* and *hypostasis* can be used in different senses, and that it is possible to speak of three *hypostases* and be orthodox.[20] This was a major breakthrough, paving the way for resolution of the crisis.

Second, Basil the Great (330–379) coined a new use for the words *ousia* and *hypostasis*, the first referring to the one being of

---

the *Councils of Nicea and Ephesus* (Basel: Friedrich Reinhardt Kommissionsverlag, 1978), 92–105.

[19] Bishops are forbidden to receive into communion clergy or laity excommunicated by another bishop (canon 5); Egypt and Libya (hotbeds of Arianism) are to submit to the Metropolitan of Alexandria (canon 6); Bishops, priests and deacons are to remain in the place where they were ordained (canon 15); Bishops are forbidden to ordain persons from another diocese without that bishop's permission, so as to prevent the poaching of clergy (canon 16); Those who had castrated themselves are forbidden to be or become clerics (canon 1); The recently baptized are forbidden to become priests or bishops (canon 2); Clergy are forbidden to have a woman live with them, except mother, sister or aunt or someone above suspicion (canon 3); The ordination of notorious sinners is forbidden, even after they had reformed their lives (canon 9); Anyone who denied their faith is to be deposed (canon 10). See Davis, *Councils*, 64–5; Percival, *Seven Ecumenical Councils*, 8–56.

[20] Athanasius, *To the Antiochenes* 5–8; *PG* 26:799–806; Hanson, *Search*, 644–5.

God, the second to the three. He insisted, in a letter to Gregory
Nazianzen, that no theological term is adequate to the thought
of the speaker for language is too weak to act in the service of
objects of thought. Yet, in turn, our thought itself – let alone
our language – is too weak for the reality. Nevertheless we
are compelled to give an answer about God to those who love
the Lord. So devote the intellectual energies God gives you to
advocating the truth, he urged his friend.[21] Basil's recognition
of the limitations of human thought and language contributed
to the relaxation of the strict semantic usage of the technical
terminology that had bedevilled the trinitarian question. As with
Athanasius he recognized that the claims of truth are paramount
and that human language and logic must bow before it.

Thus, he made the vital move of disengaging *ousia* and
hypostasis.[22] He wrote to Count Terentius that '*ousia* has the
same relation to *hypostasis* as the common has to the particular'.
Ousia is common, like goodness or Godhead, 'while *hypostasis* is
contemplated in the special property of Fatherhood, Sonship,
or the power to sanctify'. These are perfect, complete and real
hypostases, while the *homoousion* is preserved in the unity of the
Godhead.[23] This was a major step forward and it was to help
in finding a way out of the conceptual maze. Basil succeeded
in disentangling language about the trinity from technical
philosophical usage, putting it on a more flexible level.

The immediate occasion of Constantinople I was the heresy
of the Macedonians or Pneumatomachi. These people held
to the deity of Christ but balked at that of the Holy Spirit.
It was in addressing this problem that the three Cappadocian
theologians (Basil, his brother Gregory of Nyssa, and Gregory
Nazianzen) led the way out of the fourth century crisis. Once
again, as Davis points out, 'since the official acts of the Council
are no longer extant, it is difficult to determine exactly what the

---

[21] Basil of Caesarea, *Letters* 7; *PG*, 32:244–5.

[22] Occasionally Basil writes of *physis* rather than *ousia*, and *prosôpon* rather than
hypostasis.

[23] Basil of Caesarea, *Letters*, 214:4; *PG*, 32:789.

fathers really did.'[24] The origin of the famous creed associated
with this council, known popularly but inaccurately as the
Nicene creed, is similarly shrouded in mystery.[25]

The new emperor Theodosius I called a council of the
Eastern Church at Constantinople early in 381 in an attempt
to unite it on the basis of the Nicene faith. The council met
in May, June, and July. Its composition was not ecumenically
representative, nor was it recognized as an ecumenical council at
once. There was no representation of the Western Church, and
in particular none from Rome. At first the only bishops present
were from Asia Minor, western Syria and Palestine, although
later some arrived from Egypt, notably Alexandria, and a few
from Illyricum. However, by 550 it was universally regarded as
ecumenical.

A crucial issue for the council was the relationship with
the Macedonians or Pneumatomachi. Some have argued that
Theodosius wanted the council to adopt a conciliatory tone
so as to secure the broadest possible unity for the Church, an
important factor in maintaining the cohesion of the Empire in
face of threats from the Goths. In the end, whether or not this
was so, conciliation proved impossible to secure. The council
passed four canons. Bishops' activities were to be limited to
their dioceses. Maximus the Cynic was condemned. The bishop
of Constantinople was proclaimed second in honor to Rome,
for 'Constantinople is the new Rome'. The rationale for this
was the Eastern practice of basing church administration on the
pattern of existing political structures. Since Constantinople
had risen to political eminence second only to Rome, this was
now reflected in the ecclesiastical realm. Constantinople's rise
was now entire, from the day Constantine moved the seat of
Empire there in 324. Davis comments that this short canon 'will
be the cause of turmoil in the Church for centuries to come'.[26]

---

[24] Davis, *Councils*, 120.
[25] See J. Kelly, *Early Christian Creeds* (London: Longman, 1972), 252–79.
[26] Davis, *Councils*, 128.

The first canon was on theology, reaffirming the dogma of Nicaea, and condemning the Eunomians, Anomians, Arians, Eudoxians, Macedonians, Sabellians, Marcellians, Photinians and Apollinarians (see glossary for details about these groups).

The creed

To this day what is popularly but wrongly called the Nicene creed, and is more accurately described as the Niceno-Constant-inopolitan creed, is recited throughout the Eastern and Western Churches. This creed (C) is associated with this council. However, it raises the vexed question as to whether the council ever produced such a creed? The first mention of C is no earlier than in 451. The minutes of the Council of Chalcedon of that year record the archdeacon of Constantinople reading it to the assembled bishops as the faith of the 150 Fathers who met at Constantinople. Until the middle of the twentieth century the great majority of scholars disputed its purported origin.[27] There is no record of it in the council of 381, although since we have no minutes extant, that proves less than at first sight might be supposed. Moreover, the church historians closest to the events – Socrates and Sozomen, of the early fifth century – do not mention it. Indeed, from 381 to 451 silence reigns, not only from councils but also theologians. Some have pointed to a virtually identical creed cited by Epiphanius in a work composed in 374 but later scholarship considers this creed to be closer to the creed of Nicaea (N) than C.

However, Kelly produces powerful countervailing reasons that support the Constantinopolitan origin of C.[28] Why, he asks, did the Fathers at Chalcedon accept the explanation of its origin presented to them by the archdeacon? They were known to be opposed to the making of unnecessary creeds. No one cast doubt on it at that time. As Hanson argues, we should expect the archdeacon of Constantinople to know what was done in

[27] Kelly, *Creeds*, 305–12.
[28] Ibid., 312–31.

the council in his own city.[29] Moreover, the hostility of Rome
and especially Alexandria to the claims of Constantinople to be
second in honor only to Rome, advanced at the council, helps
explain why its creed may have been suppressed for a time by
its jealous rivals. The expression 'the faith of Nicaea', used
pervasively down the years, was not always applied to the council
of Nicaea as such but to all who followed in the general orbit of
its teaching. Given this practice, it is easy to see why a formulary
that followed in the ethos of Nicaea might have remained in
the background for a while. The council of Constantinople
would not have seen itself as promulgating a new teaching, but
rather endorsing Nicaea, only with a different formulary. The
teaching of Nicaea, rather than the precise words, was what
was considered of importance.[30] It could well be that C may
have already been in existence – the flow of language suggests
liturgical use – and the council then adopted it, perhaps using
it at the baptism of Nectarius, Gregory Nazianzen's successor
at Constantinople. Kelly suggests the Nicene faith was ratified
in the shape of C, arguing it was used to try to win over the
Macedonians while at the same time endorsing Gregory's
doctrine of the Holy Spirit in all but words. I might also suggest
that there is a hint of a very early reference to C in the third
book of Gregory of Nyssa's *Against Eunomius*, where he refers to
the phrases 'light of light, true God of true God' in 'our simple
and homespun statement of faith' as confessing the identity of
substance of the Son with the Father. These phrases are present
in both N and C but two factors may point to a reference
to C. We know that Gregory read parts of this work to a select
gathering immediately before the council but this consisted of
the first two books, for he did not write the rest until two years
afterwards. Additionally, Gregory omits the phrase 'God of
God' from N, which is also left out by C. If so, this is the very
earliest attestation we have for C, and it would be a most reliable

---

[29] Hanson, *Search*, 813.
[30] Hanson, *Search*, 820 agrees.

one, for Gregory was present throughout the council and played a leading role in it.[31]

What is the connection of C to the synodical letter issued the following year? The principal difference is the moderate tone of C concerning the Holy Spirit – there is no reference to his being *homoousios* with the Father and the Son, nor is he called God – compared with the clear and unambiguous assertions of the letter, which state precisely these points that C sidestepped. The most common thesis is that the council attempted to secure as wide acceptance as possible and so held back on terms that might offend some, particularly the Macedonians. The following year, so the theory goes, these people had shown themselves so hostile to the council that further temporizing was unnecessary and so the need for restraint no longer existed. This is based on the assumption that C is an attempt to win over the Macedonians or Pneumatomachi. There are good reasons why this is a misreading of the creed. It also forgets that the Macedonians left the council early, rejecting the course it was taking. The breach between them and the Nicenes had already occurred and was not postponed until after the council had ended.[32]

From another angle, what is the relationship between C and N? C has often been thought to be simply an expansion and updating of N. This is not so. C omits a wide range of words and phrases in N, while introducing a further series of statements that have no counterpart in its predecessor. Only about one-fifth of the words of C can be traced to N. The biggest difference is a larger section in C on the Holy Spirit. Kelly is correct that C is an entirely new document, not merely a revision, although its compilers would not have thought of it as new, since they were concerned less with verbal precision and more with theological

---

[31] Gregory of Nyssa, *Against Eunomius*, 3:4, my translation. See J. A. McGuckin, *St. Gregory of Nazianzus: An Intellectual Biography* [Crestwood, New York: St Vladimir's Seminary Press, 2001], 349–50; J. Quasten, Volume III: The golden age of Greek Patristic literature from the Council of Nicea to the Council of Chalcedon, *Patrology* [Westminster, Maryland: Christian Classics, Inc, 1992], 254–96.

[32] Hanson, *Search*, 817–18.

compatibility.[33] The two key formulae of N are omitted: 'from the *ousia* of the Father' and 'God from God'. Some of the words and phrases introduced by C are important. For instance, the phrase 'whose kingdom shall have no end' is clearly to counter Marcellus of Ancyra's Sabellian-sounding idea that the Son's kingdom would end when he hands over the kingdom to the Father. There are also a large number of trivial differences between the two creeds that could hardly have been made if the compilers of C had simply wanted to update N. In short, the council either constructed or adopted as its own the only creed that is truly ecumenical, confessed in both Eastern and Western Churches, 'one of the few threads by which the tattered fragments of the divided robe of Christendom are held together.'[34]

The following are the words of the Niceno-Constantinopolitan creed, probably dating from the Council of Constantinople (AD 381), which brought to a resolution the convulsions of the fourth century:

> We believe in one God the Father Almighty, maker of heaven and earth and of all things visible and invisible;
> And in one Lord Jesus Christ the Son of God, the Only-begotten, begotten by his Father before all ages, Light from Light, true God from true God, begotten not made, consubstantial with the Father, through whom all things came into existence, who for us men and for our salvation came down from the heavens and became incarnate by the Holy Spirit and the Virgin Mary and became a man, and was crucified for us under Pontius Pilate and suffered and was buried and rose again on the third day in accordance with the Scriptures and ascended into the heavens and is seated at the right hand of the Father and will come again with glory to judge the living and the dead, and there will be no end to his kingdom;
> And in the Holy Spirit, the Lord and life-giver, who proceeds from the Father, who is worshipped and glorified together with the Father and the Son, who spoke by the prophets;

---

[33] Kelly, *Creeds*, 301–5, 325; Ibid., 820.
[34] Kelly, *Creeds*, 296.

And in one holy, catholic and apostolic Church;
We confess one baptism for the forgiveness of sins;
We wait for the resurrection of the dead and the life of the
coming age. Amen.

The theology of the creed

We noted that C is significantly different from N. In the first
place, there are a number of additions. For the phrase 'from
the Holy Spirit and the virgin Mary' there is no ready explanation other than that the words may have been in a pre-
existing formula that the council adopted. The expression
about Christ 'whose kingdom shall have no end' was directed
against Marcellus of Ancyra's idea that Christ's kingdom is
temporary. The other additions, with one exception, are all
trivial and so point to a different base for this creed than N.
The one non-trivial addition is the third article, on the Holy
Spirit. This is explained by the controversies caused by the
Macedonians.

The omissions from N require some comment. The single
most obvious one is the phrase 'from the substance (*ousia*)
of the Father' with reference to the Son. On the basis of
this omission, Harnack claimed that C was not prepared to
assert that the Son is of the identical substance (*homoousios*)
to the Father. However, the most reasonable conjecture for
the omission is that C may have originated as a formula for
liturgical purposes – it has a rythmic flow to it – and so the
council may not have considered it necessary to repeat the
precise phraseology of N.

The needs of the time required a more extensive reference to
the Holy Spirit. We are sceptical about the council's adopting,
whether under imperial pressure or by design, a conciliatory line
towards the Macedonians on this issue. The following year the
homoousion of the Spirit is clearly asserted in the synodical letter.
As Hanson suggests, the clause on the worship of the Holy
Spirit together with the Father and the Son was unacceptable
to the Macedonians. They considered the Spirit to be a kind of

creature and so not to be worshipped. The clause in question was designed to exclude them, not conciliate them.[35]

Overall, however, C intends to teach the deity of the Holy Spirit in guarded language, giving as little offence as possible. A number of factors support this. First, the title 'Lord' is applied to the Spirit, 'the Lord and giver of life.' *Kurios* is the Greek word customarily used for YHWH, the God of Israel. Second, the statement that the Spirit is 'worshipped together with the Father and the Son' reproduces Athanasius' comments in his letters to Serapion.[36] The phrase highlights the real personal distinctions but unites the worship, which is one and the same. It places the Holy Spirit without question on the side of deity. While he is not specifically called *homoousios* as such, all that goes with that term is present, whether explicitly or by direct entailment.[37] While not all in the orthodox ranks as yet felt completely at ease about calling the Holy Spirit God in so many words, the synodical letter in 382 removed all ambiguity. It said 'there is one Godhead, Power, and Substance (*ousia*) of the Father and of the Son and of the Holy Ghost ... in three perfect *hypostases*, i.e. three perfect persons (*prosopa*).'[38]

The creed asserts indirectly the monarchy of the Father, since the Holy Spirit proceeds from the Father.[39] At the same time, this statement counters and contradicts the Macedonians, who maintained that the Spirit was a creation of the Son. That he is said to proceed from the Father – and by implication from the Father's *ousia* – places him completely outside those things

[35] Hanson, *Search*, 818.

[36] Athanasius, *Letters to Serapion on the Holy Spirit* 1:31, PG 26:601. See also Basil of Caesarea, *Letters*, 90:2, PG 32:473.

[37] B. de Margerie S.J., *The Christian Trinity in History* (E. J. Fortman S.J.; Petersham, Massachusetts: St. Bede's Publications, 1982), 105–6; B. Studer, *Trinity and Incarnation: The Faith of the Early Church* (ed. M. Westerhoff; A. Louth; Collegeville, Minnesota: Liturgical Press, 1993), 157.

[38] Percival, *Seven Ecumenical Councils*, 189.

[39] B. Bobrinskoy, *The Mystery of the Trinity: Trinitarian Experience and Vision in the Biblical and Patristic Tradition* (A. P. Gythiel; Crestwood, New York: St. Vladimir's Seminary Press, 1999), 249–50.

made by the Son.[40] In addition, the personality of the Spirit is implied in his speaking through the prophets.[41] As de Margerie indicates, the creed places failure to teach that the Spirit is to be worshiped together with the Father and the Son outside the pale of the Christian faith.[42]

The Holy Spirit is also coordinate with the Father and the Son in creation and grace. The Father is the maker of all things, while the Lord Jesus Christ is the one through whom all things came into existence, and the Holy Spirit is the Lord and giver of life. Creation is a work of the whole trinity, all three persons actively involved in the creation of all that is made. Moreover, in being the Lord and giver of life, together with the Father and the Son creating all things, the Spirit is again placed unequivocally in the category of what is God.

If Kelly's thesis is correct, we must conclude that the council was not going out of its way to be innovative. It was content to adopt a previous formula. Constantinople I resolved the issues at stake and developed the theology of Nicaea I, applying the homoousial status of the Son to the Holy Spirit. It continued the Eastern practice of accommodating church organization to the civil organization of the Empire, 'sowing the seeds of discord among the four great sees of East and West by raising the ecclesiastical status of Constantinople.' Here is the root of one of the bones of contention between East and West. Whereas the prominence of Constantinople is based on conciliar canons, the claims of Rome are based on its interpretation of Jesus' words to Peter (Matt. 16:13-19). Whatever Protestants – or the Orthodox – might think of these claims, in the eyes of Rome they are founded on the words of Jesus himself.[43] The question of the trinity was resolved but other issues were brewing. In particular, having struggled with the question of the relation of Jesus Christ to God, the Church – and note again, in particular

---

[40] Studer, *Trinity*, 157.

[41] Ibid., 157–8; Bobrinskoy, *Mystery*, 249–50.

[42] de Margerie S.J., *Christian Trinity*, 107.

[43] Davis, *Councils*, 128–30.

the *Eastern* Church – was now to be faced by the matter of the relation of his deity to his humanity.[44]

---

[44] Again, a number of disciplinary and administrative canons were issued, anathematizing various heresies, reaffirming the faith of Nicaea, restating the Nicene prohibition on bishops going beyond their dioceses unless invited, how to deal with penitent heretics, and the declaration that the Bishop of Constantinople shall have the prerogative of honour after the Bishop of Rome; see Percival, *Seven Ecumenical Councils*, 161–90.

2

On to Chalcedon

Ephesus 431

The next major theological crisis arose over the identity of Jesus Christ. Since he was and is the eternal Son of God, how does this relate to the fact – obvious from the Gospels – that he is also human? Flowing from this, what significance do these things have for our salvation? These questions were thrust into the foreground in the year 428 by Nestorius, the Bishop of Constantinople.[1] He began to attack the term *theotokos* (God-bearer), a popular title for Mary. Following the dominant stress in the Christology of Antioch,[2] which distinguished sharply between the deity of Christ and his humanity, Nestorius held that Mary could only strictly be called mother of *the man* Jesus. She could be termed *christotokos* (Christ-bearer) with no qualms, since there was no danger then of confusing deity and humanity. Nestorius' problem was that, while he had a firm

---

[1] On Nestorius, see G. Prestige, *Fathers and Heretics* (London: SPCK, 1940), 120–49; J. Kelly, *Early Christian Doctrines* (London: Adam & Charles Black,1968), 310–17.

[2] See D. Wallace-Hadrill, *Christian Antioch: A Study of Early Christian Thought in the East* (Cambridge: Cambridge University Press, 1982).

grasp of the distinctiveness of Christ's divinity and humanity,
he was less sure of the unity of his person. Talk of Mary as
theotokos conjured up in his mind the spectre of Arianism. Arius,
and his more influential successor Eunomius, had reduced the
Son's deity to creaturehood. Nestorius feared that use of this
term *theotokos* would lead to a blurring of the creator–creature
distinction. He wanted to avoid any notion of a mixture of deity
and humanity, and so preserve the integrity of the human nature.
He was also alert to the danger of Apollinarianism. Apollinaris
(c.315–before 392), a strong supporter of the Council of Nicaea,
had wandered into heresy in his old age by teaching that the
Logos took the place of a human soul in the incarnate Christ.
The Word assumed flesh – a body – only. He was condemned by
Constantinople I. The problem with Apollinaris' teaching, in
Gregory Nazianzen's words, was that 'whatever is not assumed
cannot be healed'. If the Son did not assume into union a full
humanity, including a soul, there was no incarnation. We
could not then be saved, since Christ would have been less than
man, since a human being minus a soul is not a human being.
Nestorius' concern was – correctly – to affirm the full integrity
of Christ's human nature. So he spoke of a 'conjunction' of the
divinity and humanity rather than a 'union', a conjunction that
resulted in a *prosopon* of union, a single object of appearance,
which was identical with neither of the two natures. The
prosopon of union, not the Logos or Word, was the subject of the
incarnate Christ.

Nestorius was vehemently opposed by Cyril of Alexandria,
who began from the premise of Christ's unity.[3] For Cyril,
Nestorius threatened not only the unity of Christ's person but

---

[3] For Cyril, see St. Cyril of Alexandria, *On the Unity of Christ* (J. A. McGuckin;
Crestwood, New York: St. Vladimir's Seminary Press, 1995); J. A. McGuckin,
*St. Cyril of Alexandria and the Christological Controversy: Its History, Theology, and
Texts* (Crestwood, New York: St. Vladimir's Seminary Press, 2004); Prestige,
Fathers, 150–79; Kelly, *Doctrines*, 317–23; N. Russell, *Cyril of Alexandria* (London:
Routledge, 2000); T. G. Weinandy, *The Theology of St. Cyril of Alexandria* (London:
T.&T. Clark, 2003), 23–74.

also the incarnation itself, for his teaching effectively denied that there was a real participation by the Son of God in our humanity. The two natures – so it seemed – were more like two pieces of board held together by glue. Cyril stressed that salvation was a work of God, that the man Jesus could not defeat sin and death by his human nature alone. To do this, the eternal Logos assumed into *union* the human nature of Christ.[4]

Nestorius did not help his cause by his apparent indifference to the teaching of Julian of Eclanum, one of the foremost advocates of Pelagianism, who had created controversy in the West by his claim that, due to free will, fallen man had the ability of himself to respond to the gospel. Julian also opposed Augustine's doctrines of original sin and predestination. Augustine had responded to Julian in great detail. Pelagius himself, the originator of the heresy, had been condemned in the West by a Council of Carthage in 418. Nestorius had sent copies of Julian's sermons to Pope Celestine, asking what the problem was with him, undermining his relations with Rome, which had fought Pelagianism for years and condemned it. This obviously lessened the chances of Rome sympathetically mediating his conflict with Cyril.[5]

Cyril's opposition to Nestorius was highly provocative. Cyril, hardly the most tactful of men, was not the most ready to reach a mutually acceptable agreement and neither, for that matter, was Nestorius. Added to this, the rivalry of Alexandria to Constantinople's upstart position as the new Rome complicated the struggle. In his *Second Letter to Nestorius* – to be adopted as definitive at the fourth ecumenical Council at Chalcedon in 451 – Cyril starts with the unity of Christ's person. The Word 'united to himself ... flesh enlivened by a rational soul, and in this way became a human being.' There is an 'unspeakable and unutterable convergence into unity, one Christ and one Son out

---

[4] See J. Meyendorff, *Christ in Eastern Christian Thought* (Crestwood, New York: St. Vladimir's Seminary Press, 1975), 18–19.

[5] L. D. Davis, *The First Seven Ecumenical Councils (325–787)* (Collegeville, Minnesota: The Liturgical Press, 1990), 140–1.

of two.' To reject this personal union is to fall into the error of positing two sons. 'We do not worship a human being in conjunction with the Logos, lest the appearance of a division creep in ... No, we worship one and the same, because the body of the Logos is not alien to him but accompanies him even as he is enthroned with the Father.' The Word did not unite himself to a human person but to flesh. The Virgin Mary is *theotokos* since it is *the Word* that united himself to this human body and soul.[6] In short, for Cyril, Nestorius' stress on the integrity and distinctiveness of Christ's humanity had jeopardized his unity.

In his *Third Letter to Nestorius*, Cyril again stresses the personal union of the Word with the flesh. All expressions in the Gospels refer to the one incarnate person of the Word. Mary is *theotokos* since she 'gave birth after the flesh to God who was united by *hypostasis* with flesh', man ensouled with a rational soul.[7] Cyril adds twelve anathemas to this letter. In these, he declares that 'if anyone will not confess that the Emmanuel is very God, and that therefore the Holy Virgin is the Mother of God (*theotokos*), inasmuch as in the flesh she bore the Word of God made flesh ...; let him be anathema.' He insists, *inter alia*, that the natures in the one Christ come together into a union, and that the Word and man are not worshipped jointly but are given one act of worship, and that it is the Word who suffered, was crucified, and died according to the flesh.[8] For Cyril, the Word who existed before the incarnation is the same person after the incarnation, now enfleshed. This union excludes division but does not eliminate difference.

---

[6] Ibid., 149–50; R. A. Norris Jr., *The Christological Controversy* (Philadelphia: Fortress Press, 1980), 131–5, esp 133.

[7] E. R. Hardy, *Christology of the Later Fathers* (The Library of Christian Classics; Philadelphia: Westminster Press, 1954), 349–54, esp 352–3.

[8] Ibid., 354; Davis, *Councils*, 150–1; H. R. Percival, *The Seven Ecumenical Councils of the Undivided Church: Their Canons and Dogmatic Decrees* (A Select Library of Nicene and Post-Nicene Fathers of the Christian Church: second series; Edinburgh: T.&T. Clark, 1997 reprint), 206.

The Council

To resolve the controversy, under pressure from Nestorius himself, Emperor Theodosius II called a council at Ephesus for Pentecost, Sunday 7 June 431.[9] Huge intrigue surrounded it. Both Nestorius and Cyril, complete with bodyguards, harangued their followers but refused to speak to each other. Kelly writes of 'an astonishing medley of rival meetings'.[10] Cyril opened a pre-emptive council himself on 22 June, which Nestorius refused to attend. There were two votes taken. Cyril's *Second Letter to Nestorius* was accepted as conforming to the Creed of Nicaea. Nestorius' reply, it was decided, was not so compatible – hardly a surprise, since those at this gathering were all staunch supporters of Cyril! Following this, Nestorius was expelled from the episcopal office and the priesthood. On 11 July, the Papal legates approved these decisions. During the confusion, 'Dalmatius, a monk who had not left his cell for forty-six years, set out to approach the emperor personally on Cyril's behalf.'[11] Meanwhile a rival council of Nestorius' supporters had met and deposed Cyril! The presence and support of the Papal legates decided the matter in Cyril's favour. They ratified Cyril's council, making Cyril the winner and securing the ecumenical status of his council in the eyes of its supporters.[12] Further corroboration came when Chalcedon accepted it and Cyril's *Second Letter to Nestorius* (although his *Third Letter to Nestorius* with the twelve anathemas did not receive such approval).

This council shows the Church at its worst. It was marked by petty intrigue, political opportunism, posturing, and personal intimidation. It was an almost complete shambles.[13] Nestorius

---

[9] See Kelly, *Doctrines*, 324–30; A. Grillmeier S.J., *Christ in Christian Tradition: Volume One: From the Apostolic Age to Chalcedon (451)* (Second, revised; J. Bowden; Atlanta: John Knox Press, 1975), 484–7; T. Ware, *The Orthodox Church* (London: Penguin Books, 1969), 32–3; J. Pelikan, *The Christian Tradition 1: The Emergence of the Catholic Tradition (100–600)* (Chicago: University of Chicago Press, 1971), 260–1.

[10] Kelly, *Doctrines*, 327.

[11] Davis, *Councils*, 154–8.

[12] Ibid., 160.

[13] On the canons of the council and other relevant documents, see Percival, *Seven Ecumenical Councils*, 191–242.

and his followers were banished, eventually retreating to the Egyptian desert. Unlike the Arians they continued in existence, as they do to this day. Their vigorous missionary activity took them to Persia and China, where they produced an extensive body of Christian writings in Chinese from 635 to 845. A famous monument discovered there in the seventeenth century testifies to their presence and impact.[14] However, their banishment returned to haunt the Eastern Church with a vengeance. During his early travels, Muhammad probably encountered merchants with a smattering of knowledge of Nestorian Christianity. It is likely that *theotokos* – or its entailments – may have cropped up on some occasion, probably in garbled fashion, and contributed to Muhammad's belief that Christians worshipped a trinity consisting of Allah, Jesus his Son, and the Virgin Mary, Jesus' mother.[15] On the other hand, the council achieved the positive effect of declaring that Christ's humanity, wholly human, was appropriated by the Word as his own, and so forms the basis for our own salvation.[16]

Chalcedon 451[17]

The Council of Ephesus did not end the Christological problems faced by the Eastern Church. It merely addressed one particular heresy. Before long a fresh crisis arose, generated by Eutyches from Alexandria, who Kelly calls an 'aged and muddle-headed archimandrite'.[18] Eutyches is an extreme exponent of Cyrilline Christology, without Cyril's theological sophistication.

Eutyches

For Eutyches, before the incarnation Christ was of two natures but after it he is one nature, one Christ, one Son, in one *hypostasis*

---

[14] S. Neill, *Christian Missions* (London: Penguin, 1964), 94–6.

[15] Abdullah Yusuf Ali, *The Meaning of the Holy Qur'an* (Beltsville, Maryland: Amana Publications) Surah 4:171.

[16] Meyendorff, *Christ*, 21.

[17] See Grillmeier S. J., *Christ*, 520–57; Pelikan, *The Christian Tradition 1*, 263–6.

[18] Kelly, *Doctrines*, 331.

and one *prosopon*. Christ's flesh was not consubstantial with ordinary human flesh, since Eutyches thought this would entail the Word assuming an individual subsistent man. Behind this, he understood nature to mean concrete existence – so Christ could not have two natures or he would have two concrete existences and so be divided.[19] Thus, he had an overpowering emphasis on the unity of Christ's person, exactly the opposite of Nestorius. Where Nestorius had sought to uphold the distinctness of the two natures and so threatened the unity of Christ, Eutyches so underlined Christ's unity that he blurred the distinctness of the two natures, Christ's humanity swamped by his deity, although to be fair Eutyches did insist on the full and complete humanity. However, his muddled thinking clouded his probable thoughts. His ideas raised similar problems to those of Apollinaris, for our salvation depends on the reality of the incarnation, on a real assumption of unabbreviated humanity by the Son of God. If Christ was not truly and fully man we could not be saved, for only a second Adam could undo the damage caused by the first.

The 'Robber Council' of Ephesus 449

In 448 the Home Synod, a semi-permanent council of bishops in Constantinople, pronounced against Eutyches, deposing him as priest and excommunicating him. Responding to the crisis, the Emperor Theodosius II called a council at Ephesus in 449. Pope Leo did not attend, citing precedent, but sent legates instead and also his famous *Tome*, summarizing the Christology of the West.[20] This letter of Leo's was to cause problems later, since it appeared to the monophysites to make large concessions to Nestorius.[21] This council, known to posterity as the 'Robber Council' of Ephesus (449), was rigged in favour of Eutyches. The bishops (forty-two of them) who had been at the Home Synod were barred from taking part, as were the Papal legates.

---

[19] See Kelly, *Doctrines*, 330–4; Davis, *Councils*, 171.

[20] Davis, *Councils*, 173–9.

[21] Norris Jr., *Controversy*, 145–55, esp 148 section (3).

Backed up by armed force and a battalion of thugs, Eutyches
was restored.[22] In retaliation, Leo gathered a synod at Rome and
annulled the robber synod's decisions, branding it a *latrocinium*
(a band of robbers, hence its permanent tag). He did not have
to wait long for the situation to be righted. Shortly afterwards,
Theodosius died following a riding accident. Following this,
the imperial court underwent major changes in personnel and
suddenly the balance of power was weighted against Eutyches.

The Council of Chalcedon

Marcian, the new Emperor, called a fresh council to be held
at Nicaea in 451. Pope Leo sent three legates.[23] However,
due to invasions by the Huns, the Emperor was unable to
leave Constantinople and so he ordered the council to move
to Chalcedon, across the Bosphorus, where it convened on
8 October. Sensing the worst, and fearing for their own positions,
Eutyches' supporters one by one withdrew their backing for
him. Much of the council's work was spent dealing with these
supporters and reinstating his deposed opponents. The bishops
reaffirmed the creeds of Nicaea and Constantinople, Cyril's
Second Letter to Nestorius and Leo's *Tome*.[24]

On 22 October, at the fifth session, on the repeated insistence
of the imperial commissioners, a commission was appointed to
draw up a doctrinal statement. It consisted of the three Papal
legates, six orientals, plus three each from Asia, Pontus, Illyricum and Thrace, which met in the oratory of the most holy
martyr Euphemis. The council presented the Creed of Nicaea
and the Creed of Constantinople as an authentic interpretation

---

[22] Kelly, *Doctrines*, 334–8.

[23] For the Council of Chalcedon, see R. Sellers, *The Council of Chalcedon: A
Historical and Doctrinal Survey* (London: SPCK, 1953), 209ff; Kelly, *Doctrines*, 338–43;
Davis, *Councils*, 180–2; Percival, *Seven Ecumenical Councils*, 243–95.

[24] After Leo's *Tome* was read, at the second session of the council, 'the most
reverend bishops cried out: This is the faith of the fathers, this is the faith of
the apostles. So we all believe, thus the orthodox believe. Anathema to him who
does not thus believe. Peter has spoken thus through Leo. So taught the apostles'
(Percival, *Seven Ecumenical Councils*, 259).

of the Creed of Nicaea, raising the Council of Constantinople to the level of what we now call an ecumenical council.[25] We saw in chapter 1 how this is the first record we have of a creed at Constantinople. The bishops affirmed their adherence to the formulas of the Council of Ephesus (431), accepting it as on the same level as Nicaea and Constantinople.[26]

In composing the Definition, the bishops drew on Cyril's *Second Letter to Nestorius*, Cyril's *Letter to the Antiochenes*, Flavian's *Confession* and Leo's *Tome*. According to Pelikan, Leo's *Tome* was the single most decisive contributor, even though there were more quotations from Cyril.[27] The Definition at last clearly distinguishes between person and nature.

> Therefore, following the holy Fathers, we all with one accord teach men to acknowledge one and the same Son, our Lord Jesus Christ, at once complete in Godhead and complete in manhood, truly God and truly man, consisting also of a reasonable soul and body; of one substance with the Father as regards his Godhead, and at the same time of one substance with us as regards his manhood; like us in all respects, apart from sin; as regards his Godhead, begotten of the Father before the ages, but yet as regards his manhood begotten, for us and for our salvation, of Mary the Virgin, the God-bearer; one and the same Christ, Son, Lord, Only-begotten, recognized in two natures, without confusion, without change, without division, without separation; the distinction of natures being in no way annulled by the union, but rather the characteristics of each nature being preserved and coming together to form one person and subsistence, not as parted or separated into two persons, but one and the same Son and only-begotten God,

[25] 'The most glorious judges and great senate said, Let there be read what was set forth by the 150 holy fathers. Aetius, the reverend deacon of Constantinople read from a book [the creed of the 150 fathers.] *The holy faith which the 150 fathers set forth as consonant to the holy and great Synod of Nicaea.* "We believe in one God," etc. All the most reverend bishops cried out: This is the faith of all of us: we all so believe' (Percival, *Seven Ecumenical Councils*, 249).

[26] Davis, *Councils*, 185.

[27] Sellers, *Chalcedon*, 209–10.

the Word, Lord Jesus Christ; even as the prophets from earliest times spoke of him, and our Lord Jesus Christ himself taught us, and the creed of the Fathers has handed down to us.

That Christ subsists in two natures is a decisive rejection of Eutyches. The Definition rejects any notion of the union that might erode or threaten the differences of the natures. At the same time, it also insists that Christ is not divided or separated into two persons, as the Nestorian heresy implied.

The anti-Nestorian stance is evident in a number of ways. The repetition of the phrase 'the same', and the reaffirmation of the Virgin Mary as *theotokos* are two obvious points. Again, towards the end, the Definition denies that Christ is parted or separated into two persons, but rather asserts that the two natures 'come together to form one person and subsistence', echoing Cyril's *Second Letter to Nestorius*. In all these ways it clearly affirms the unity of the person of Christ. On the other hand, the Definition equally repudiates the Eutychian heresy, which had occasioned the Council in the first place. Christ is 'complete in manhood', so much so that he is 'of one substance with us'. The distinction of natures is in no way annulled by the union. There are also clear restatements of opposition both to Apollinarianism, in the point that Christ has 'a reasonable soul and body', and also to Arianism in that Christ is 'of one substance with the Father'.

Above all, the famous four privative adverbs together form the central hinge of the Definition. The incarnate Christ is '*in two natures, without confusion, without change.*' Here is an explicit rejection of Eutyches. The union neither changes Christ's humanity into anything else, nor absorbs it into the divinity. The humanity remains fully humanity. On the other side of the spectrum, the natures are '*without division, without separation.*' By this it is declared impermissible so to focus on either nature of Christ that the personal union is undermined in the manner Nestorius had done. These four adverbs outlaw both Nestorianism and Eutychianism.

The Council also anathematizes those who talk of two natures of the Lord before the union but only one afterwards. This is directed at Eutyches, probably at the behest of Pope Leo and the Papal legates.[28] It would cause problems later for the monophysites, who were accustomed to think of 'nature' as synonymous with what we would now call 'person' and for whom Chalcedon seemed an unwarranted capitulation to Nestorius. However, the problem was more a lack of knowledge of Greek by the Latins, who had pressed this point. Taking *physis* (Greek) to mean *natura* (Latin), it seemed to Leo and his legates that the Alexandrian mantra of one incarnate nature (*physis*) of the Logos was a heretical belief in only one *natura*. It betrayed a failure to appreciate that at this time the Greeks were using *physis* and *hypostasis* interchangeably. These were similar problematics to the situation at and after Nicaea. It would be another century before Emperor Justinian I brought about a clear distinction between these two terms. In reality, the real objection in this anathema is, as Sellers observes, to Eutyches' false interpretation of the formula, not to Cyril's position, which was not in view at the time.[29]

Assessment of Chalcedon

Chalcedon failed to do justice to some real concerns of the Cyrillians. The point that 'the distinction of natures being in no way annulled by the union but rather the characteristics of each nature being preserved and coming together' could be taken to mean that human attributes must be predicated only of the human nature, and the divine of the divine. This sounded Nestorian to these people. It gave the impression that Christ was some form of schizoid, for whom some things could be related only to one part of him and other things to another part. Their strong concern for the unity of Christ seemed to have been given short shrift. It seemed as though the idea that salvation

---

[28] Ibid., 224–6.
[29] Ibid., 226.

begun by the union of the human nature of Christ with the divine was under attack. Chalcedon certainly allows the deity and humanity to be seen as two each in its 'ownness'.[30]

Moreover, Chalcedon left the concept of the hypostatic union unclear. For instance, it did not specify who exactly it was who had suffered and been crucified. Nor did it say that the deification of man began in the union of Christ's humanity with his divinity. The monophysites later thought that Chalcedon was soft on Nestorianism by asserting 'two natures after the union', precisely because it made no mention of the hypostatic union, refusing to include the confession 'out of two'. Chalcedon satisfied the West but not the East.[31]

Furthermore, two passages in Leo's *Tome,* effectively canonized by Chalcedon, were held by the monophysites to be indisputably Nestorian, where 'Leo so separates, and personalizes, what is divine and what is human in Christ that the hypostatic union is dissolved.'[32] Leo states that the properties of both natures are kept intact so that 'one and the same mediator between God and human beings, the human being who is Jesus Christ, can at one and the same time die in virtue of the one nature and, in virtue of the other, be incapable of death.'[33] In the absence of mention of the hypostatic union, followers of Cyril were loath to accept Chalcedon. Moreover, they strongly held to the personal identity of the incarnate Christ with the pre-existent Son, and this the Council did not affirm.[34]

Chalcedon was not the final definitive verdict on Christology. As Sellers points out, 'it allows deductions to be made from its dogmatic decisions, and, in effect, encourages enquiry into the mystery.'[35] 'It is intended to explain just one definite question of the church's christology, indeed the most important one.

---

[30] Ibid., 224.
[31] Ibid., 256–60; Davis, *Councils*, 187; Meyendorff, *Christ*, 28; Pelikan, *The Christian Tradition 1*, 265–6.
[32] Sellers, *Chalcedon*, 266.
[33] Norris Jr., *Controversy*, 148.
[34] Davis, *Councils*, 196–7.
[35] Sellers, *Chalcedon*, 350.

It does not lay claim to having said all that may be said about Christ.' It was far from innovative but, rather, was in line with the preceding tradition. The idea of doctrinal development was alien to the assembled bishops. 'Few councils have been so rooted in tradition as the Council of Chalcedon. The dogma of Chalcedon is ancient tradition in a formula corresponding to the needs of the hour. So we cannot say that the Chalcedonian Definition marks a great turning point in the christological belief of the early church.'[36] At the same time, it left a good deal of unfinished business on the table.

Administrative and disciplinary canons of the Council of Chalcedon

The Council also issued thirty disciplinary canons.[37] Three of these were controversial. Canons 9 and 17 gave Constantinople certain rights over other sees as a court of appeal but the most problematic was Canon 28. This canon granted Constantinople equal privileges with 'elder Rome' as 'new Rome'. Constantinople thereby gained equal ecclesiastical privileges to Rome, and was placed second to Rome only in honour. The basis for this decision was the standing of the respective cities in civil affairs, normal thinking in the East. 'For the fathers rightly granted privileges to the throne of old Rome, because it was the royal city. And the one hundred and fifty most religious bishops [Constantinople I], actuated by the same consideration, gave equal privileges to the most holy throne of new Rome, justly judging that the city which is honoured with the sovereignty and the Senate, and enjoys equal privileges with the old imperial Rome, should in ecclesiastical matters also be magnified as she is, and rank next after her.'[38] In keeping with this new and grand status, the Patriarchate of Constantinople was extended. The metropolitan bishops in the Pontic, Asian, and Thracian dioceses were from now on to be ordained by the Bishop of

---

[36] Grillmeier S.J., *Christ*, 550.

[37] Davis, *Councils*, 189–94; Ware, *Orthodox Church*, 33–6.

[38] Percival, *Seven Ecumenical Councils*, 287.

Constantinople. The intent of the canon was to keep the peace of the Church in the East but it did so at the expense of peace with the West. Almost incidentally, Jerusalem was proclaimed as a fifth patriarchate – with Rome, Constantinople, Alexandria, and Antioch.

Pope Leo refused to accept the twenty-eighth canon. The basis for Rome's position was the words of Jesus to Peter (Matt. 16:13ff), which – according to its claims – referred to his role as the first Bishop of Rome. The other patriarchates were of apostolic origin, and so could also claim roots in Scripture and the earliest tradition. Constantinople, on the other hand, had risen to prominence because the East based ecclesiastical jurisdiction on civil pre-eminence. In this the Eastern Church had transparently followed the Empire. Here was a crucial principial difference between East and West that would plague the church down through the subsequent centuries, exacerbate East–West tensions, and so play a role in the eventual schism. Leo, for his part, accepted the faith of Chalcedon but not the canons. This twenty-eighth canon was only recognized officially by the East in the sixth century. In the West it received recognition at the Council of Lyons in 1274.

The twenty-eighth canon also signalled the defeat of Alexandria. Along with what Alexandrians considered a strong theological rebuff in the Definition's implicit support for Nestorian teaching, here was an obvious ecclesiastical blow. By its recognition as second only to Rome, Constantinople had usurped the place Alexandria coveted. The Pentarchy was now complete – Rome, Constantinople, Alexandria, Antioch, and Jerusalem. While Ware describes this as a simple matter of ecclesiastical organization, Rome having the primacy but not the supremacy, a presidency of love, the first among equals, with the equality of bishops maintained, these jostlings for precedence were real and insidious, sowing discord between Alexandria and Constantinople in the East, and between Constantinople and Rome looking toward the West.

Bewildering intrigue was to follow for a century or so, much of it utterly confusing. From 476 the reaction of the West mattered less, since the Roman Empire proper ceased to exist from that date. With that far-reaching event the balance of power shifted decisively eastwards. The decisions at Chalcedon were now reinforced by *realpolitik*. Meanwhile, theological confusion resulted from the unfinished business of Chalcedon. In 484 ecclesiastical confusion arose from outright schism between East and West when Acacius erased the name of Pope Felix II from Constantinople's diptychs (see glossary), a breach lasting until 518.[39] To the resolution of the theological disorder in the East we now turn.

---

[39] Davis, *Councils*, 204–6.

3

Constantinople and Nicaea Again

Constantinople II 553[1]

The monophysites

Davis comments aptly that 'the period following the Council of Chalcedon was much like that following the Council of Nicaea: at both councils a basically Western solution to an Eastern problem had been intruded into the theological diet of the East. After both councils it took the East considerable time and effort

---

[1] A. Grillmeier, S.J., *Christ in Christian Tradition: Volume Two: From the Council of Chalcedon (451) to Gregory the Great (590–604): Part Two: The Church of Constantinople in the Sixth Century* (trans. T. Hainthaler, J. Cawte; London: Mowbray, 1995), 438–75, 503–13; R. Sellers, *The Council of Chalcedon: A Historical and Doctrinal Survey* (London: SPCK, 1953), 254–350; H. M. Relton, *A Study in Christology: The Problem of the Relation of the Two Natures in the Person of Christ* (London: SPCK, 1917); T. Ware, *The Orthodox Church* (London: Penguin Books, 1969), 37; J. Pelikan, *The Christian Tradition 2: The Spirit of Eastern Christendom* (Chicago: University of Chicago Press, 1974), 49–61; J. Pelikan, *The Christian Tradition 1: The Emergence of the Catholic Tradition (100–600)* (Chicago: University of Chicago Press, 1971), 277, 337–41; W. Frend, *The Rise of the Monophysite Movement* (Cambridge: Cambridge University Press, 1972); J. Meyendorff, *Christ in Eastern Christian Thought* (Crestwood, New York: St. Vladimir's Seminary Press, 1975).

to digest and assimilate an alien morsel.'[2] As a consequence of Ephesus and Chalcedon, sections of the church went into a schism that still continues. This breakup occurred over whether the Chalcedonian formula, by its stress on the integrity of the two natures and the appropriate attributions to be made to either one, actually left the door open to a Nestorian interpretation that undermined the unity of Christ's person. Many followers of Cyril thought this was exactly what it did do. They were disconcerted that not nearly enough emphasis was laid on Christ's unity and on his personal identity with the eternal, pre-existent Logos. These people, known as *monophysites* (those who held to 'one nature'), took as their lodestar Cyril's phrase 'the one incarnate nature of the Word made flesh'. The resulting schism was to haunt the East in the seventh century, for the areas of monophysite strength were geographically adjacent to Arabia and provided a soft underbelly for the forces of Islam to invade. In many cases, the monophysites were treated better by their Islamic invaders, to whom the niceties of Christian orthodoxy were alien and who regarded all Christians alike, than they had been by the Orthodox Christian Byzantine Empire, to which they were little short of pariahs.

The foundational disagreement between the monophysites and the Chalcedonians surrounded the unity of Christ and the place accorded his human nature. The monophysites insisted on the absolute unity of the person of Christ and his continuity with the pre-incarnate Logos. The Chalcedonians, on the other hand, were fearful of minimizing the humanity of Christ and could never accept that Christ's manhood was merely a 'state' of the Logos. While this was a further time of controversy, it will help to keep it in perspective. For all that we have just said, the Chalcedonians did not regard the monophysites as heretics, and the latter were committed to maintain the central concerns of Chalcedon.[3] For instance, John of Damascus treats them as

---

[2] L. D. Davis, *The First Seven Ecumenical Councils (325–787)* (Collegeville, Minnesota: The Liturgical Press, 1990), 207.

[3] Sellers, *Chalcedon*, 269–71.

simply erring and muddled.[4] In general, they followed Cyril, not the heretic Eutyches.[5]

Severus[6]

Severus, one of the leading and most rigorous of the mono-physites, thought that Chalcedon was weak in its Christology. For him, it took far too inadequate account of the unity of Christ's person. He held that Chalcedon's treatment of the two natures entailed two separate beings. Chalcedon did not emphasize the hypostatic union, he concluded, with the result that it failed to safeguard the identity of the incarnate Christ with the pre-existent Logos. He insisted that, after the union, there is only one countable entity.[7] What Severus wanted was a commitment to the basic premise of Alexandrian–Cyrilline Christology. From within that framework it would be possible to speak of two natures, but not without those safeguards.[8]

Severus held to what today would be called a Christology from above, dominantly so. This is an understanding of who Christ is that begins from the basic premise of his eternal deity and oneness with the Father, rather than from his humanity. John 1:14 – 'the Word became flesh' – was a key text in his arsenal. It taught that the incarnation was an action stemming from God. In Severus' mind, an approach to the person of Christ via the earthly Jesus was gravely suspect. This did not

---

[4] A. Louth, *John Damascene: Tradition and Originality in Byzantine Theology* (Oxford: Oxford University Press, 2002), 172.

[5] Meyendorff, *Christ*, 37.

[6] For Severus, see Grillmeier, *Christ in Christian Tradition*, 2:2, 148–75; V. Samuel, 'The Christology of Severus of Antioch,' *Abba Salama* 4 (1973), 126–90; V. Samuel, 'Further Studies in the Christology of Severus of Antioch,' *Ekklesiastikos Pharos* 58 (1976), 270–301; N. Zabolotsky, 'The Christology of Severus of Antioch,' *Ekklesiastikos Pharos* 58 (1976), 357–86; I. R. Torrance, *Christology After Chalcedon: Severus of Antioch and Sergius the Monophysite* (Norwich: Canterbury Press, 1988).

[7] See Davis, *Councils*, 214–5.

[8] Sellers, *Chalcedon*, 262–4.

mean he was in any way docetic,[9] for he gladly accepted the
reality of Christ's humanity. He was no Apollinarian, for he
clearly believed and taught that Jesus had a human soul.[10] He also
opposed Eutychianism, with its swamping of the humanity by
the divinity. The important point was that he rejected the word
phusis (nature) to describe Christ's humanity. This was more
than anything due to its identification at the time with *hypostasis*
(person), from which talk of two natures in the incarnate Christ
seemed to Severus to imply two persons. As he saw it, only the
Logos is *phusis*.[11] He feared that an excessive stress on Christ's
humanity would lead to its being seen as equally eternal with the
divine being. Severus argued that, since Christ was the eternal
Logos enfleshed, he was originally not a human being. From this,
it is clear that Severus was not, strictly speaking, a monophysite
– *mia phusis*, one nature, was the result of the incarnation, the
one *phusis* being the united divinity and humanity.[12] He did not
deny that Christ had a human nature, but he did not want to use
the word 'nature' to describe it.

In Severus' thought, Jesus Christ is a constant symbiosis of
divinity and humanity. However, the divine has clear priority.
As Davis comments there is for him 'a clear Logos-hegemony in
Christ. The subordinate part is the *sarx* [flesh] of Christ.'[13] Every
activity flows from above, from the Logos, even if the humanity
is involved. This is in obvious contrast to Pope Leo, whose *Tome*
spoke of two activities, deity and humanity. 'Severus finds it
difficult to recognize and appreciate the genuine activity of the
human willing of Christ and to reconcile it with the *mia-physis*
formula.'[14] He was afraid that, in Arian fashion, the Logos might

---

[9] Docetism is the earliest Christological heresy. It claimed that Christ's humanity
was not real but only apparent. It derives its name from the Greek verb *dokein*, to
seem or appear; Christ, according to this thinking, only *seemed* to be human.

[10] Apollinaris taught that the Logos provided the soul of Jesus, so that he did not
have a specifically *human* soul.

[11] Grillmeier, *Christ in Christian Tradition*, 2:2, 152–5; Sellers, *Chalcedon*, 263.

[12] Grillmeier, *Christ in Christian Tradition*, 2:2, 156–8.

[13] Ibid., 163.

[14] Davis, *Councils*, 163–6.

be made a receptive principle. He was also concerned that, as with Nestorius, Christ's humanity be made an autonomous principle of salvation alongside the Logos.[15] In line with Severus' concerns, the Scythian monks drew up a formula intended to smoke out all Nestorians – 'one of the trinity was crucified in the flesh' – an enlargement of Cyril's twelfth anathema.[16]

In opposing Severus, the neo-Chalcedonians appealed to Cyril's *Third Letter to Nestorius* to show that, had he lived, Cyril would not have opposed Chalcedon. From Cyril they showed that flesh is flesh and the Logos is Logos, Godhead is one thing and manhood another, that Cyril opposed a mixture of Godhead and manhood in Jesus Christ. So they argued that Cyril would have agreed with Chalcedon's central claim that Christ is one person in two natures after the union.[17]

Having posed the problem that emerged in the wake of Chalcedon, we must ask now how it was resolved. Here there are three figures who, each in his own way, contributed to the overcoming of this dilemma. The identity of the third of these might seem rather surprising.

Leontius of Byzantium[18]

For Leontius of Byzantium the starting point was not, as with Severus, the eternal Logos but Jesus Christ. This raises the question of whether for him the Christ-subject is a *tertium quid* in addition to the deity and the humanity. The answer to this is definitely no.[19] The point is that he was preoccupied with contrasting nature and hypostasis so as to justify Chalcedon.[20] In contrast to Severus, Leontius started with *ousia* (being). The divinity communicates itself to the humanity and vice-versa, in unmediated reciprocity.

---

[15] Ibid., 169.

[16] Sellers, *Chalcedon*, 305.

[17] Davis, *Councils*, 218; Ibid., 284ff.

[18] Grillmeier, *Christ in Christian Tradition, 2:2*, 181–229; Relton, *A Study in Christology*, 69–83; B. Daley, 'Leontius of Byzantium: A Critical Edition of His Works, with Prolegomena' (D.Phil. dissertation, Oxford University, 1978).

[19] Grillmeier, *Christ in Christian Tradition, 2:2*, 187–8.

[20] Ibid., 192.

However, there is not exactly an even playing field between the divinity and humanity, for this mutual communication occurs from the side of the Logos rather than vice versa.[21]

Leontius shared the Alexandrian stress on Christ's unity but he was also concerned to preserve the true humanity.[22] He came up with the idea of Christ's humanity as *enhypostatos* (existing in a *hypostasis* of another nature). Nature situates a being in a genus, whereas *hypostasis* denotes individuality; a *hypostasis* always has a nature but a nature does not always have a *hypostasis*. Christ's human *hypostasis* subsists in the *hypostasis* of the divine nature. Thus, the human nature in Christ is *enhypostatos* – existing in something, subsisting in a *hypostasis* of another nature. The single *hypostasis* of Christ is the eternal Word in which subsist two natures, divine and human. All operations of both natures are attributed to the *hypostasis* of the divine Word.[23] Grillmeier considers this the work of Leontius of Jerusalem, further developed by Emperor Justinian. Both Relton and Sellers take the older view that Leontius of Byzantium propounded *enhypostasia*.[24] For Leontius of Byzantium, we have translated extracts from *Three Books against the Nestorians and Eutychians* (his chief work).[25]

Leontius of Jerusalem[26]

The other Leontius, whose contribution to this debate occurred between 532 and 536, was emphatic that the one subject in Christ is clearly the *hypostasis* of the Logos. This was, of course, something to which Chalcedon could not have aspired.[27] Grillmeier comments that 'there is thus complete identity of the *prosopon*, of the person, of the subject before and after the

[21] Ibid., 209.

[22] Davis, *Councils*, 221.

[23] Ibid., 234; Meyendorff, *Christ*, 61–8.

[24] Sellers, *Chalcedon*, 308–20, esp 316–19; Relton, *A Study in Christology*, 69–83.

[25] E. R. Hardy, *Christology of the Later Fathers* (The Library of Christian Classics; Philadelphia: Westminster Press, 1954), 375–7.

[26] Grillmeier, *Christ in Christian Tradition*, 2:2, 276–312.

[27] Ibid., 277.

incarnation. The pre-existent *hypostasis* of the Logos himself is the
subject of the incarnation who assumes a human nature, which
neither is nor has its own *prosopon* ... Because the one *hypostasis*
has entered into this entitative relationship with the *prosopon-
less sarx*, it can bear both series of 'physical names,' that is, the
predicates of both divine and human natures.'[28] He continues,
'Thus it follows that the acknowledgement of divinity and
humanity in Christ as *enhypostata* does not mean that they are
idiohypostata, that is, that each constitutes its own proper *hypostasis*.
For Leontius of Jerusalem, Christ is only one *hypostasis* in the
real two natures.'[29] Indeed, he wrote that the Word hypostatized
human nature into his own hypostasis.[30] Leontius of Jerusalem
makes a real contribution insofar as the concept of *enhypostasis*
or insubsistence emerges formally and is used to explain the
unity of the subject in Christ.[31] Moreover, Meyendorff sums up
by explaining Leontius' meaning as 'a hypostasis that, instead of
being another isolated and individualized hypostasis among all
the hypostases that constitute the human nature, is the hypostatic
archetype of the whole of mankind, in whom "recapitulated"
mankind, and not merely an individual, recovers union with
God. This is possible only if Christ's manhood is not the human
nature of a mere man but that of a hypostasis independent of the
limitations of created nature.'[32] In this, Leontius was providing
the foundations for a coherent doctrine of union with Christ
and deification. The assumed humanity of Christ, deified in
and by the Word, becomes the source of divine life, since it is
the Word's own flesh. Because Christ's humanity has divine life
hypostatically, we can – in union with Christ – receive divine
life by grace and participation.[33]

---

[28] Ibid., 279.

[29] Ibid., 285.

[30] Cited in Meyendorff, *Christ*, 74.

[31] Grillmeier, *Christ in Christian Tradition*, 2:2, 289.

[32] Meyendorff, *Christ*, 75.

[33] Ibid., 78–9. *Against Nestorius* 1:49, *PG* 86:1512b. But see comments by
Louth, 160–1.

Justinian I

The third contributor to the resolution of the post-Chalcedon Christological problem was the Emperor Justinian I (483–565, Emperor from 527). In many ways, he is the principal architect of the conclusion of this conflict at Constantinople II. His interest in theology propelled him on to the stage in a big way as a force to be reckoned with theologically as well as politically. He was certainly no mere dilettante. He was a man 'orthodox and deeply pious with a taste for theological discussion'. He intervened forcefully in ecclesiastical matters more than any Emperor before. He recognized that the formula of the Scythian monks 'one of the trinity suffered for us' (designed to smoke out any with Nestorian sympathies) was true to Chalcedon and at the same time likely to win over Cyril's supporters among the monophysites. Moreover, the Pope approved it, effectively providing the backing of the Western church.[34]

Between 532 and 536, Leontius of Jerusalem had insisted on identifying the *hypostasis* of union in the incarnate Christ with the pre-existent *hypostasis* of the Word. As a direct corollary, Christ's manhood had no pre-existence for 'the *hypostasis* of Christ is the Divine Logos, One of the Holy Trinity'.[35] Following this, for Justinian Jesus is the second person of the trinity, who is incarnate.[36] Thus *hypostasis*, not nature, is the foundation of being. This means that there is a personal foundation of reality and it follows that God is primarily love.[37] It also entails that the single *hypostasis* in Christ was the *hypostasis* of *both* the divine *and* human natures. Christ's humanity had no separate *hypostasis* of its own, so as a consequence Christ unites all mankind – not merely a single human being – to the divinity.

---

[34] Davis, *Councils*, 225–9.

[35] K. P. Wesche, *On the Person of Christ: The Christology of Emperor Justinian* (Crestwood, New York: St. Vladimir's Seminary Press, 1991), 12.

[36] Wesche, *The Christology of Justinian*, 31, from Justinian's 'Letter to the monks of Alexandria against the Monophysites.'

[37] Wesche, *The Christology of Justinian*, 13–14.

Justinian established the distinction between *hypostasis* and nature. This clarified Chalcedon (the union of two natures in one *hypostasis*) by identifying the *hypostasis* of Christ as the pre-existent *hypostasis* of the divine Word.[38]

The Edict of Justinian: 'The Edict on the True Faith' (551)

In this Edict, Justinian explained his own view. It also presents the reasoning behind the fifth council's decisions. The Emperor set forth the orthodox doctrine, stating that 'we confess that our Lord Jesus Christ is one and the same Divine Logos of God who was incarnate and became man.'[39] In this he affirms the central point of the Cyrilline Christology and its development along the lines of the two Leontii. He enlarges on this by saying that 'the *hypostatic* union means that the Divine Logos, that is to say one *hypostasis* of the three divine *hypostases*, is not united to a man who has his own *hypostasis* before [the union], but that in the womb of the Holy Virgin the Divine Logos made for himself, in his own *hypostasis*, flesh that was taken from her and that was endowed with a reasonable and intellectual soul, i.e. human nature.'[40]

Justinian argues that Cyril maintained the integrity of the two natures but that he used nature as a synonym for *hypostasis*. Instead, the Emperor clearly distinguishes between the two terms. We cannot talk of Christ having one nature and one hypostasis; instead 'we speak of one *hypostasis* and of a union of two natures' since the Logos of God was united to human nature and not to a particular *hypostasis*. So the one hypostasis of the Logos was incarnate and is recognized in both natures.[41] So 'we never refer to the human nature of Christ by itself, nor did it ever possess its own *hypostasis* or *prosopon*, but it began to exist in the *hypostasis* of the Logos.'[42] On the other hand, those who

---

[38] Davis, *Councils*, 232.
[39] Wesche, *The Christology of Justinian*, 165.
[40] Ibid., 166.
[41] Ibid., 178.
[42] Ibid., 179.

forbid talk of two natures after the union – like Apollinaris and
Eutyches – confuse the issue.[43]

Synthesis is the key to Justinian's Christology, union according to the *hypostasis*.[44]

He says the divine *hypostasis* created this spiritually ensouled
human nature for himself so as to be *hypostasis* for it and to exist
humanly in it as divine *hypostasis*. In contrast to Chalcedon, which
used *hypostasis* to refer to the outcome of the two natures coming
together into one Christ, Justinian used it of the pre-existent Logos.
The assumed human nature thus participates in a *hypostasis* only
by inexisting in the *hypostasis* of the Logos, by virtue of a creative
act of the Logos himself.[45] Grillmeier remarks that Justinian had
'a commendable understanding of the problems of incarnational
theology' and that 'in Justinian we find for the first time the sketch
of a complete interpretation of Christ's person and its union of
divine and human nature in the one divine *hypostasis* of the Logos.'[46]
While he bases his Edict on Chalcedon, he has a stronger grasp of
the union, due to the presence of Cyrilline elements and the model
provided by Leontius of Jerusalem.

Justinian shared with the monophysites the principle that Jesus
Christ is the divine Logos. The main problem was that the monophysites used nature as a synonym for *hypostasis* when talking of the
particular but used nature as a synonym for essence (being) when
talking of the universal. Justinian's achievement was to distinguish
nature and hypostasis according to the trinitarian distinction of the
Cappadocians. Hypostasis refers to the one Logos who becomes
man and nature to the mystery that he became fully man.[47]

The Second Council of Constantinople
Justinian called the Council, explaining its purpose in a letter
read at its first session as 'to unite the churches again, and to

---

[43] Ibid., 180.

[44] Grillmeier, *Christ in Christian Tradition*, 2:2, 435–6.

[45] Ibid., 436–7.

[46] Ibid., 438.

[47] Wesche, *The Christology of Justinian*, 19–20.

bring the Synod of Chalcedon, together with the three earlier, to universal acceptance.'[48] Most of its time was taken up with the condemnation of 'the three chapters,' teachings of Theodore of Mopsuestia, Theodoret of Cyrus, and Ibas, all with a strongly Nestorian ring to them. The Council then confessed the faith and Creed of Nicaea, and its explanations and the further defini- tions of Constantinople, Ephesus, and Chalcedon.[49] A series of anathemas stressed the unity of Christ, and another series defended the distinction (but not separation or division) of the natures. All heretics of the previous three hundred years were condemned. Fifteen anathemas were issued against the Origen- ists, although no one is sure how these anathemas got to be assoc- iated with this council and it has been strenuously debated as to whether these are actually doctrines of Origen. Sellers argues that the condemned Christological doctrines seem to be from Evagrius of Pontus (346–399), not Origen.[50]

Opposition to the Council was strong and widespread in the West, for Origen was more accepted there than in the East. Various Popes including Gregory the Great (590–604) accepted the Council with but a few reservations, and Constantinople III affirmed it as ecumenical.[51]

Grillmeier bemoans the fact that the twenty-eight paragraphs of the *Sententia Synodica* contain 'hardly one positive dogmatic explanation.'[52] Interest lies mainly in the Canons appended to the *Sententia Synodica*. Canon I distinguishes *phusis* from *ousia*, and *hypostasis* from *prosōpon*, in line with Justinian. Canon II ascribes two births to the God-Logos, the one from eternity from the Father, without time and without body, and the other his being made flesh of the holy and glorious Mary, Mother of God. The next

---

[48] H. R. Percival, *The Seven Ecumenical Councils of the Undivided Church: Their Canons and Dogmatic Decrees* (A Select Library of Nicene and Post-Nicene Fathers of the Christian Church: second series; Edinburgh: T.&T. Clark, 1997 reprint), 302.

[49] Ibid., 307–10; Davis, *Councils*, 241–3; Sellers, *Chalcedon*, 329.

[50] Davis, *Councils*, 244–6; Sellers, *Chalcedon*, 330; Hardy, *Later Fathers*, 378–81.

[51] Davis, *Councils*, 253.

[52] Grillmeier, *Christ in Christian Tradition, 2:2*, 444.

three Canons are all strongly anti-Nestorian. Canon III says that the God-Logos who works miracles and the Christ who suffered should not be separated, for it is one and the same Jesus Christ our Lord, the Word, who became flesh and a human being.[53] Canon IV rejects the notion of an accidental and not substantial unity of Christ as in the classic interpretation of Antiochene Christology. Behind this is the fact that Christ's unity is a true union, not a mingling or division. Canon V asserts that there is only one subsistence or person. The incarnation is to be seen solely from the hypostasis of the Son who is one of the trinity. Thus 'one of the trinity has been made man.' Canon VIII, on the other hand, guards against monophysitism, pronouncing that both natures remain what they were. In other words, the *mia-phusis* formula is not granted equal rights with the Chalcedonian Definition's insistence on the integrity of both natures in the union, nor is it regarded as a necessary interpretation of the Definition. 'For in teaching that the only-begotten Word was united hypostatically [to humanity] we do not mean to say that there was made a mutual confusion of natures, but rather each [nature] remaining what it was, we understand that the Word was united to flesh.'[54] Canon IX declares that the worshipping of Christ in two natures is in fact one act of worship directed to the incarnate God-Logos with his flesh. Canons XI–XIV condemn the three chapters – Theodore of Mopsuestia, Theodoret of Cyrus, and Ibas.[55] Grillmeier concludes that Constantinople II is 'not a weakening of Chalcedonian terminology, but its logical clarification.... Nevertheless the use and application of the main concepts were clearer and more unambiguous than at Chalcedon.'[56] The Council was overshadowed by the controversy over the three chapters and posthumous condemnations. On the positive side the most valuable contribution was by the Emperor Justinian.[57]

---

[53] Ibid., 446; Percival, *Seven Ecumenical Councils*, 312.

[54] Percival, *Seven Ecumenical Councils*, 313.

[55] Ibid., 314–16; Grillmeier, *Christ in Christian Tradition*, 2:2, 447–53.

[56] Grillmeier, *Christ in Christian Tradition*, 2:2, 456.

[57] Grillmeier, *Christ in Christian Tradition*, 2:2, 461. For an evaluation of the Council, see Sellers, *Chalcedon*, 331–45.

Constantinople III 680–681[58]

Monotheletism

The repercussions of the Christological debates had not entirely died down. Under Emperor Heraclius I (610–41), the Empire recovered after a time on its knees. Greek replaced Latin as the official administrative language. The educated elites of East and West now spoke and read different languages and increasingly only one of them.[59] The impact on the church and theological discussion was to become ever more clear. The interests of the Eastern and the Western churches diverged. There was still sufficient contact for there to be two further ecumenical councils but the West's contribution was to wither.

That the declarations of Constantinople II did not stifle the debate on Christ's humanity is evident by the issue of whether he had two wills or only one. Theodore of Pharan argued that there was in the incarnate Christ only one energy and one will, that of the Word. 'The Incarnate Word was thus the agent and subject of all action, whether this was appropriate to his divine or human nature.'[60] The Syrians accepted monoenergism (the claim that Christ had only one energy) and later monotheletism (the teaching that Christ had only one will). This, again, was an extreme version of the Alexandrian stress on the oneness of Christ's person. All action was attributed to the person of Christ, not the natures. It seemed to be a belated triumph and vindication of the monophysites.[61]

However, Sophronius of Jerusalem, in opposition, insisted that action springs from the natures. He convened the Home Synod of Constantinople which ruled that though all actions are those of the one agent, there should be no numbering of activities. Later, at a synod in Jerusalem in 634, the doctrine of two wills or operations was defined. According to this declara-

---

[58] Pelikan, *The Christian Tradition 2*, 62–90; Meyendorff, *Christ*; Davis, *Councils*, 260–89.

[59] Davis, *Councils*, 258–60.

[60] Ibid., 261.

[61] Ibid., 262–3.

tion, either nature works what is proper to itself. But Sophronius insisted that while there are two operations there is only
one agent; this statement was limited to a rebuttal of monoenergism. Nowhere does Sophronius speak of two wills in Christ.
As yet, the question of wills had not surfaced. It was in 636 that
Sergius (Bishop of Constantinople), a monoenergist, issued an
edict, the Ecthesis, (signed by Pope Honorius in 638), to the effect that there is one Christ who works both divine and human
effects, with one will. This moved discussion to the question of
the single will. According to Sergius the human nature is merely
a docile instrument with no initiative of its own.[62]

At this point, a dramatic force explosively transformed the
scene. In 638, the Muslims invaded. Damascus had already fallen
in 634. But to prove this was no isolated or localized accident, in
638 both Antioch and Jerusalem, bastions of the Eastern church,
capitulated to the Arab hordes, to be followed in lightning
succession by Caesarea in Palestine, in the following year, and
in 642 by Alexandria and Persia. Since the Muslims treated all
Christians equally, there was no longer any pressure on Christian
heretics to conform to a prescribed standard of orthodoxy. At
once monophysitism, rejected by Constantinople II but now
freed from the restraints of the Byzantine Empire, spread from
Syria into Persia and Mesopotamia, while the monophysite
church in Armenia remained staunchly so. The Nestorians
remained strong in Persia and engaged in missionary activity
beyond its borders, reaching China, central Asia and south
India. Orthodoxy shrank to the Byzantine lands, Greek in
language, under the Patriarch of Constantinople. Many Greek
monks fled to the West, including most notably Maximus the
Confessor who had already moved to Carthage in 628. The
territory under the Eastern church's jurisdiction, operating
within the boundaries laid down by the ecumenical councils,
contracted greatly.[63]

[62] Ibid., 264–8.
[63] Ibid., 269–71.

For Maximus, the incarnation is the central factor in deification. Christ is the meeting point of God's reaching down to man, and of man's God-given tendency towards the divine. If the natures of Christ are two, Maximus concluded that the operations of those natures must be two. Consequently, Christ has two natures, operations, and wills. His wills proceed from the divine and human natures, but always act in harmony because the single divine person assures their goodness of choice.[64]

In 649 Pope Martin I called a council at the Lateran Palace (his official residence) in Rome, with Maximus present, which adopted a clear dyothelite position (the idea that in Christ there are two wills), in harmony with Maximus' teaching. However, he – the Pope – was later captured by the forces of the Emperor, fiercely monothelite, taken to Constantinople, degraded from office amid the insults of the mob, and exiled. He died shortly afterwards in 655. Later Maximus himself was captured, taken to Constantinople, mutilated by having his tongue and right hand cut out, and exiled to the Caucasus, where he died in 662.[65]

The Council

Eventually with a new Emperor and Patriarch, the situation changed. The Emperor Constantine IV summoned a council to meet at Constantinople in 680. The Pope's reply affirmed Rome's unswerving fidelity to the apostolic teaching and its confession of two natures of Christ and two wills. The Papal legates arrived in Constantinople on 10 September 680. They convinced George of Constantinople of the dyothelite position by a range of patristic citations. The single most crucial element in this was a pellucid[66] letter from Pope Agatho to Emperor Constantine read at the fourth session on 15 November. In it he affirmed the following:

---

[64] Ibid., 272–3; Maximus the Confessor, *On the Cosmic Mystery of Jesus Christ: Selected Writings from St. Maximus the Confessor* (P. M. Blowers; Crestwood, New York: St. Vladimir's University Press, 2003), 173–6.

[65] Davis, *Councils*, 275–8.

[66] clear, transparent

this then is the status [and regular tradition] of our evangelical
and apostolic faith, to wit, that as we confess the holy and inseparable Trinity, that is, the Father, the Son, and the Holy Ghost
to be of one deity, of one nature and substance or essence, so
we will profess also that it has one natural, will, power, operation, domination, majesty, potency, and glory. And whatever
is said of the same holy Trinity essentially in singular number
we understand to refer to the one nature of the three consubstantial persons, having been so taught by canonical logic. But
when we make a confession concerning one of the same three
persons of that Holy Trinity, of the Son of God, or of God the
Word, and of the mystery of his adorable dispensation according to the flesh, we assert that all things are double in the one
and the same our Lord and Saviour Jesus Christ according to
the evangelical tradition, that is to say, we confess his two natures, to wit, the divine and the human, of which and in which
he, even after the wonderful and inseparable union, subsists.
And we confess that each of his natures has its own natural propriety, and that the divine has all things that are divine, without
any sin. And we recognize that each one (of the two natures)
of the one and the same incarnated, that is, humanated (*hu-
manati*) Word of God is in him unconfusedly, inseparably and
unchangeably, intelligence alone discerning a unity, to avoid
the error of confusion. For we equally detest the blasphemy of
division and of commixture. For when we confess two natures
and two natural wills, and two natural operations in our one
Lord Jesus Christ, we do not assert that they are contrary or
opposed one to the other ... nor as though separated ... in two
persons or subsistences, but we say that as the same our Lord
Jesus Christ has two natures so also he has two natural wills and
operations, to wit, the divine and the human: the divine will
and operation he has in common with the coessential Father
from all eternity: the human, he has received from us, taken
with our nature in time. This is the apostolic and evangelical
tradition ... This is the pure expression of piety. This is the true
and immaculate profession of the Christian religion, not in-
vented by human cunning, but which was taught by the Holy
Ghost through the princes of the apostles.[67]

---

[67] Percival, *Seven Ecumenical Councils*, 330–1.

Agatho bases much on Jesus' prayer to the Father in Gethsemane, where he says 'not my will, but yours be done.' Here he sees the distinctness of the human will of Jesus from his divine will but is equally quick to point out that the two act in perfect harmony. He is unequivocal that the monothelites have introduced a novelty, and that he is affirming 'the living tradition of the apostles of Christ, which his church holds everywhere.'

The Council declared the synodal letters of the dyothelite Sophronius orthodox. At the seventeenth session on 16 September 681, the Council adopted a definition, signed by 174 bishops. This accepted the decisions of the five ecumenical councils and adopted the creeds of Nicaea and Constantinople I. The council was conscious simply of repeating the faith handed down from the apostles; the monothelites had introduced the novelty. All Patriarchs of Constantinople from 610 to 666 were anathematized, as was Pope Honorius (d. 638) and Theodore of Pharan.[68] The definition produced by the Council, clearly borrowing language from Agatho, specified that in Christ there are 'two natural wills and two natural operations, indivisibly, incontrovertibly, inseparably, inconfusedly.' These two wills 'are not contrary the one to the other ... but the human will follows ... as subject to his divine and omnipotent will.'[69] With similar language, the council affirmed two natural operations in the one Lord Jesus Christ, divine and human. As Sellers points out, 'For as his most holy and immaculate animated soul was not destroyed because it was deified, but continued in its own measure and order ... so also his human will, though deified, was not suppressed but rather preserved.'[70] So close was the harmony in which the natures acted together that the human will 'willed of its own free will those things which the divine will willed it to will.'[71] This was not a parallelism, in which the two wills

---

[68] Davis, *Councils*, 279–82.

[69] Ibid., 283; Percival, *Seven Ecumenical Councils*, 345.

[70] Sellers, *Chalcedon*, 346.

[71] John of Damascus, *On the Orthodox Faith*, 3:18.

willed separately but in agreement. Rather, it was a synthesis, concurring into the one *prosopon* of Jesus Christ.[72]

Ultimately, monotheletism was defeated for much the same reasons as monophysitism. To deny the existence of a human will, it was concluded, was to adopt a truncated view of Christ's humanity. The lack of a human will would raise huge questions over the reality of whether Christ was truly human, and consequently over the gospel itself. Thus, the will is a predicate of the nature and, since Christ has two natures, he also has two wills. However, since his two natures are not separate but in union, so his two wills will in harmony and synthesis. Hence, although the monothelites accepted Chalcedon, while the monophysites did not, John of Damascus was to treat them more sternly, since their error struck more closely at the heart of Christ's humanity and so of salvation itself.[73] The ecumenical nature of the decision is seen in that Pope Leo II approved the Definition, had it translated into Latin and distributed it to all bishops in the West.[74] Eleven years after the council, the Quinisext Council in Trullo carried forward the work of the fifth and sixth ecumenical councils by passing some disciplinary canons, and is held to share Constantinople III's ecumenical status.

What these Christological debates show us is that, in the words of Meyendorff, 'Ephesus, Chalcedon and the two Byzantine councils (553 and 681) *together* represent the great Byzantine Christological synthesis: the later developments of Orthodox theology must be approached in the light of this synthesis.'[75]

Nicaea II 787[76]

Iconoclasts and iconodules

A further controversy, a long and bitter one, erupted in the early eighth century. It concerned the legitimacy of icons. However, the real issue was again Christological. Emperor Leo III began his

---

[72] Sellers, *Chalcedon*, 346.

[73] Louth, *John Damascene*, 172.

[74] Davis, *Councils*, 284.

[75] Meyendorff, *Christ*, 14.

attack on icons in 726, and it was not until 780 that the Empress
Irene suspended the persecution of the iconophiles (the supporters
of icons). Irene summoned a Council to Nicaea in 787, which
upheld her iconophile decree. Later, in 815, a new attack on icons
was launched by Leo V the Armenian, until in 843 the Empress
Theodosia ended it, an action that continues to be celebrated as
a feast day called The Triumph of Orthodoxy. John of Damascus
was the chief defender of icons. Since John was living in Islamic-
controlled territory, and had been an employee of the government,
this was 'not the last time that Islam acted unintentionally as the
protector of Orthodoxy'.[77] However, Louth points out that John's
defence of icons played little part in the controversy, since he was
living outside the Byzantine Empire, within which the possession
of his books would have been a capital offence due to the dominance
of the iconoclasts and his condemnation by the iconoclast Synod
of Hiereia in 754. Moreover, travel and communication at the time
were difficult, slowing the transmission of ideas from Islamic lands
to the Empire.[78]

After Justinian I, attitudes to images had begun to change.
Hitherto they were regarded as teaching aids. Now, however,
increasingly they were believed to possess links to the spiritual
world, offering aid and protection. Images, formerly seen on
the walls of churches, increasingly were to be found in private
homes. In particular, icons depicting Christ and the saints became
objects of private devotion. At the same time, the church began
actively to promote icons. The Quinisext Council of 692 decreed
that Christ was not to be depicted as a lamb but in human form
'so that we may perceive through it the depth of the humiliation
of God.'[79] Here is a combination of an icon as a teaching aid and
an icon as a means to perceive realities depicted by it, as a means
through which we are enabled to penetrate beyond.[80]

---

[76] Ibid.; Davis, *Councils*, 290–322; Pelikan, *The Christian Tradition 2*, 91–132.

[77] Ware, *Orthodox Church*, 39.

[78] Louth, *John Damascene*, 197–8.

[79] Davis, *Councils*, 293–4; Percival, *Seven Ecumenical Councils*, 401.

[80] See E. Kitzinger, 'The Cult of Images in the Age Before Iconoclasm,' *Dumbarton Oaks Papers* 7 (1954), 83–150.

A considered justification of images was made by Leontius of Neapolis, who saw images of Christ as an extension, a re-enactment, of the incarnation.[81] Battle began in 726, when Emperor Leo ordered the destruction of the image of Christ over the doors of the Imperial palace; a riot ensued. The Pope reacted vehemently against this development – a huge rift was created between the Pope and the Emperor.[82]

From 726 to 730 John of Damascus emerged as the most influential spokesman for images, as the chief iconophile theologian.[83] At the heart of his apology was a Christological argument. He carefully distinguishes between adoration – due to God alone – and veneration in its various degrees. If an image of the invisible God were made, it would be a serious error. However, an image of the incarnate God is no such error, for Christ assumed human flesh. For John 'appeal to the Incarnation in defence of icons is something more developed ... than in his predecessors or contemporaries.'[84] Angels can also be pictured since they are not simple beings but are finite and limited to space. Christians do not live under the Old Testament, which prohibited images, but under the new age of grace. Man himself is the image of God. For John, to argue that images are impermissible is to fall into Manichaeism, as if matter were evil. Yet adoration must be given only to God, while veneration is given to persons of great dignity. Sacred images are means of instruction in the faith, memorials of Christian lives, incitements to lead a good life. They are channels of grace – they have sacramental power. For John the whole world is iconic.[85]

After 740 the new Emperor Constantine V outlined the case for iconoclasm. If an image pictures only Christ's human nature it severs his humanity from his person. If the attempt is to portray Christ according to both natures, the deity is

[81] Davis, *Councils*, 295.
[82] Ibid., 297–8.
[83] Louth, *John Damascene*, 193–222.
[84] Ibid., 218.
[85] Ibid., 213–19; Davis, *Councils*, 298–9.

circumscribed and brought down to the level of humanity. Therefore Christ cannot be pictured. The only real image of Christ is the one he gave us, the eucharist. He called a Council, at Hiereia, near Chalcedon, in 754, which condemned images as blaspheming the incarnation and contrary to the six ecumenical councils. Images fell into the heresy of either Nestorianism or Eutychianism.[86] The controversy aroused violent passions. Monks died under the lash in the public circus, a leading monk was torn to pieces by a mob, the Patriarch Constantine of Constantinople – although an iconoclast himself – was publicly beheaded, monks had their nostrils slit.[87] The conflict forced the Papacy to ally itself with the Franks, rather than the East, for the dominant iconoclasm was alien to the West. Questions have been raised as to whether the iconoclasts were influenced by Islam. The Islamic revulsion against images may well have encouraged this movement. Some have suggested that it was an Asiatic protest against the Greeks.[88] However, both of these suggestions ignore the obvious theological and Christological case made by the council in 754.

The council

In 780 the Empress Irene came to *de facto* power and called a general Council, with the agreement of Pope Hadrian. The Council opened on 24 September, 787. It accepted the previous six ecumenical Councils. It also decreed that the images were to be restored. This it justified on the grounds that images showed that the incarnation was real and not fantastic. Images were to be given 'due salutation and honourable reverence, not indeed that true worship of faith which pertains only to the divine nature ... for the honour which is paid to the image passes on to that which the image represents, and he who reveres the image reveres in it the subject represented.'[89] In keeping with

---

[86] Percival, *Seven Ecumenical Councils*, 545–6.

[87] Davis, *Councils*, 301–5.

[88] Ware, *Orthodox Church*, 38–9.

[89] Davis, *Councils*, 306–10; Percival, *Seven Ecumenical Councils*, 550.

this edict, the Council anathematized those who equated images with idols.

The Council also passed twenty-two canons. Ecclesiastical appointments made by princes are invalid. Clear requirements were laid down for bishops: they must know the Psalter by heart, read the canons and Scriptures, and live according to the commandments of God. Simony should cease. Bishops who consecrate churches without relics are to be deposed. A non-ordained person must not read from the pulpit.[90]

Sequel in East and West
The most immediate effect of the seventh ecumenical Council was to arouse intense opposition from the newly powerful Kingdom of the Franks. Charlemagne had Theodulf draw up the *Libri Carolini*, which argues that only God can be adored. The principle that veneration can be given to the image because of its relationship to the original is false and misleads simple people into venerating the image itself, Theodulf pointed out. The book also attacked the ecumenical claims of Nicaea II, since the Franks, now the dominant force in the West, were not represented. The *Libri Carolini* rejected both the iconoclast council of 754 and the iconophile Nicaea II. The Empress Irene as a woman had no right to teach men or to call a council. However, there are many foundational errors in these books, not least a failure to appreciate the iconophile distinction between *latreia* (worship, adoration), owed only to the holy trinity, and *proskunesis* (veneration), directed towards images. In this, Latin had but one word to translate both terms, *adoratio*, which in untutored minds immediately conjured up the idea of idolatrous worship.[91] On the other hand, a Western ally of Nicaea II was the Pope.[92] A rift now existed in the West, only resolved by the continued political dominance of Charles and future Popes' dependence on him.

---

[90] Davis, *Councils*, 310–11.

[91] See Percival, *Seven Ecumenical Councils*, 532–38.

[92] Davis, *Councils*, 312–13.

When Pope Leo III crowned Charles Roman Emperor on Christmas Day, 800, relations between East and West deteriorated further. There were now two hostile Christian empires. Constantinople, digging in its heels, refused to recognize Charles as Roman Emperor until in 812 he seized the Byzantine city of Venice.[93] Later conflicts over images were ended in 843 when the Patriarch Methodius declared sacred images lawful and condemned iconoclasm. The First Sunday of Lent was declared the Feast of Orthodoxy.

We shall discuss the question of icons critically from both Biblical and theological perspectives in chapter 6. For now we simply report the findings of Nicaea II, the one ecumenical council with which conservative Protestants might find some difficulty.

The Council the Eastern church missed
The East is deeply shaped by these Councils. Insofar as Eastern Christianity has a doctrinal foundation these seven ecumenical Councils provide it. That is why we have begun with such a concentration on them, the conflicts that brought them about, and the consequences they had. However, there is one important Western council that impinged little on Eastern Christianity, in consequence of which the two branches of the church began to drift in different directions. In 418 a Council of Carthage rejected Pelagianism. Pelagius, a British layman who lived in Rome and moved in prominent circles there, called for dedicated Christian living, supported the monastic movement, and stressed human freedom. He was understood by his opponents to minimize the need for the grace of God since he argued that sinful man had the freedom to do what is right and to respond of himself to the Christian message. After the Council's condemning verdict Pelagius went into exile, probably in Egypt. Augustine wrote many of his later works against the Pelagians, especially Julian of Eclanum.[94] The controversy concerned the respective roles of

---

[93] Ibid., 313.

[94] P. Brown, *Augustine of Hippo: A Biography* (London: Faber and Faber, 1967), 340–407; G. Bonner, *St. Augustine of Hippo: Life and Controversies* (Norwich:

God's grace and human freedom, the effects of sin – Pelagius and
Julian opposed Augustine's doctrines of original sin – and the
nature of salvation, with Augustine's doctrine of predestination
also strongly attacked.[95] Canon IV of the Council of Ephesus
(431) orders deposition for any of the clergy who consent to
Celestine, presumably a reference to Celestius, who shared
Pelagius' views. In this the Eastern church formally aligned
itself with the Council of Carthage. However, the reference to
this heresy is almost incidental.[96]

This highlights questions that concerned the West but
bypassed the East – questions of sin and grace, free will and
predestination. In time, these fed into matters relating to law
and gospel, atonement and justification. The East found these of
lesser interest, since they had not been a cause of trouble and so
did not need addressing. Moreover, the East had a strong stress
on free will and the co-operation of fallen man in salvation;
synergism is characteristic of the Eastern view of salvation. This
goes all the way back to these early days, no doubt facilitated by
the fact that a controversy of this nature did not emerge in the
East. Chrysostom, for one, is clear on the point.[97] So too, well
over three centuries later, is John of Damascus.[98]

The West, partly due to the impact of Rome, had a more
practical bent. Even in the matters at stake in the ecumenical

---

Canterbury Press, 1986), 312–93; S. Lancel, *Saint Augustine* (A. Nevill; London:
SCM Press, 2002), 323–46, 413–38.

[95] P. Brown, 'Pelagius and His Supporters: Aims and Environment,' *JTS* 21
(1970), 56–72; G. Bonner, 'How Pelagian Was Pelagius?' *StPatr* 9 (1966), 350–8;
F. Refoulé, 'Julien d'Éclane: Théologien et Philosophe,' *RechScRel* 52 (1964), 42–
84, 233–47; J. Ferguson, *Pelagius: A Historical and Theological Study* (Cambridge:
Cambridge University Press, 1956); G. Bonner, *Augustine and Recent Research on
Pelagius* (Villanova: Villanova University Press, 1972).

[96] Percival, *Seven Ecumenical Councils*, 229.

[97] See, *inter alia*, Chrysostom, Homily III on The Epistle to the Romans in
NPNF[1], 11:355, 11:365. See also Homily VIII on Philippians (2:12ff), in NPNF[1],
13:220; Homily IX on Thessalonians (1 Thess. 5:6-8) in NPNF[1], 13:362; Homily
XII on Hebrews (Heb. 7:8), in NPNF[1], 14:425.

[98] John of Damascus, *On the Orthodox Faith*, 2:25-30, in NPNF[2], 9:2:39-44;
and ibid., 3:14; in NPNF[2], 9:2:58-59; ibid., 2:30, NPNF[2] 9:2:42, 43.

Councils, a considerable difference of outlook between the Latins and the Greeks is clear. The Greeks were more speculative, intellectually brilliant and versatile. The Western contributors, such as Pope Leo I, were more pastoral, less creative. Rome held tenaciously to the central points, the East seemed to come up with a successive array of brilliant but speculative heresies that needed answering. We shall see in chapter 9 that the great divide over the *filioque* arose from different ways of understanding the trinity. These are early hints at significant differences of outlook and interest that later would move from seed form to full flower.

4

Fathers of the Church

Athanasius (c295–373)

Alexandria was a cosmopolitan city, at the centre of both ideas and commerce, in a strategic position on major trade routes between Rome, Africa and Asia. The Jewish scholar Philo (c.20 BC–c.AD 50) and the Christian theologian Origen (c.185–c.254) had been based there. It was the religious capital of Egypt, the bishop appointing all other Egyptian bishops and with absolute authority over them. According to Pettersen,[1] by AD 300 approximately 50% of the Egyptian population was Christian. In Athanasius' day, a dispute lingered over those who lapsed during the Diocletianic persecution. Melitius, a rigorist, had not wanted them back. Monks in Upper Egypt had withdrawn from church life. Inland, the Coptic church, more simple and rigorist, contrasted to the Greek-speaking church in the coastal area.

Athanasius had a restricted formal education but his life was full of action and intrigue. Appointed a deacon, he accompanied Bishop Alexander to Nicaea in 325, where Arius was condemned.

---

[1] A. Pettersen, *Athanasius* (London: Geoffrey Chapman, 1995), 5.

Elected bishop in 328 on Alexander's death, his authority was soon challenged by the Melitian clergy who Melitius ordained on his own authority to replace the lapsed ones. Melitian groups were also adamant against receiving Arius back.

By 332, Arius persuaded Emperor Constantine of his orthodoxy but, contrary to imperial orders, Athanasius refused to restore him. Nor did he follow Nicaea's requirement to reconcile with the Melitians. In 334 charges were brought against him: that (1) he raised a tax on linen garments – a right belonging to the pagan priesthood, (2) his presbyter Macarius had desecrated a Melitian church and broken a chalice, (3) he had organized the kidnap and murder of a Melitian bishop and used his severed hand for magical purposes. On the last charge, Athanasius' supporters produced the bishop alive and well, hand intact, but the others were more difficult to refute. Constantine summoned a council, but Athanasius refused to attend, not expecting an impartial hearing. He was present at the Council of Tyre in 335 but, since it was stacked against him, he left for Constantinople, and was deposed on disciplinary grounds. Then new charges were filed – he had delayed the vital corn shipments to Constantinople, it was alleged. He was exiled from 335 to 337 but not replaced.

In 337 Constantine died and the Empire split. Constantine II recalled Athanasius and he returned in November. Opposition at fever pitch, and accused of embezzling corn, the Council of Antioch deposed him early in 339. He withdrew in March to Rome, where he had more support, especially from Pope Julius. This second exile lasted seven years.

In 341 a Council at Rome cleared him of all charges and admitted him into communion as a lawful bishop. Rival theories of church authority were competing with one another. Rival councils sprang up in both east and west. Eventually after his replacement in Alexandria died, the Emperor Constans (his supporter) persuaded his brother Constantius II to be reconciled to him and so, to a hero's welcome, he returned again in October 346.

Nevertheless, from 350 the situation took another down-turn. Constans was assassinated in 350 and by 359 Constantius was the sole emperor, with semi-Arians and Arians in the ascendancy supporting him. By then, he had turned against Athanasius. On the night 7/8 February 356, troops surrounded Athanasius' church during a service and entered the building. Athanasius managed to escape by another exit. He fled to the monks of Upper Egypt, to be replaced by a pork salesman, George of Cappadocia. This third exile lasted until 362.

George provoked opposition by favoring the Arians and was forced to withdraw in 358. However, Julian (known as 'the apostate' as he favored paganism) became emperor in 361, and George returned to Alexandria, only to be murdered by the mob. Julian recalled Athanasius in February 362, only for him to flee to the desert again in October!

The next year, Julian died, to be replaced by Jovian, who recalled Athanasius. But Jovian himself died early in 364 and was succeeded by Valentinian, a supporter of Nicaea but who appointed his brother Valens (an Arian) in control of the east. Valens tried to force Arian creeds on the eastern bishops. A fifth exile ensued for Athanasius from October 365 to February 366. In February 366 Valens rescinded his edict and Athanasius returned. The last seven years of his life were comparatively uneventful. Of his forty-six years as a bishop, seventeen were in exile.

Writings
(1) Dogmatic and apologetic – *Oratio contra Gentes* and *De incarnatione*, possibly originally a two-volume work; and anti-Arian works, *Orationes contra Arianos*, three extended discourses – a fourth is by someone else. Another work *De incarnatione et contra Arianos* is not to be confused with the two earlier mentioned works of similar name.

(2) Spurious – there are many documents claiming to be by Athanasius that are not genuine, including two volumes written against the Apollinarians, and the famous Athanasian creed.

(3) Polemical – *Apologia contra Arianos*; and a history of the Arians.

(4) Sermons – most purporting to be by Athanasius are known to be spurious.

(5) Commentaries (fragments) on the interpretation of the Psalms, on the Psalms, on Ecclesiastes and the Song of Solomon, and a few isolated fragments on Genesis.

(6) Ascetic treatises – notably a life of St. Anthony, and one on virginity.

(7) Letters – (i) Festal letters, written to his diocese each Easter; of note is no. 39 (367) on the Biblical canon, a list identical with Codex Vaticanus, with the deutero-canonical literature (the apocrypha) considered useful for the edification of new converts but not part of the canon; (ii) Synodical letters including *Ad Antiochenos*; (iii) Encyclical letters; (iv) Dogmatic and pastoral letters, including *Ad Serapionem* on the Holy Spirit, and *Ad Epictetum* concerning the relation between the historical Christ and the eternal Son.

Thought

Incarnation

In *De incarnatione*, a masterpiece written sometime before 340, Athanasius unfolds the purpose, necessity, and truth of the incarnation. A number of features are prominent. First is the close link between creation and redemption (1:14). Salvation in Christ is equivalent to the renewal of creation. This is a striking difference from conservative Protestantism, where the focus has been the deliverance of the individual from sin and corporate elements are often restricted to the church.

Athanasius develops this in a number of ways. He has *a trinitarian view of creation and providence,* in which the Word, Jesus Christ our Lord, was the agent in making all things out of nothing (3, cf. 5, 11-12). Athanasius brings together creation, providence, the trinity, man, Christ, and salvation into an integrated whole in the first few pages!

That, of course, was not the whole story, for sin entered and death gained a legal hold over us that is impossible to evade (6). We could not regain the former position by repentance alone, for that is insufficient to guard the just claim of God (7). The incarnation of the Word was needed, the same Word who made all things out of nothing. Again, salvation is the recreation of everything.

He explains the purpose of the incarnation (8). The Word (Christ) was not far from us before; he has filled all things everywhere, remaining present with his own Father. In his incarnation, he takes to himself a body just like ours. Because we all were under the penalty of corruption and death he gave his body over to death in place of all, and offered it to the Father so that, since all died in him, the law involving our ruin might be undone and that, secondly, he might turn men to incorruption, and quicken them from death by the appropriation of his body and by the grace of the resurrection. Since it was impossible for the Word *qua* Word to suffer death, he takes to himself a body capable of death. So, by offering to death the body he had taken, he put away death from us all by the offering of an equivalent. He satisfied the debt by his death and, united with all people by nature, clothed all with incorruption by the promise of his resurrection (9).

The incarnate Christ was not circumscribed in the body, nor while present in the body was he absent elsewhere, nor while he moved the body was the universe left void of his working and providence but, Word as he was, so far from being contained by anything, he rather contained all things himself. Thus, even while present in a human body and himself quickening it, he was quickening the universe as well. He was in every process of nature, and simultaneously outside the whole. He was not bound to his body but himself wielded it so he was not only in it but also in everything and, while external to the universe, abode in his Father only (17). This is the Catholic teaching that the person of the incarnate Christ was and is not confined to the humanity he had assumed but remains transcendent. Later, in post-Reformation disputes Lutherans were to call it the *extra-Calvinisticum*.

The deity of Christ

This is the issue for which Athanasius is most noted. He was at the forefront in the battle against Arianism. Arius argued that the Son was not co-eternal with the Father and was lesser in being and status. He was the first of God's creatures, brought forth out of nothing and not of the same being as the Father. This provided a simple, rational answer to complex questions. Yet it attacked the whole of salvation, for Jesus could not be the true revelation of God if he was merely a creature, nor could he accomplish salvation for the human race. The Council of Nicaea maintained that the Son was of the same being as the Father. Athanasius' *Orationes contra Arianos* contain his most rigorous defence of Nicene theology. He marshals a range of theological and biblical arguments against the 'Ariomaniacs', as he calls them. Additionally, the first two of his letters to Serapion stress this essential point.

Exchange in the incarnation – and deification

Protestants are accustomed to think of an exchange occurring at the cross where Christ took our sins and we receive his righteousness. For Athanasius, an exchange of a different – although related – kind took place in the incarnation. In becoming man, Christ received and assumed what is ours and, in doing so, sanctified it, making it fit for fellowship with God. In turn, he imparted to humanity the grace of being partakers of the divine nature. This exchange in the incarnation is the basis for Athanasius' teaching on deification (*theosis*). The Word was made man that we might be made God (54). At the back of this lies New Testament teaching such as 2 Peter 1:4 and much in the writings of John. Athanasius no more means that we cease to be human and become God ontologically than he implies that the Word ceased to be God and changed into man. Rather, the idea is that of union and communion, just as the deity and humanity in Christ remain such but are in unbreakable personal union. Thus in *Orationes contra Arianos*, 2.70. Similarly he comments in Letter 60.4 'he has become man that he might deify us in himself' and in Letter 61.2 'we are deified ... by receiving the body of the Word himself in the eucharist.'

The trinity

The *Letters to Serapion on the Holy Spirit* are important. In these letters, Athanasius deals at length with the trinitarian relations. The Son is of the same being as the Father.[2] The trinity is indivisible, so wherever the Father is mentioned the Son should also be understood and – by the same token – where the Son is the Holy Spirit is in him.[3] The Spirit is never apart from the Son, a point Athanasius repeats time and time again.[4] The Son is in the Father and the Father is in the Son, and so also the Holy Spirit is in the Son and the Son is in the Holy Spirit. Thus, the Spirit cannot be divided from the Word.[5] So also the Spirit is in God the Father and from the Father.[6] As the Son comes in the name of the Father, so the Holy Spirit comes in the name of the Son.[7] There is one efficacy and action of the Holy Trinity, for the Father makes all things through the Word by the Holy Spirit.[8] Nothing could be clearer than the intimate, unbreakable relation between the Son and the Holy Spirit in Athanasius' thought.[9]

---

[2] Athanasius, *Ad Serapionem*, 2.5, PG 26:616.

[3] Athanasius, *Ad Serapionem*, 1:14, PG 26:566.

[4] Athanasius, *Ad Serapionem*, 1:14, 17, 20, 31, 3:5, 4:4; PG 26:565-6, 572, 576-7, 601, 632-3, 641.

[5] Athanasius, *Ad Serapionem*, 1:20-21, PG 26:580.

[6] Athanasius, *Ad Serapionem*, 1:25, PG 26:588.

[7] Athanasius, *Ad Serapionem*, 1:20, PG 26:580.

[8] Athanasius, *Ad Serapionem*, 1:20, 28, 30, PG 26:580, 596, 600.

[9] A. Grillmeier S.J., *Christ in Christian Tradition: Volume One: From the Apostolic Age to Chalcedon (451)* (Second, revised; J. Bowden; Atlanta: John Knox Press, 1975); J. Quasten, Volume III: The golden age of Greek Patristic literature from the Council of Nicea to the Council of Chalcedon, *Patrology* (Westminster, Maryland: Christian Classics, Inc, 1992); A. Petterson, *Athanasius* (London: Geoffrey Chapman, 1995); G. Prestige, *God in Patristic Thought* (London: SPCK,

The Three Cappadocians

Basil the Great (330–379)

As Anthony Meredith points out, we know more about Basil than any other ancient writer, with the exception of Cicero and Augustine.[10] He studied under his father, a teacher of rhetoric – his brother was Gregory of Nyssa – and then Libanius of Antioch, a celebrated pagan rhetoric teacher, who later taught Chrysostom. Further studies followed at Athens, in the company of his friend, Gregory Nazianzen. His writings suggest he also studied science.

Baptized in 357, he was strongly drawn to asceticism, influenced by his sister, Macrina. In 360 he attended, and played a leading part in, a synod in Constantinople, where he opposed Eunomius, a powerful advocate of a theology close to Arius. At this time, he trod a middle path between Eunomius – who held that the Son came into being at a particular point, was created and so of a different being than the Father – and Athanasius, who supported the Creed of Nicaea which affirmed that the Son is of the same, identical being as the Father. The group with which Basil was connected were known as the *homoiousians*, since they taught that the Son is of a like being to the Father, neither identical to him nor different from him.

On his consecration as bishop of Caesarea in 370, Basil tried to remove Eunomius' followers from influence – a difficult task, since the Emperor Valens actively encouraged the preferment of Arians. At the same time, Basil modified his thoughts on the trinity and moved towards an accommodation with Athanasius. This he did by a significant development in the use of language. The fourth-century trinitarian crisis had been bedevilled by technical and philosophical terminology. Frequently, antagonists

---

1952); J. Kelly, *Early Christian Doctrines* (London: Adam & Charles Black, 1968); F. Young, *From Nicea to Chalcedon: A Guide to the Literature and Its Background* (London: SCM, 1983).

[10] A. Meredith, *The Cappadocians* (Crestwood, New York: St. Vladimir's Seminary Press, 1995), 20.

spoke past each other, for they were using words that had as yet no fixed meaning, and were using them in strikingly different ways. Athanasius paved the way for a breakthrough when, in his *Tomus ad Antiochenos* (362), he argued that what was important was not the precise words that were used but the meaning that was attached to the words. This helped the various participants in the debate to ask what others intended by their language. Basil took the matter a vital step further. The terms *ousia* and *hypostasis* were used in various ways up to this point, often as synonyms. Basil proposed that *ousia* be reserved for the one being of God, while *hypostasis* be used for the way he is three. By this coining of new language, the door was opened to think of God as he is one in distinction from the way he is three. Moreover, Basil's innovation freed trinitarian discussion from the straightjacket of philosophical terminology and granted it the flexibility needed for the crisis to be resolved.

Basil wrote voluminously. We have a large collection of his letters extant, interacting with a range of figures in the church. Of particular importance is his treatise *De Spiritu Sancto*, the first on the Spirit in church history, although Athanasius had written an important series of letters to Serapion on the Holy Spirit. It is a landmark in the development of trinitarian doctrine. Basil's thought on the Spirit emerged from worship; the trinitarian formula he used in the liturgy had aroused criticism from his opponents, and he defended and explained it here. It has been suggested that Basil was reluctant to call the Holy Spirit 'God'; some claim he did not regard him as God, while others consider – with far more justification – that he was cautious on the matter, preferring to preserve the unity of the church as far as possible. However, Basil writes so strongly of the Holy Spirit that it is difficult to make a case for his seeing the Spirit as anything less than God; the terms he uses for the Spirit demand nothing less than full deity.

In another way, Basil is important for the future development of the Eastern church. In opposing Eunomius' rationalism, he taught the incomprehensibility of God, drawing a distinction between the being of God (who God is), which is beyond our capacity to know, and the actions of God, which we can know. In this, he has been accused of agnosticism, a charge we will consider later in the book.

Basil attended closely to his own diocese. The Arian sympathizer, the Emperor Valens, in attempting to curtail Basil's growing influence, cut the diocese into two, leaving him with the smaller part, so reducing the number of bishops Basil could appoint. However, as R.P.C. Hanson — himself at one point a bishop — remarks, parting a bishop from his diocese is like trying to tear a dog from a bone. In response, Basil simply doubled the number of episcopal positions under his jurisdiction!

We have examples of Basil's preaching, in his *Hexaemeron*, on the six days of creation, a series of homilies on the first chapter of Genesis, in which he not only expounds the chapter but interacts with the science of his day. He established hospitals for the poor, and promoted monasticism. His monastic rule greatly influenced the later work of St. Benedict, who urged his monks to read it in addition to the Bible.[11] Basil was not a supporter of solitary monasticism, of the forms of withdrawal commonly associated with the Egyptian monks. For him, the life of a community was essential, with manual labour an integral part, and care for the poor central to its operation. As Meredith indicates, both Gregory of Nyssa and Gregory Nazianzen wrote on love for the poor, and it is not difficult to trace the impact of Basil at this point.[12]

Gregory of Nyssa (d. c.394)

Gregory was Basil's brother. It is probable that he married, although the experience seems to have been a far from happy one. Unlike Basil, he did not travel to receive a wide-ranging education. Instead, he attributed his learning to Basil's own teaching. Nevertheless, he is generally recognized as the

---

[11] Ibid., 24.
[12] Ibid., 27.

most brilliant of the three Cappadocians. Basil was definitely responsible, however, for his brother's ecclesiastical appointments, although Gregory was singularly ill-suited to the position he occupied. After Valens' division of his diocese, Basil appointed Gregory in 372 to one of the new jurisdictions he created to circumvent the Emperor's move – the tiny and unpretentious see of Nyssa. Three years later, due to Arian intrigues, Gregory was forced into exile, to return in 378.

Around this time, Gregory composed his vast refutation of Eunomius, *Kata Eunomiou (Against Eunomius)*. It seems that the first two books of this enormous work were written before the Council of Constantinople (381) and read to a select gathering before the Council met, while the remainder were completed a couple of years later. He preached the funeral orations for Meletius, the first moderator of the Council who died shortly after it began, for the Emperor's wife in 383 and younger daughter two years later.[13] He wrote a large number of treatises and homilies, and shared many of his brother's concerns.

In his criticism of Eunomius, Gregory stressed the point – also asserted by Basil – that the being of God is beyond our capacity to define. God is infinite and beyond the grasp of the human mind. By his hair-splitting rationalism, Eunomius was destroying the Christian faith. In contrast, human beings live by faith, dependent on God's revelation. In this, Gregory prepared the ground for the apophatic approach that has come to be characteristic of Eastern theology, especially in the writings of Dionysius the Areopagite. This is the idea that knowledge of God is not primarily to be found in positive affirmations about him but by way of negation through prayer and contemplation.

Gregory was strongly influenced by Platonism, yet not so much as is sometimes thought. He had a strong grasp of the materiality of creation, and man as both body and soul. He emphatically teaches the bodily resurrection of Christ. Evil is a privation of the good, as Plotinus argued and as Augustine was

---

[13] Ibid., 52–3.

famously to teach. Thus, when redemption has run its course, evil will disappear and all things will be restored. Redemption itself must display the justice of God and it does so by tricking Satan, who had first tricked man. Thus, as Adam was deceived into eating the fruit, so the devil was deceived by the humanity of Christ as bait, his deity being concealed. The devil fell for the bait and swallowed it, and was destroyed in the process.

For Gregory, the ultimate end of redemption is our deification. This occurs by our bodies being transformed by the body of Christ, by coming into contact with the author of eternal life, which takes place in the eucharist. There Christ unites us with himself so that we may share in incorruptibility and immortality. This is what deification means, not any absorption of humanity into God but its partaking of bodily immortality.

Gregory Nazianzen (c.330–391)
Life
Gregory is called by the Eastern church 'the theologian', a title he shares with the apostle John alone. He was born at Arianzus, a country estate belonging to his father, near Nazianzus, probably around 330. His father – also Gregory – had been a member of an obscure heretical sect before becoming a Christian through the influence of his wife, Nonna. Shortly afterwards he was made bishop of Nazianzus. Our Gregory was born after his father's ordination, for the father frequently urged him to ordination saying, 'You have not been so long in life as I have spent in sacrifice' – a blow to Roman arguments for the antiquity of the requirement of celibacy!

Gregory had a wide-ranging education. When thirteen, he and his brother (who became a doctor in the imperial court at Constantinople) were sent to Caesarea, where he met Basil, who became a lifelong colleague. Later, he went to Palestinian Caesarea, to study rhetoric, and then to the University at Alexandria, while Athanasius was bishop, although there is no evidence that they ever met, for his time there probably coincided with

Athanasius' second exile (339–346). For a longer time Gregory was in Athens.

At Athens from the age of 18 to past 30, he renewed acquaintance with Basil. They agreed to renounce the city's attractions and to devote themselves to the church. Basil returned sooner to Cappadocia and monastic seclusion. When Gregory went back, his parents were still alive, his father bishop. He divided his time between helping his father with his episcopal duties and the mountains, at Basil's monastic base, in prayer, meditation, study, and manual labour.

Probably at Christmas 361, Gregory was ordained, against his will but with the acclamation of the people of Nazianzus. Oppressed by what he called this 'tyranny' he fled to Pontus. He returned by the following Easter but when he preached his first sermon many stayed away in protest. Later he wrote an apology for his flight, saying he shrank from the huge responsibilities thrust upon him against his will.

In 370 Basil was elected bishop of Caesarea, a metropolitan see. When Basil doubled the number of bishops under his jurisdiction, he found something for Gregory. The something was a tiny obscure backwater called Sasima, at a road junction, without water or grass, full of dust, noise and vagabonds. Gregory was furious – but, due to military occupation of the area, he very likely never took charge. His father required his assistance at Nazianzus and Gregory himself helped to resolve the dispute that gave rise to the matter. After his parents' death in 374 he went into seclusion for the rest of his life, except for a short but unhappy spell as Bishop of Constantinople during which he presided briefly at the ecumenical council. While at Constantinople the Arians even hired a contract killer to murder him. Jerome (translator of the Vulgate) was there at the time and greatly appreciated his preaching and learning.

Gregory died in 391, the same year as Augustine was ordained presbyter of Hippo. Contemporaries described him as of medium height, pale, with thick hair and a short beard, and conspicuous eyebrows. He had a scar on his right eye. His knees were worn out by excessive kneeling. His asceticism was considered overdone. He was cut off from the world and lacked experience of human nature. His love of solitude prevented him from producing the theological output he could have done. What he did write stands any test. He is the single most quoted author in the East, after the Bible.[14]

Thought

At Constantinople, Gregory's main theme was worship of the trinity. Between 379 and 381 he preached five sermons (the *Theological Orations*) that permanently established his reputation. As one critic put it, 'Critics have rivalled each other in the praises they have heaped upon them, but no praise is so high as that of the many theologians who have found in them their own best thoughts.'[15] Gregory's principal opponent in these sermons were the Eunomians.[16] Rationalists, with a strong belief in the capacities of human logic, they maintained we are capable of comprehending God. They assumed there to be a univocal relation between the divine and human mind (an identity of meaning for both God and man). For them, the Son is absolutely unlike the Father. God is absolute being, and generation cannot be predicated of him. Because of the correspondence between the mind of God and human reasoning, generation attributable to the Son is to be understood in terms of generation as we know it on the human level. Thus, eternal generation is inconceivable. The generation of the Son must have had a beginning. Therefore, there was a time when the Son did not exist. The Son is the first

[14] J. Binns, *An Introduction to the Christian Orthodox Churches* (Cambridge: Cambridge University Press, 2002), 72.

[15] P. Schaff, *A Select Library of the Nicene and Post-Nicene Fathers of the Christian Church: Second Series 7: Select Orations of Saint Gregory Nazianzen* (Edinburgh: T.&T. Clark, 1989) 333–6; B. Studer, *Trinity and Incarnation: The Faith of the Early Church* (ed. M. Westerhoff; A. Louth; Collegeville, Minnesota: Liturgical Press, 1993), 143–4.

[16] For what follows, see R. Letham, *The Holy Trinity: In Scripture, History, Theology, and Worship* (Phillipsburg, New Jersey: Presbyterian & Reformed, 2004), 157–64.

to be created and is the instrument by which God created the world. The Holy Spirit is even further removed from God.

In contrast, Gregory follows the stress of the other two Cappadocians on the incomprehensibility of God. It is impossible for anyone fully to grasp God's nature. We can only speak in negatives. It is difficult to conceive God but to define him in words is an impossibility. It is one thing to be persuaded of God's existence and quite another to know what he is. On the other hand, God has revealed himself, to Abraham, Manoah, Isaiah, and Paul. This is true knowledge but it is not direct knowledge of God's essence (from *esse*, to be) (3.12). In the same way, our bodily existence prevents us grasping spiritual realities.

Gregory then unfolds his own teaching. He starts by affirming the monarchy (the principle of unity in God). The Cappadocians have been (wrongly) taken to task by some for making the Father the cause of the deity of the Son and the Holy Spirit, by arguing that the Father is the source of the divine essence. Nothing could be further from Gregory's mind. The monarchy is not limited to one person so that, although the persons are numerically distinct, there is no severance of essence. The Father is the begetter and emitter, the Son is the begotten, and the Holy Spirit the emission, but this is so in the context of equality of nature, a union of mind, an identity of motion (3:2). The begetting of the Son and the procession of the Spirit took place beyond time and above reason, for there never was when the Father was not, nor was there such with respect to the Son and the Holy Spirit. The Son and the Spirit are from the Father but not after the Father (3:3). To be begotten and to proceed are concurrent with to be (3:9). All this is, of course, beyond our comprehension. Yet this does not negate it, any more than we reject God's existence because we cannot comprehend him (3:8). The begetting of the Son by the Father establishes their identity of nature, for the offspring is of the same nature as the parent (3:10). The thing to note, he says, is that the begetting and being begotten (and, we may add by inference, procession) is a property of the persons (the *hypostases*), not the one essence

(3:12). In the same way, Father does not denote the essence of God but the relation in which the Father stands to the Son, which also denotes the identity of nature between the Father who begets and the Son who is begotten (3:16). Thus, there was never a time when the Father was without the Son, nor the Son without the Father (3:17). Since his opponents were accustomed to cite Biblical passages attributing weakness and subordination to the Son, Gregory points to the incarnation as the occasion for such descriptions. What is lofty you are to apply to the Godhead ...but all that is lowly to the composite condition of him who ...was incarnate (3:18). He remained God while adding human nature (3:19), while his humanity was united to God and became one person so that we might be made God so far as he is made man.

On the question of the Holy Spirit the *Pneumatomachi* (fighters against the Holy Spirit) were the problem. They were followers of Macedonius, a deposed bishop, and were also known as Macedonians. They denied the deity of the Holy Spirit, considering him even more removed from God than the Son. For his part, Gregory makes a point from the theology of deification. In salvation we are made God. But if the Holy Spirit is not from eternity, how can he make me God, or join me with the Godhead? (5:4) Gregory points to the confusion that currently existed over the status of the Spirit (5:5):

> But of the wise men among us, some have conceived of him as an activity, some as a creature, some as God; and some have been uncertain which to call him, out of reverence for Scripture, they say, as though it did not make the matter clear either way. And therefore they neither worship him, nor treat him with dishonor, but take up a neutral position, or rather a very miserable one, with respect to him.

His opponents were asking Gregory to make clear definitions, since they supposed human logic capable of unfolding the truth about God. He replies by saying that with respect to the procession of the Spirit, as with the begetting of the Son, human

language about God is not to be understood in a univocal sense
(5:7). Thus we are unable to define the procession of the Spirit
and the generation of the Son (5:8):

> What then is procession? Do you tell me what is the
> unbegottenness of the Father, and I will explain to you the
> physiology of the generation of the Son and the procession of
> the Spirit, and we shall both of us be frenzy-stricken for prying
> into the mystery of God.

How, then, does the Spirit differ from the Son? The difference
of manifestation, or the difference in relations, gives rise to
the difference of their names (5:9). Their respective properties
(unbegotten, begotten, proceeding) have given them their
respective names (Father, Son, Holy Spirit) 'that the distinction
of the three persons may be preserved in the one nature ...of the
Godhead.'

Appropriately, Gregory turns to a consideration of worship.
The Spirit is the one in whom we worship and in whom we pray.
Thus, prayer to the Spirit is, in effect, the Spirit offering prayer
or adoration to himself. The adoration of the one is adoration
of the three, because of the equality of honor and deity between
the three (5:12). The questions of the deity of the Son and the
Holy Spirit are connected – once the former is acknowledged
the other follows (5:13). 'To us there is one God, and all that
proceeds from him is referred to one, though we believe in three
persons. For one is not more and another less God; nor is one
before and another after; ...but the Godhead is ...undivided in
separate persons... When we look at the Godhead, or the first
cause, or the monarchia, that which we conceive is one; but
when we look at the persons in whom the Godhead dwells ...
there are three whom we worship' (5:14). 'Each of these persons
possesses unity, not less with that which is united to it than with
itself, by reason of the identity of essence' (5:16).

Gregory points to the historical and progressive outworking
of revelation to explain the comparative reticence of Scripture
on the Spirit. 'The Old Testament proclaimed the Father openly,

and the Son more obscurely. The New manifested the Son, and suggested the deity of the Spirit. Now the Spirit himself dwells among us, and supplies us with a clearer demonstration of himself. For it was not safe, when the Godhead of the Father was not yet acknowledged, plainly to proclaim the Son; nor when that of the Son was not yet received to burden us further ...with the Holy Spirit...' (5:26). 'Now, worship and baptism establish the Spirit's deity for we worship God the Father, God the Son, and God the Holy Spirit, three persons, one Godhead, undivided in honor and glory ... for if he is not to be worshipped, how can he deify me by baptism? But if he is to be worshipped, surely he is an object of adoration, and if an object of adoration he must be God' (5:28). Gregory, then, has a clear grasp of the distinct persons while holding firmly to the unity of the undivided Godhead. For him, the trinity was not an abstract puzzle but the heart of the Christian faith and the center of true worship. 'But when I say God, I mean Father, Son, and Holy Spirit' (*Oration 38 on the Theophany, or Birthday of Christ*, 8).

John Chrysostom (c. 349–407)[17]

John was born into an affluent family in Antioch. His father died soon after he was born and he was raised by his mother, a devout Christian. He received the best education Antioch could offer and was taught in rhetoric by the renowned Libanius. John was soon enamoured with the ideal of an ascetic life as a monk. In the mountains around Antioch were large monastic colonies, while many hermits used the caves that abounded in the hills.

In his twenties, John himself took to the hills, living for several years in a group of monks and then spending two more years as a recluse. His diet was sparse and he stood on his feet continuously, without sleeping, for the two years of his eremetic existence. As a result his health, and especially his digestive system, was irreparably damaged; he had stomach trouble and

---

[17] See J. Kelly, *Golden Mouth: The Story of John Chrysostom – Ascetic, Preacher, Bishop* (Grand Rapids: Baker, 1995).

insomnia for the rest of his days, besides acute sensitivity to cold.

Returning to Antioch, he was eventually ordained. His outstanding oratorical skill opened for him a role as the *de facto* chief assistant to the bishop, Flavian. For ten years he was the outstanding preacher in Antioch. It was then that he was given the nickname Chrysostom (golden-mouth). He is widely considered to be among the greatest – if not the greatest – preachers in the history of the Christian church.

John's preaching was reduced to writing by stenographers. Many of his homilies show spontaneity, with reproofs, ripostes and other asides that are obviously those of a preacher in dynamic contact with his congregation. He often preached consecutively through books of the Bible. His method was to stick close to the text. Since he was in Antioch, he followed the more rigorous, literal method of exegesis associated with that place, in contrast to the fanciful allegorical method that had been spearheaded by Origen. His preaching often addressed pressing social and political matters. John became known as a champion of the poor and was a frequent thorn in the flesh of the rich and privileged.

In 397, on the death of Nectarius, bishop of Constantinople, John was unexpectedly made bishop by imperial appointment. There he continued his preaching but now in the midst of a cauldron of political intrigue. For the first few years he had a cordial relationship with Emperor Arcadius and his more powerful wife, the Empress Eudoxia. However, the patriarch of Alexandria, Theophilus, was opposed to John since he preferred his own man, the octogenarian Isidore, through whom he would have been able to exercise real power; moreover, his ire was already aroused by the decree of Constantinople I, declaring Constantinople the new Rome, second only to Rome, supplanting Alexandria from its ancient place.

John's trenchant attacks on the privileged in Constantinople soon earned him serious opposition. The monks were largely his enemies too, and since there was a strong residual Arian element in Constantinople, John was constantly walking a political

tight-rope. On a trip to Asia in 402, he intervened in a controversy surrounding allegations of corruption against the bishop
of Ephesus. In the course of this he deposed and consecrated
a number of bishops, contrary to the canons of Nicaea, which
forbad a bishop to intervene outside the bounds of his jurisdiction. Moreover, on his return, he antagonized the powerful
bishop Severian. His fatal error was to receive a group of monks
– the Long Brothers – who were fleeing abuse from Theophilus
and his accusations of Origenism. He granted them sanctuary,
awaiting clarification of the issues. To cap it all, he made sweep-
ing and implied criticisms of Eudoxia in a sermon, apparently
likening her to Jezebel. This concatenation of errors, allied to
John's notorious tactlessness, was his undoing. Theo3philus,
summoned to Constantinople to defend himself against charges
of oppressing the monks, travelled by land, gathering increasing
support from a range of bishops who joined his entourage. On
reaching Constantinople he turned the tables on John, and had
him tried at the Synod of the Oak in 403. John was sent into
exile, despite the huge popular unrest this generated. Realizing
her mistake, Eudoxia had him restored to the city. However, no
synod reversed the decree of the Synod of the Oak and so John's
renewed episcopal activities were regarded by his opponents as
invalid. Further tactless errors on John's part gave his enemies
occasion a few months later to ensure a second and permanent
exile. In rapidly declining health, John was banished to the
mountains of Armenia. After his place of exile became a place
of pilgrimage, he was sent further afield to the east of the Black
Sea, but died before arrival.

Cyril of Alexandria (378–444)[18]

Cyril was Theophilus of Alexandria's nephew and was with
him at the Synod of the Oak in 403, which condemned John

---

[18] See N. Russell, *Cyril of Alexandria* (London: Routledge, 2000); J. A.
McGuckin, *St. Cyril of Alexandria and the Christological Controversy: Its History,
Theology, and Texts* (Crestwood, New York: St. Vladimir's Seminary Press, 2004);

Chrysostom. Born in lower Egypt, his uncle became Patriarch when Cyril was only seven. Theophilus took ~~John~~ Cyril and his sister under his wing after they were orphaned at an early age, and may have supervised his education, which followed the conventional pattern for the privileged classes, including grammar, logic, classical literature, and rhetoric. However, he showed no evidence of an extensive philosophical education, although he did have a good knowledge of Aristotelian logic. He developed a thorough grasp of the theological writings of the Cappadocians and – hardly surprisingly – Athanasius. He may well have functioned as Theophilus' assistant in the same way as Theophilus had done to Athanasius.

On Theophilus' death in 412, Cyril replaced him, despite military support for a rival. His uncle's interference in church affairs throughout the East, often accompanied by large-scale political manoeuvrings, had aggravated the political elite, who had thrown their weight against a perceived continuation under his nephew. However, widespread rioting occurred in Alexandria in support of Cyril and in the end the authorities were forced to back down in his favour.

As a bishop Cyril followed his uncle's policies. He brought relentless pressure on heretics, pagans, and Jews; sought support from Rome; and was constantly seeking to thwart the ambitions of Constantinople. With help from the monks and the mob, Cyril shrewdly built a secure power base. Knowing how to manipulate popular sentiment, and prepared to use rioting and violence for his own ends, he connived in the brutal public murder of the pagan philosopher Hypatia, a woman, who was stoned to death and hacked to pieces in a former pagan temple.

Early in his career, Cyril wrote extensively against the Jews. In this, he reflected at length on the relationship between the two Testaments. He argued that it is the Christians, not the Jews, who are the heirs to the promises God made to the patriarchs. He

T. G. Weinandy, *The Theology of St. Cyril of Alexandria: A Critical Appreciation* (London: T.&T. Clark, 2003).

built on the recapitulation theory of Irenaeus, who saw Christ as the second Adam who restores humanity to the favour of God lost by the first Adam. With Christ's incarnation – central to his thought – the time of the Jews has passed. This emphasis went together with a strongly Christocentric method of Biblical interpretation. The goal of the whole Bible is to point to Christ. Thus Moses points to Christ and, in doing so, he is superceded by Christ. The church, which has replaced Israel, has received the Holy Spirit. Thus, there are two key moments in salvation – the incarnation of Christ and the descent of the Spirit. Moreover, the Spirit, who deified the humanity of Christ, heals our broken humanity and lifts us up to deification. He restores the divine image in us and transforms us through the sacraments, enabling us to live in communion with the holy trinity.

Like the Cappadocians, Cyril opposed the followers of Eunomius. Cyril, in opposition, grappled with the problem of how we can talk about a transcendent God. He shared the Cappadocian distinction between the essence (or being) of God – who he is – and his works. We know he exists and we can see his works, while his essence is not fully comprehensible.

It was the controversy with Nestorius that gave rise to Cyril's most lasting fame. Nestorius, a monk, was installed as bishop of Constantinople early in 428. Soon he and some colleagues questioned the accepted teaching that Mary was *theotokos*, the mother of God. Nestorius considered that, while this was not wrong in itself, it was preferable to call her *Christotokos*, mother of Christ, since this did more justice to Christ's humanity. For Cyril, this was like a red rag to a bull. Two factors spurred him to action. The theological point was that Nestorius appeared to jeopardize the unity of Christ's person.

For Cyril, Christ is not simply an amalgam of two natures but is the eternal Word who has added humanity in an unbreakable union. Thus *theotokos* expresses the truth about the child Mary bore – he was the Son of God. These concerns were borne out by Nestorius' apparent teaching that the union occurred at the level of the two natures, which seemed to imply to the Alexandrians that there were two persons.

The second factor was the intense rivalry between Alexandria and Constantinople aroused by the canon at Constantinople I declaring Constantinople 'second Rome.' Here was a chance for Cyril to cut the upstart see down to size. In chapter 2 we discussed the details surrounding the eventual Council of Ephesus (431) and the deposition and exile of Nestorius, so we will not go over the ground again here. Suffice it to say that Cyril was not only Nestorius' leading opponent and the foremost exponent of the hypostatic union at that time but he also overshadowed the events of the next hundred years, for the debates and controversies that followed Ephesus and Chalcedon were largely attempts to grapple with his Christology. His central theme was, in his own words, 'the one incarnate nature of the Word made flesh.' This was not heretical, as it might seem to the casual reader. Cyril understood *phusis* (nature) and *hypostasis* (person) to be virtual synonyms. In this, he merely affirmed the unity of Christ's person; that the Word, now made flesh, was one. At the same time his answer to the question of who was Christ, was the Word. This was to receive conciliar approval at Ephesus and Chalcedon and especially at Constantinople II.

There is little doubt that Cyril was a militant theological and ecclesiastical fighter. He made plenty of enemies along the way. Indeed, one bishop is on record as passing this far from complimentary comment on hearing of his death:

At last with a final struggle the villain has passed away.... His departure delights the survivors, but possibly disheartens the dead; there is some fear that under the provocation of his company they may send him back again to us.... Care must therefore be taken to order the guild of undertakers to place a very big and heavy stone on his grave to stop him coming back here.[19]

---

[19] Attributed to Theodoret of Cyrrhus, Ep. 180, *PG* 83:1489c-1491a: G. Prestige,

Dionysius the Areopagite (Pseudo-Dionysius, possibly early sixth-century Syria)

This unknown author wrote as if he were the convert of the apostle Paul recorded in Acts 17:34. His writings were cited as greatly authoritative by Gregory Palamas (1296–1359) and, more recently, by Vladimir Lossky (1900–58). Indeed, both Palamas and his chief opponent, Barlaam, both quote Dionysius, although from radically different perspectives.

One of the chief points made by Dionysius – influential down the centuries – concerns apophatic theology. In this, he effectively identifies theology with contemplation. In relation to God, we are to proceed not by positive statements but negation. In Lossky's words:

> Dionysius distinguishes two possible theological ways. One – that of cataphatic or positive theology – proceeds by affirmations; the other – apophatic or negative theology – by negations. The first leads us to some knowledge of God, but is an imperfect way. The perfect way, the only way which is fitting in regard to God, who is of His very nature unknowable, is the second – which leads us finally to total ignorance. All knowledge has as its object that which is. Now God is beyond all that is inferior to Him, that is to say, all that which is. If in seeing God one can know what one sees, then one has not seen God in Himself but something intelligible, something which is inferior to Him. It is by *unknowing* ... that one may know Him who is above every possible object of knowledge. Proceeding by negations one ascends from the inferior degrees of being to the highest, by progressively setting aside all that can be known, in order to draw near to the Unknown in the darkness of total ignorance. For even as light, and especially abundance of light, renders darkness invisible; even so the knowledge of created things, and especially excess of knowledge, destroys the ignorance which is the only way by which one can attain to God in Himself.[20]

Fathers and Heretics (London: SPCK, 1940), 150; cited by Russell, *Cyril*, 3, and by Binns, *Orthodox Churches*, 72–3.

[20] V. Lossky, *The Mystical Theology of the Eastern Church* (London: James Clarke & Co. Ltd, 1957), 25.

God thus transcends all affirmations and negations. One can have no concepts relating to God, only signs.[21] This apophatic approach to *theologia* means that knowledge of God is not knowledge as we usually understand it, but rather total ignorance. It is not intellectual knowledge at all but mystical ecstasy. As Lossky insists, theology and mysticism go together.[22]

For Dionysius, central to theology is that God draws us into union with himself in deification, already a theme right at the heart of the Eastern church, and one to which Dionysius gave added impetus by his influential writings.

Maximus the Confessor (580–662)[23]

Although it is impossible to be certain, Maximus was probably born and raised in Constantinople. Appointed to the imperial court, he left to become a monk. His monastic life began in Asia Minor but later he moved eastwards. However, following the Arab invasions, he – together with many other monks – fled to north Africa, to the Carthage area. His mentor, Sophronius, abbot of Eukratos, near Carthage, later became Bishop of Jerusalem, and influenced Maximus greatly in his opposition to monotheletism. The earlier Latin culture, which flourished until the time of Augustine, had been overrun. The Byzantines had moved in during the sixth century, ousting the Vandals. However, the autocratic doctrinal impositions of Justinian, especially Constantinople II's rejection of the three chapters, alienated large sections of the population. At the time Sophronius and Maximus fled there, the Emperors were strongly monothelite and were imposing this view on the church in north Africa, as elsewhere. This was fertile soil for the dyothelite position.

In 645, Maximus defeated a leading monothelite, the former patriarch Pyrrhus, in a public debate. Much church opinion

---

[21] A. Laats, *Doctrines of the Trinity in Eastern and Western Theologies: A Study with Special Reference to K. Barth and V. Lossky* (Frankfurt am Main: Peter Lang, 1999), 83–4.

[22] Lossky, *Mystical Theology*, 7–22.

[23] See A. Louth, *Maximus the Confessor* (London: Routledge, 1996).

in north Africa swung to his support. In 649, he attended the
Lateran Council in Rome, bringing north Africa behind Rome
in opposition to the monothelite East. However, on his return
to Constantinople in 655 he was put on trial and exiled. Worse
followed. After cross-examination, he was retried and publicly
mutilated. His tongue and right hand were cut off. Exiled again,
he died shortly afterwards. For this, he is known as the Confessor.
He was posthumously vindicated by Constantinople III, which
anathematized monotheletism. Maximus had straddled East and
West and had pointed the way to the truth.

Maximus left a significant body of writings. His vast
theological vision integrated cosmic and redemptive motifs into
a coherent Christocentric and Trinitarian whole. His vividly
clear thinking and exacting logic was integrally connected with
a stress on spiritual experience. As Blowers and Wilken put it:

> To be sure, Maximus' theological reasoning at times comes to
> expression in an exacting logic and use of syllogisms, and he
> is often meticulously precise in the nuances of his theological
> language. Yet all the while *theologia* – as the aspiration to
> intimate knowledge of the Holy Trinity that must always
> remain grounded in, and integrated with, the contemplative
> and ascetic life of the Christian – entails for this Byzantine
> sage an intensive, ongoing, multifaceted 'intellectual quest' ...
> into the foundations and future of the world created by God,
> recreated through the work of Jesus Christ, sanctified by the
> Holy Spirit, and summoned to an unprecedented and glorious
> deification.[24]

Maximus did not write in the systematic form familiar to Western theology but in a series of aphorisms, or answers to questions. He was, after all, a monk and was dealing with issues of
concern to other monks. Living at a time of great insecurity,
following the eruption of Islam, he found the bedrock of his

---

[24] P. M. Blowers, *On the Cosmic Mystery of Jesus Christ: Selected Writings of St.
Maximus the Confessor* (Crestwood, New York: St. Vladimir's Seminary Press,
2003), 16–17.

theology in the Definition of Chalcedon, which he staunchly defended against the monothelite implication that attentuated or eradicated the humanity of Christ. The incarnation is central. The Logos, in becoming man, reveals the Father and the Holy Spirit. The incarnation opens the world for its ultimate deification, for Christ is the mediator of humanity, which in turn is the central part of the entire created order. We share in his ministry through ascetic practice, prayer and meditation. Creation and deification on the one hand, redemption on the other, are both parts of the one work of God, the mystery which is Jesus Christ.

In terms of salvation, Adam's fall plunged the race into slavery to sin, with its entailments – passibility, corruption, and mortality. In his incarnation, Christ assumed the natural human capacity to suffer and liability to deviant passions – without sin – but not the sinful propensities that came into existence after the fall. Thus he overcomes the effects of the fall and forms a new humanity. Each individual Christian is a microcosm of this great cosmic salvation. Baptism is connected with this as one of the three births the Christian undergoes – his natural birth, rebirth in baptism, and the final resurrection.

John of Damascus (c. 675–c. 749)

John produced the most systematic compendium of theology in the Eastern church. Yet we know little about his life, and uncertainty even surrounds the dates of his birth and death. We know that he died by 750, but his birthdate is less clear. It is certainly during the last half of the seventh century, but suggestions that it was c. 650–60 may be unduly early. He lived his entire life under Muslim rule, during the period of the Umayyad caliphate (651–750). Born in Damascus, the capital, later he moved to Palestine as a monk. His family were leading officials in the fiscal administration of Syria, which it retained under Arab rule, for the Muslims generally left the civil administration of conquered territories intact.

Following a classical education and an extended period of government service, John resigned early in the eighth century, probably before 710, to become a monk somewhere near Jerusalem, the exact location of which is again uncertain. He was probably ordained as a priest, and had a considerable reputation as a preacher, being called John Chrysorrhoas (flowing with gold).[25] Equally difficult is the task of tracing a reliable chronology of John's life and writings. However, his works against the iconoclasts are most likely to have been composed after 726.

His central concern was the need for doctrinal orthodoxy. Christology was a constantly recurring theme, and much of his corpus is directed to counter the major Christological heresies – Nestorianism, Eutychianism, monophysitism, and monotheletism. Since the areas conquered by the Arabs proved a haven for Christian heretics, freed from the persecuting power of the Byzantine Empire, John spent a good deal of energy defending the teaching of the great councils against opposition – especially monophysite – in the region. Occasionally, he addressed the challenge posed by Islam, and typical Muslim objections to Christianity. His most famous work is *The Orthodox Faith*. Later Western translations have divided this into four sections, corresponding with typical divisions in Latin scholastic theology. However, this was not the context in which John wrote. The final stage of the original work, called *The Fountainhead of Knowledge*, was a sequence of three sections – philosophical foundations, exploration of heresy, defence of orthodoxy – consisting of a hundred short chapters each (three centuries), an established genre at the time. It was intended for John's fellow monks. The third century is now, in translation, what we know as *The Orthodox Faith*. It was a monastic work, rather than – as translations imply – a systematic precursor of Western scholasticism. Throughout John avoids any thought of

---

[25] A. Louth, *John Damascene: Tradition and Originality in Byzantine Theology* (Oxford: Oxford University Press, 2002), 4–6.

originality, as we in the West understand it. For him, originality means faithfulness to the sources.

The process of refining, defining, and celebrating Orthodoxy that John took part in was the work of Palestinian monks, living and working almost literally in the shadow of the mosques of the Dome of the Rock and of Al-Aqsa, newly built on the temple mount in Jerusalem and overshadowing the Christian Holy Sites.[26] Palestinian monks also belonged to a minority with diminishing power, attacked by other Christians, and open to attack once again from Jews, Samaritans, Manichees, and eventually Muslims. This Christian Orthodoxy was not the expression of human triumphalism, but something fashioned in the crucible of defeat.[27]

John had a strong belief in the incomprehensibility of God, and saw the apophatic approach to God as basic. The idea that reality is basically personal – or hypostatic – lies at the heart of John's theology and of Greek patristic theology in general.[28]

The trinity

In *The Orthodox Faith*, John starts right away with God, and moves without delay to talk of the trinity – in stark contrast to the Western tradition, which since Aquinas has delayed the discussion of the trinity until after prolonged consideration of the existence, nature and attributes of the one God. John's placement demonstrates its centrality. Nothing emphasizes more strongly the dominant position the trinity should occupy in the faith and worship of the church, and presents a huge contrast to the Western church.[29]

---

[26] Ibid., 7.

[27] Ibid., 14.

[28] Ibid., 51.

[29] On John of Damascus, see J. Bilz, *Die Trinitätslehre Des Johannes von Damaskus* (Paderborn, 1909); Prestige, *God*, 263–4, 280; M. C. O'Carroll, *Trinitas: A Theological Encyclopedia of the Holy Trinity* (Collegeville, Minnesota: The Liturgical Press, 1987), 139–40.

The knowledge and incomprehensibility of God

God is ineffable and incomprehensible. No one has ever known him except insofar as he has revealed himself. However, he has not left us in ignorance. He has implanted the knowledge of his existence in all nature. More than that, in the law and the prophets and, later, in Christ he disclosed himself as far as it is possible for us to grasp. Therefore we seek for nothing further than those things delivered to us in Scripture.[30]

Thus, not all things about God are knowable, neither are all things unknowable. What God is in his being and nature (essence) is incomprehensible and unknowable. We know he does not have a body, that he is infinite, invisible, simple and not compound, immutable, and fills the universe. But these things give an idea only of what he is not, not of what he is. To explain the essence of anything we must speak in positive terms, but in the case of God it is impossible to explain what he is. So, all we can affirm concerning God 'does not show forth God's nature, but only the qualities of His nature. For when you speak of Him as good, and just, and wise, and so forth, you do not tell God's nature but only the qualities of His nature.'[31]

John follows in the next section with an extensive exposition of the doctrine of the trinity. Most noteworthy is the fact that John is the first to use the term *perichoresis* in trinitarian theology. It refers to the mutual indwelling of the three persons in the one being of God. The subsistences, or persons, are *in* each other.[32] In this, we recognize the indivisibility and unity of God. 'For they are made one not so as to commingle, but so as to cleave to one another, and they have their being in each other (*perichoresin*) without any coalescence or commingling.... For the Deity is undivided amongst things divided ...and it is just like three suns cleaving to each other without separation and giving out light mingled and conjoined into one.' This is an important stage in

---

[30] John of Damascus, *The Orthodox Faith* 1:1. See also 1:3. PG 194:789–97.

[31] John of Damascus, *The Orthodox Faith* 1:4. PG 194:797-800.

[32] Cf., Gregory Nazianzen, *Orations* 1, 37; PG 35:395-402, 36:279-308.

the history of the doctrine. The idea was present earlier but John gives it a more developed treatment.[33] This exposition of the trinity, together with his defence of icons (see chapter 6), is perhaps John's greatest single contribution to theology.

Gregory Palamas (1296–1359)

Born in Constantinople, Palamas was a monk – at Mount Athos and then Thessalonica – who was ordained a priest at the age of thirty. After lengthy spells in solitude, much of his time was taken up by polemics, in the face of ecclesiastical turmoil. In 1347 he was elected Archbishop of Thessalonica. In 1354 he was captured and imprisoned by the Turks for about a year. After his death, he was proclaimed a saint by the Synod of Constantinople in 1368. Palamas wrote his *Triads* against Barlaam, a Byzantine philosopher with a positive estimate of Greek philosophy who regarded education and human knowledge as necessary to know anything about God. For Barlaam, God's essence is unknowable. His energies are created and so what is left to man is a dialectical knowledge that stops short of a knowledge of God himself in his essence. Direct knowledge of God is not possible to the human mind. He can only be known indirectly by contemplation of his works in nature. He was strongly intellectualist and believed it necessary to mortify all passions, rather than to transform them and devote them to the service of God, as Palamas maintains.[34] Barlaam's views were condemned by successive councils in Constantinople in 1341. Following this, he went into exile in Italy. Gregory, in opposing these ideas, supports the hesychasts, hermits who engaged in continuous prayer and contemplation. The famous Jesus prayer – 'Lord Jesus Christ, Son of God, have mercy on me' – was central to their spirituality. From their

---

[33] V. Harrison, 'Perichoresis in the Greek Fathers,' *StVladThQ* 35 (1991), 53–65; V. S. Conticello, 'Pseudo-Cyril's De Sacrosancta Trinitate: A Compilation of Joseph the Philosopher,' *OCP* 61 (1995), 117–29; W. Kaspar, ed., *Lexicon Für Theologie und Kirche* (Freiburg: Herder, 1999), 8:707–8.

[34] J. Meyendorff, ed., trans., preface by, *Gregory Palamas: The Triads* (New York: Paulist Press), 154, n119.

practice of gazing downwards at their bodies while repeating
the prayer over and over again, Barlaam mockingly called
these monks 'people-whose-soul-is-in-their-navel'.[35] Gregory's
defence of the hesychasts was accepted by the Orthodox at the
1341 council. He was canonized in 1368 and since then he has
been commemorated on the second Sunday in Lent.

The essence and energies of God

For Gregory, as for the East in general, deification is central to
the Christian message, for the saints are made partakers of the
divine nature, as Peter says in 2 Peter 1:4. This, as Meyendorff
observes, Gregory sees as given to all Christians through baptism
and continuous participation in the eucharist.[36] The incarnation
is crucial for this. In becoming flesh, the Son of God united to
himself human nature. It became God's humanity, filled with
the divine energy. In union with Christ we in our humanity
are transformed, body as well as soul. A real knowledge of God
is possible in Christ through communion with his *uncreated*
energies.

Gregory's major contribution is the distinction he draws
between the one unoriginated and eternal essence of God, and
the energies of God. While certain divine powers and also some
works of God have no beginning – his providence, will, and
foreknowledge –these are not identical with the essence of
God.[37] God himself infinitely transcends his uncreated works
– whether his uncreated goodness, holiness, or virtue. These are
what he calls the energies of God. Perhaps the best way for us
to understand what he means is to think of these energies as

---

[35] J. Meyendorff, ed., trans., preface by, *Triads*, 8. For this reason it is mystifying
to read Bray's comment that what constitutes the difference between Eastern and
Western concepts of man and his salvation is, on the part of the East, 'a denial of
the Son's saving love in the life of the Christian, or at best a relegation of that love
to second place' (G. Bray, 'The Filioque Clause in History and Theology,' *TB* 34
[1983], 128).

[36] J. Meyendorff, *Byzantine Theology: Historical Trends and Doctrinal Themes* (New
York: Fordham University Press, 1979), 77.

[37] Gregory Palamas, *The Triads,* III.ii.6.

'existentially perceivable manifestations' in an Aristotelian sense, but applied here as the appearance of the coinherent (*perichoresis*) tri-personal life of God. Thus, since God is entirely present in each of the divine energies we name him from each of them although it is clear that he transcends them all.[38] However, there are some energies of God that have both a beginning and an end. All the divine energies are uncreated but not all are without a beginning. These are those energies that are directed towards created things. Since creation had a beginning so do those energies of God related to creation. Here the distinction between the energies and the essence of God is most clear. Thus the divine essence transcends all energies whatsoever and transcends them to an infinite degree and an infinite number of times.[39] Essence and energy are therefore not totally identical in God. So, the energies exist not in him but around him.[40] Consequently, it is impossible, as the Fathers have said, to find a name to express the nature of the uncreated trinity. Rather, the names belong to the energies. He who is beyond every name is not identical with what he is named.[41] Hence, we have knowledge not of the essence of God, but of his energies. We shall critically consider this teaching in more detail in chapter 9.

Nicholas Cabasilas (1322–?)

Cabasilas lived at a time of uncertainty and upheaval in the declining Byzantine Empire of the fourteenth century. Educated at Thessalonica, where he was born, and also at Constantinople, he rose to high office in the imperial court, helped by being the personal friend of Emperor John VI Cantacuzenus. Loyal to the emperor, he was sent on several important diplomatic missions. However, in 1354 John VI Cantacuzenus abdicated and became a monk. Probably in connection with this, Cabasilas disappeared from public life from this point, and his literary output was at its

---

[38] Ibid., III.ii.7; J. Meyendorff, *Byzantine Theology*, 185–6.
[39] Gregory Palamas, *Triads*, III.ii.8.
[40] Ibid., III.ii.9.
[41] Ibid., III.ii.10.

height hereafter. It seems probable that he entered a monastery but its identity is uncertain. The most likely candidates are Mount Athos or Constantinople. It is known that Cabasilas survived the capture of Thessalonica by the Turks in 1387 but the date and place of his death are unknown. He is best known for a work on the divine liturgy and another entitled *Life in Christ*. The former is a detailed exposition of the symbolism of the liturgy, explaining point by point how it portrays the work of redemption. The latter is a classic manual of the Christian life, an Orthodox counterpart to Thomas à Kempis' *Imitation of Christ*. It is a work of great value to Christians today, whatever their background.

5

The Eastern Church from the Seventh Century

The advent of Islam

By 650, the progress of the church in the East was rudely interrupted. In 610, deep in the Arabian peninsula, a man called Muhammad began to have visions. In the ensuing years, despite intense opposition, he gathered together a group of followers. Through a number of fierce and portentous battles they began to unify a disparate and disunited group of tribesmen. Muhammad died in 632 but within ten years his band had swelled in numbers and power, bursting the boundaries of Arabia and rampaging through the eastern Mediterranean. In 634, Damascus fell. To prove this was no isolated or localized accident, in 638 both Antioch and Jerusalem, bastions of the Eastern church, capitulated to the Arab hordes, to be followed in lightning succession by Caesarea in Palestine, in the following year, and in 642 by Alexandria and Persia.

Since the Muslims treated all Christians equally, there was no longer any pressure on Christian heretics to conform to a prescribed standard of orthodoxy. At once monophysitism, rejected by Constantinople II but now freed from the restraints of the Byzantine Empire, spread from Syria into Persia and Mesopotamia, while the monophysite church in Armenia remained staunchly committed to its beliefs. The Nestorians remained strong in Persia and engaged in missionary activity beyond its borders, reaching China, central Asia and south India. Orthodoxy shrank to the Byzantine lands, Greek in language, under the Patriarch of Constantinople. Many Greek monks fled to the West, including most notably Maximus the Confessor who had already moved to Carthage in 628. The territory under the jurisdiction of the Eastern church, operating within the boundaries laid down by the ecumenical councils, contracted greatly.[1]

As Islam burst on the scene, it met a receptive population – in Egypt the monophysites had been maltreated by the Byzantine Empire, excoriated as heretics. For the Muslims, with little interest in the niceties of Christian theology, they were simply Christians; as a consequence they were treated better by the Islamic invaders than by the Christian Empire. So the monophysites found their circumstances improved under Muslim rule. Moreover, the once-thriving church in North Africa had neglected to evangelize the native Berber population. These people proved a thorn in the flesh to the church and the Roman Empire in the late fourth and early fifth centuries.[2] Once the Romans were driven out by the Vandals, the church was reduced to a pitifully low level, with the Berbers welcoming the Arab invaders in the seventh century – their language had striking similarities to Arabic.[3]

Islam's theory of *jihad* (holy war) transformed the traditional Arab raid into a religious duty, as a means to spread Islam.[4] With its practice of *dhimma*, Islamic rulers granted a legally protected

---

[1] L. D. Davis, *The First Seven Ecumenical Councils (325–787)* (Collegeville, Minnesota: The Liturgical Press, 1990), 269–71.

[2] See especially S. Lancel, *Saint Augustine* (A. Nevill; London: SCM Press, 2002).

[3] P. G. Riddell, *Islam in Context: Past, Present, and Future* (Grand Rapids: Baker, 2003), 70.

but subordinate place to defeated peoples, including Jews and Christians, whom the Qur'an considered 'people of the Book'. The Muslims, in practice, gave the subjugated populations a range of choices: to convert to Islam; to accept *dhimmi* status, as second-class citizens subject to punitive taxation; or death. Dhimmitude entailed payment of the *jizya* tax, the level of which was left to the discretion of individual rulers but could be as high as fifty per cent of the harvest. In return, the rulers offered military protection. Normally, these agreements were honoured. Often the tax brought in extensive revenue and so rulers were loathe to encourage mass conversion to Islam, preferring to secure the economic benefit. However, in Syria, Iran and Asia Minor, the Caliph Walid I (705–15) attempted to eradicate the church. He demanded it use Arabic instead of Greek.[5]

Under the Abbasid dynasty (750–945), the centre of Islamic rule moved from Damascus to near present-day Baghdad, and Christians experienced fluctuating fortunes. At times, especially under the enlightened caliph al-Ma'mun (813–33), Baghdad became a prosperous city, Arabic culture, science, and scholarship flowered, and Christians rose to positions of considerable prominence. One such figure, Hunayn ibn-Ishaq (809–73), who has been described as one of the most outstanding intellects in history, certainly among the greatest figures – if not the greatest – of the ninth century, was superintendent of the library in Baghdad. This was a time when the great works of Greek and Latin culture were translated into Arabic and preserved for future generations while the West was relapsing into barbarism. Hunayn was a Nestorian, and we noted how the Nestorians spread eastward so vigorously.

At other times, the Abbasids introduced open anti-Jewish and anti-Christian discrimination. Christians were forced to wear

---

[4] J. Binns, *An Introduction to the Christian Orthodox Churches* (Cambridge: Cambridge University Press, 2002), 170.

[5] Riddell, *Islam in Context*, 73.

distinctive clothing identifying them as non-Muslims, were forbidden to engage in public displays of religion, to ride horses, or handle weapons, while church buildings were allowed to fall into disrepair. Earlier, in Egypt, the governor Abu Ja'far al-Mansur (750–4) ordered the destruction of many monasteries.[6] Nevertheless, the position of the Christians was superior to those of religious minorities in the Christian Empire or in Western Europe, which was at this time in a state of major decline.[7] On the other hand, Islamic rule was generally totalitarian, calculated to create an inbuilt slavish mentality in the subjected groups, milking the prosperity and hard work of the Christian communities, for the rulers knew that without the tax revenues they produced their rule was hardly sustainable economically. Hence, the relationship was symbiotic; the Christians and Jews enjoying a degree of autonomy within strict limits in return for protection from attackers, the Muslims receiving revenue necessary to maintain their power.

Yet, due to Muslim dependence on Christians to run the economy and civil service, one finds theologians like John of Damascus writing and flourishing under Islamic rule. By a strange irony, John's grandfather had handed Damascus over to the Muslims in 635. John himself was employed by the Muslim rulers. He was an official in the Ummayad court before he became a monk, possibly at the monastery of St. Sabas, near Jerusalem, in an area under Arab rule.

This was the position of the Christian churches in the East beyond the bounds of the Byzantine Empire, living under the yoke of Islam. Most of these were heretical churches, anathematized by the ecumenical councils. However, some churches of the pentarchy – Alexandria, Jerusalem, and Antioch – were under this rule too. Pelikan notes that this forced them on to the defensive. Prohibited from evangelism they went into their shell and sought simply to preserve what they already had.

---

[6] Binns, *Orthodox Churches*, 174.
[7] Riddell, *Islam in Context*, 88–91.

As a result they eventually froze into a time warp. There was a drought of ideas, a dearth of theological or spiritual creativity. Since theological scholarship had been integrated into the heart of the Empire, once the imperial culture went into decline theological activity atrophied too.[8] On the other hand, the churches did receive protection and in the long run managed to survive for centuries under this arrangement. Indeed, when in later years the equivalent status of *millet* was withdrawn by the Ottomans in Turkey in the nineteenth century, the church was exposed to violent persecution and plunged into terminal decline.[9]

The Greek church in the Byzantine Empire to 1453

How about the Eastern church outside Islamic rule? How did the depredations of the Arab invaders impact the Greek church, for instance?

Development of the dyarchy: Emperor and Patriarch

Theoretically, between the civil government and the church in the Byzantine Empire there existed a harmonious relationship, based on both empire and church being ordained by God. In the imperial palace a throne containing an open gospel book showed the source of the emperor's authority.[10] However, practice was often different. The emperor Justinian I had authority over all aspects of church administration. He appointed and deposed patriarchs, summoned an ecumenical council, and established the qualifications for bishops and ordination. He could preach to the congregation, and administer the eucharist after the elements had been consecrated by a priest. What in theory was a harmonious dyarchy appeared to Western observers to be a form of Caesaropapism, with the emperor firmly in charge. Several emperors tried to define dogma, particularly during the

---

[8] See Binns, *Orthodox Churches*, 78–80.

[9] Binns, *Orthodox Churches*, 171–2.

[10] Binns, *Orthodox Churches*, 164.

iconoclast controversy. This may have been encouraged by the fact that Justinian had been a powerful theologian in his own right.

However, the patriarch, for his part, had a role in civil affairs. On the death of the emperor he was in charge of administration, and could serve as regent should the emperor be a minor. Photius, in his *Epanagoge Aucta*, defines the powers of the patriarch, reserving to him authority over full ecclesiastical matters, and comparing his relationship to the emperor to that between the soul and the body.[11] Photius relates that the clergy were banned from engaging in certain activities: civil bureaucracy, banking, and the ownership of private estates.

By the end of the fourteenth century the relationship between emperor and patriarch was almost completely reversed; the Empire was now so weak that the patriarch often represented the Empire to foreign rulers.[12] The crucial point is that the power politics of Byzantium meant that there was no single settled centre of power. As Binns recounts, in the case of Emperor Constantine VI's notorious divorce and remarriage in 795, 'The Patriarch turned a blind eye (a strategy often resorted to and justified under an "economy" or an act of discretion exercised in the administration of temporal responsibility), but punished the priest who officiated at the wedding. The monks were furious at this convenient overlooking of Christian standards, and so the Emperor exiled some of them. Then the Emperor's mother caused her son to be blinded and reinstated the monks. The officiating priest's fortunes went up and down, being excommunicated, reinstated, and excommunicated again, depending on who was in power. Within the power politics of the Byzantine court, it would be rash to claim either that the Emperor had supreme power and controlled the Church, or that he bowed to the authority of the Patriarch in matters

---

[11] D. J. Geanakoplos, *Byzantium: Church, Society, and Civilzation Seen Through Contemporary Eyes* (Chicago: University of Chicago Press, 1984), 137.

[12] Ibid., 143.

ecclesiastical.'[13] This inherent instability is clear from the chilling fact that of the eighty-eight emperors from Constantine I to the fall of Constantinople in 1453, half either died a violent death or had to flee to a monastery for protection from the mob. Even so, mutilation was the most popular punishment, stopping short of death.

The Church in the Byzantine Empire

The Eastern church in the Byzantine Empire had no systematic ecclesiology. Unlike the West, there was no coherent body of canon law, due to the fact that the Byzantines never considered the church in a juridical manner.[14] This flowed from the differences between East and West over authority. The West, with the strategic centrality of Rome and its history of law, had a clear source of authority and, although this was radically challenged at the time of the Reformation, both Catholics and Protestants agreed that the question of where authority lay was a crucial one, whether it resided in Scripture or the church, or some combination of the two. In the East, however, the issue never arose. The church simply recognized the single living tradition, of which Scripture and the liturgy were key parts. Councils did not meet to hand down freshly authoritative decrees binding on all; they gathered to recognize the living apostolic tradition. Hence, the church was not a legal or juridical body in the East as it was in the West. This allowed for the phenomenon of *oikonomia*, by which political or ecclesiological decisions could be made arbitrarily so as to suit the exigencies of the time.

Eventually, the Greek church suffered a major body blow when Constantinople fell to the Turks (now Muslim) in 1453. The great cathedral, Hagia Sophia, was turned into a mosque. Greece was to remain under Muslim rule until the nineteenth century.

---

[13] Binns, *Orthodox Churches*, 164–5.
[14] Meyendorff, *Byzantine Theology*, 79.

Monasticism in the Byzantine Empire[15]

Monasticism in the East was more faithful to the ascetic ideal than the corresponding movement in the West. In the East most monks were, and are, laypeople. There was only a single order – the 'Basilians', reflecting the seminal place of Basil the Great in the development of Eastern asceticism. In the two centuries after Basil monasticism took off. The monks were crucial in the defence of icons, and various groups of monks played decisive roles in the Christological controversies. Significant in the movement were hermits and recluses, who separated themselves from normal human interaction to devote themselves to the contemplation of God. The stylites lived at the top of poles, while David the tree-dweller, in the early sixth century, lived for three years in an almond tree so as to avoid the large crowds that flocked to him for spiritual advice. A key figure in the development of the monastic movement was Theodore of Studion (759–826), who had a stormy relationship with the political establishment, experiencing frequent exiles and mal-treatment, but whose writings and ascetic example proved an immense stimulus.

In general, Eastern monks have not been noted for learning, seeing it as inimical to mystical contemplation. When a theological seminary was founded on Mount Athos in the eighteenth century the monks burned it to the ground![16] While a more vigorous study of pagan authors developed among the monks in the ninth century, centred at the University of Constantinople, this lacked the dynamism and creativity of the later humanism of the West.[17] This is, of course, a striking contrast to much Western monasticism, in which scholarship was prized. One only has to think of medieval figures such as Bede, Anselm and Aquinas to realize that Western asceticism was a far more varied creature than its counterpart in Orthodoxy.

---

[15] See E. Benz, *The Orthodox Church: Its Thought and Life* (Garden City, New York: Doubleday, 1963), 89–93.

[16] Benz, *Orthodox Church*, 98–9.

[17] Ibid., 55ff.

One of the most prominent features of the contemplative and mystical nature of Eastern monasticism was *hesychasm*. Originating in the monastery of St. Catherine of Sinai, it became prominent in the thirteenth century, promoted by the monastery of Mount Athos. It entailed silent prayer and contemplation, with constant repetition of the Jesus prayer – 'Lord Jesus Christ, Son of God, have mercy upon me a sinner' – prayed while gazing downwards towards one's navel. Its goal was, through union with Christ, to rise to union with God and a vision of the divine light that surrounded Christ on the mount of transfiguration.[18] A great defender of hesychasm was Gregory Palamas (1296–1359). For Gregory, knowledge of God is an experience given to all Christians through baptism and the eucharist. God is totally inaccessible in his essence, man being deified only by grace or by divine energy. This tension highlights the distinction between essence and energy in God. Its origins lie with the Cappadocians, developed by John of Damascus and Dionysius the Areopagite. However, there are grounds for seeing it as at variance from Athanasius. The eventual victory of Palamism was the victory of a God-centred humanism that asserted that deification makes man truly human.[19]

Schism with the West

Communion between East and West was ruptured in 1054 when papal legates deposited a Bull of Excommunication in the Church of Hagia Sophia in Constantinople. Many years later, this was confirmed after the collapse of the Byzantine empire in 1453. However, the estrangement did not occur overnight. It was the result of a long process in which both parts of the church drifted into a state of virtual mutual incomprehension. A number of serious ecclesiastical and theological disagreements had developed, the most portentous relating to the jurisdiction

---

[18] Ibid., 100–1; D. J. Geanakoplos, *Byzantium*, 182–3.

[19] J. Meyendorff, *Byzantine Theology: Historical Trends and Doctrinal Themes* (New York: Fordham University Press, 1979), 77–8.

of the Roman church and papal authority, and to the *filioque* clause the West had inserted in its liturgical use of the Niceno-Constantinopolitan creed.

The end of the Roman Empire, officially dated from 476, had the effect of fragmenting the unity of the Mediterranean world. This process accelerated in later years. Greek and Latin, hitherto widely used throughout the area, became more or less regional languages, diminishing mutual understanding. Photios, indisputably the greatest scholar in ninth century Constantinople, could not read Latin.[20] From the seventh century, with the Persian wars immediately preceding the emergence of Islam, the Greek church looked eastwards, away from Rome. Islam only accentuated this trend. For its part, from the late eighth century Rome, deprived of the protection of the Byzantine Empire, looked west for political support from the Franks under Charlemagne. As a result 'the two halves of the Christian world began to speak different languages, and their frames of reference in theology began to diverge more sharply than before.'[21]

An acute source of conflict was the tension between the Greek theory of the pentarchy and Rome's claim to universal jurisdiction. The Greek church held to the parity of bishops, and indeed of all church members; the centres of ecclesiastical jurisdiction were based on the leading centres of political power – hence the rise of Constantinople. Many of these centres had a pedigree reaching back to the apostles. The West's insistence on the primacy of Rome, as expounded by the reformed Papacy in the eleventh century, was grounded on the claim that Jesus had entrusted such power to Peter, and so to the church of Rome, since – so the claim goes – Peter became its first bishop. It was a conflict between a collegial and an hierarchical view of the church.[22]

---

[20] T. Ware, *The Orthodox Church* (London: Penguin Books, 1969), 53.

[21] Meyendorff, *Byzantine Theology*, 50.

[22] See O. Clément, *You Are Peter: An Orthodox Theologian's Reflection on the Exercise of Papal Primacy* (New York: New City Press, 2003).

According to the Byzantines, Peter was the rock on which Christ built his church (Matt. 16:18) because he made the true confession of Christ's deity. The significance was soteriological not institutional. Others, following Cyprian, understood the passage less individualistically but avoided the Roman church's conclusions by applying it collegially; the office of Peter belongs to the bishop in each local church.[23] The Byzantines refused to recognize that one church had more of a corner on catholicity than any other or all others. Rome, on the other hand, held that Jesus addressed Peter specifically – in distinction from the rest of the apostles – and so gave him a universal pastoral jurisdiction over the whole church. Moreover, Rome argued, this bequest came to him as bishop of Rome and is transmitted to all his successors in that office. The East could allow Rome a primacy of honour, even a primacy in the pentarchy, but consistently rejected the claim to universal oversight. It was a conflict between pragmatism (adjusting to the secular realities of power) and the attribution of absolute dogmatic significance to a particular apostolic criterion of primacy.[24]

What precipitated this particular crisis were the German reforms of the Papacy in the late tenth and eleventh centuries made by Popes Leo IX (d. 1054) and Gregory VII (Hildebrand) (1073–84). This movement had an exalted view of Papal authority allied with an ignorance of Byzantium. The Byzantines, in turn, had not paid too close attention to the German reforming party. Certain liturgical and canonical practices in the West were also seen by the East as contentious – priestly celibacy and shaving of facial hair, to name but two. Patriarch Michael Cerularius' spokesman criticized Latin religious practices, especially the

---

[23] 'And although to all the apostles, after his resurrection, he gives an equal power ... yet, that he might set forth unity, he arranged by his authority the origin of that unity, as beginning from one. Assuredly the rest of the apostles were also the same as was Peter, endowed with a like partnership both of honour and power; but the beginning proceeds from unity.... The episcopate is one, each part of which is held by each one for the whole' (Cyprian, 'On the Unity of the Church,' *ANF* 5:422-23).

[24] Meyendorff, *Byzantine Theology*, 100.

use of unleavened bread (*azyma*) in the eucharist, and the observation of the Sabbath, both of which he condemned as Jewish, a remnant of the Mosaic law. Christ inaugurated a new practice for us, he urged. Those who use *azyma* and keep the Sabbath are not good Christians, since yeast in the dough is like life in the body and to use unleavened bread symbolizes death rather than life.[25]

In a debate in 1136 in Constantinople, Anselm of Havelburg argued for Roman primacy on the basis of Jesus' words in Matthew 16. The Greek bishop of Nicomedia, Nicetus, replied in eirenic spirit: 'But the Roman Church to which we do not deny the Primacy among her sisters, and whom we recognize as holding the highest place in any general council, the first place of honor, that Church has separated herself from the rest by her pretensions.'[26]

In 1054, the Papal bull excommunicated only Michael Cerularius and his followers and did not, of itself, signify a breach between Rome and Constantinople. The schism of 1054 was hardly noted by contemporary Byzantine historians. Traffic between East and West continued. The name of the Pope had been removed from the diptychs of Hagia Sophia as long ago as 1009. This was an altercation, not a schism. The crusades proved more damaging. In the fourth crusade in 1204 the crusaders, diverted from their original itinerary, detoured via Constantinople, invading and ransacking the city, remaining there until it was recovered in 1261 by Emperor Michael Palaeologus. This deliberate policy of vandalism and subjugation was fatal to the unity of the churches.

Despite even this, the Byzantine emperors of the final two centuries repeatedly tried to restore union. At the Council of Lyons in 1274, agreement was reached on the *filioque* but it was unacceptable to the populace – it was met with violence, robbing the Council of any pretence of ecumenicity. Crowds hooted at the envoys on their return.[27] It was an agreement driven largely

---

[25] Ibid., 94–5; Geanakoplos, *Byzantium*, 207.

[26] Geanakoplos, *Byzantium*, 215.

[27] Ibid., 219.

by political motives, with Emperor Michael VIII needing Papal support against the attacks of Charles of Anjou. Meanwhile, the East was coloured in its theology and liturgy by the patristic era, while the West had developed with the passing of time into the world of scholasticism, in which theology and philosophy were combined.[28]

In 1965, as a sign of a new movement in a long path towards rapprochement Pope Paul VI and Patriarch Athenagoras I withdrew the anathemas of 1054. However, since the altercation of 1054 was largely personal, this action was essentially symbolic and had no theological or canonical significance.

The filioque clause

Of all the matters that divided, by far the most important single question of all was, and is, the *filioque* clause added by the West to the Niceno-Constantinopolitan creed (C).[29] C states that the Holy Spirit 'proceeds from the Father'. There is no mention of his proceeding from the Son as well. However, in Spain due to the threat of a continued Arianism, in localized liturgies an addition crept in – *a patre filioque* – 'from the Father *and the Son.*' This addition spread and was adopted by local councils, particularly the Council of Toledo (589),[30] was accepted by the

[28] Ware, *Orthodox Church*, 71.

[29] The best place to begin consideration of this important matter is, in support of the East, the excellent article by N. Needham, 'The Filioque Clause: East or West?' *SBET* 15 (1997), 142–62 and in support of the *filioque*, G. Bray, 'The Filioque Clause in History and Theology,' *TB* 34 (1983), 91–144. Bray's article is an extensive historical discussion with penetrating theological comment. A valuable collection of essays, from Orthodox, Roman Catholic, and Protestant perspectives is L. Vischer, ed., *Spirit of God, Spirit of Christ: Ecumenical Reflections on the Filioque Controversy* (London: SPCK, 1981). The most comprehensive and recent work on the whole issue is B. Oberdorfer, *Filioque: Geschichte und Theologie Eines Ökumenischen Problems* (Göttingen: Vandenhoeck & Ruprecht, 2001).

[30] But see R. Haugh, *Photius and the Carolingians: The Trinitarian Controversy* (Belmont, Massachussetts: Norland, 1975), 160–1, who questions this explanation and argues that it 'first entered the Ecumenical Creed in the Latin West by a simple method of transposition and not by any willful act of interpolation in conscious violation of the Ecumenical decrees.' Sergei Bulgakov rightly argues that the phrase was unnecessary, for Arianism could have been rebutted quite

French church in the late eighth century, but was not inserted into the Creed by Rome until 1014 under Pope Benedict VIII. The fourth Lateran Council of 1215 mentioned it and the Council of Lyons in 1274 proclaimed it as dogma.

The East objects to this development on ecclesiastical grounds. Such a change (more a development, since C did not deny the *filioque* but simply did not comment as it was not an issue) should require an ecumenical council akin to Nicaea I, Constantinople I and Chalcedon, it maintains. As Stylianopoulos puts it, 'Can a clause deriving from one theological tradition simply be inserted in a creed deriving from another theological tradition without council?'[31]

The East also objects on theological grounds. We shall examine the reasons for this in detail in chapter 9, so for now we shall simply summarize the main areas of contention. Since East and West understand the trinity differently, on Eastern premises this Western development appears to undermine heretically the church's teaching on the trinity in a modalist direction by confusing the Father and the Son. The East has held that the Father is the basis of the unity of the trinity, and so is the single source of the generation of the Son and the procession of the Holy Spirit. For the West, following Augustine, to say that the Spirit proceeds from the Father and the Son – 'as from a single source' in Augustine's words – is to undermine the indivisible unity of the trinity and to blur the personal distinctions.

The Greek church under Ottoman rule from 1453

The final collapse of Byzantium and the fall of Constantinople in 1453 was an overwhelmingly tragic moment for the Eastern church. Threatened by the Turks for several centuries and progressively weakened, it capitulated. The Greek church was

---

readily without it; 'pour rejeter l'arianisme et reconnaître l'équi-divinité et la consubstantialité du Fils au Père, on n'a nul besoin de cette surérogation' (S. N. Bulgakov, *Le Paraclet* [C. Andronikof; Paris: Aubier, 1946], 125).

[31] T. Stylianopoulos, eds, *Spirit of Truth: Ecumenical Perspectives on the Holy Spirit. Communion on Faith and Order, NCCCUSA October 24–25, 1985 – Brookline, Massachusetts* (Brookline, Massachusetts: Holy Cross Orthodox Press, 1986) 32.

now at its lowest ebb. Binns comments that 'as Islamic influence grew, so Christian theological creativity declined.'[32] This was not a sudden, overnight event, like a massive heart attack – it was rather a slow ebbing of a chronic invalid in a nursing home. The Turks were generally tolerant, regarding Christians as 'people of the Book'. Worship continued. But the definitely second-class status, together with enforced recognition of Islamic rule and proscriptions on missionary activity, had a debilitating effect. The patient was on drip-feed, movement restricted, communications monitored. Taxes were heavy, distinctive clothing required. 'The survival of Christian theological writing after the Islamic conquests should be seen as an indication of the slowness of the advance of Muslim cultural infiltration. As this process continued, so educational and other institutions of the Church declined and with them the vitality of the theological tradition of Orthodoxy.' This was due not to any prohibition of thinking, praying, writing or debating but to the fact that in the Byzantine Empire theological scholarship had been thoroughly integrated into general life. Once the Empire was dismantled all aspects of Christian life went into decline, so much so that it is estimated that when Turkish rule was ended and the church re-established in 1850 only one per cent of the clergy could even write their own name.[33] Moreover, the Turks made the Church the basis of organization for the Christian Greeks, the Patriarch of Constantinople becoming a government official as well as a church leader. Not only was Christianity subservient but it was also implicated in the political structure of the nation, with the inevitable entanglement in corruption that went with it. In the long-term, the Greeks found it difficult to distinguish the two elements, instead tending to identify the Christian faith with the nation.[34]

As standards of theology declined in the East, many went West. Many in the East saw Rome as a predator, seeking to

---

[32] Binns, *Orthodox Churches*, 79.

[33] Ibid., 79–80.

[34] See Ware, *Orthodox Church*, 97–9.

convert the Orthodox. This became so much of an issue that, after the Reformation, Protestants were seen as allies. Both had been removed from Rome in some way or other; they had a common enemy. For Reformed Christians, one of most striking events in the Eastern church was the rise of Cyril Lukaris (1572–1638), Patriarch of Constantinople from 1620 until his tragic death. One of the most brilliant minds the East has produced, Lukaris was sent to Poland in 1596 to strengthen the Orthodox against the new Greek Catholic Church, brought about by Jesuit intrigue. There he was confirmed in his distrust and hostility towards Rome. In Poland, he worked alongside Lutherans and Calvinists and eventually, between 1615 and 1618, became convinced of Calvinism. He was consecrated Patriarch of Alexandria in 1601, and then in 1620 Patriarch of Constantinople. In 1629 he wrote a *Confession of Faith* teaching predestination and justification by faith. Deposed and reinstated six times, hugely popular with the populace, he was eventually murdered by Turkish emissaries, his body tossed into the Bosphorus.[35]

The Russian church[36]

Although Constantinople fell in 1453, bringing to an end the Christian Empire of Byzantium, the ideal of a Christian empire persisted, since at the same time Russia had emerged from Tatar domination and was now the only Orthodox area to remain free.

Orthodoxy spread to Russia in the late tenth century and took firm root. At first, Kiev became the center of gravity of Orthodoxy but eventually the balance swung to Moscow. Orthodoxy in Russia was affected surprisingly little by several centuries under domination by the Mongols. Genghis Khan's policy was universal religious toleration, the state committing itself to no one religion. He granted tax-exempt status to all religious institutions and priests. This policy led to an increase

---

[35] Binns, *Orthodox Churches*, 81–2; G. A. Hadjiantoniou, *Protestant Patriarch: The Life of Cyril Lukaris (1572–1638) Patriarch of Constantinople* (Richmond, Virginia: John Knox Press, 1961).

[36] See G. P. Fedotov, *The Russian Religious Mind* (New York: Harper, 1946).

in the wealth and status of the church, a development of icon painting, and the rapid growth of monasteries.

The development of Christianity in Russia led to the conviction that Moscow was the third Rome, the inheritor of the Empire, an idea that gained ground after the fall of Byzantium. The first Rome had fallen, due to heresy. Constantinople, the second Rome, had similarly been subjugated; this time its capitulation to the Papacy at the Council of Florence in 1439 had come under divine judgment. Moscow was left, the centre of a now autocephalous jurisdiction, alone the bastion of the Orthodox faith. This idea is sometimes overstated; the Patriarch of Moscow never claimed it, only that Moscow had replaced Rome in the pentarchy, from which it had fallen.[37]

Russian monasticism

Two different types of monasticism emerged in Russia. They differed over their attitude to the State and to monastic property. Skete monasticism was eremitic. As hermits, these monks avoided politics and preached a gospel of love. On the other hand, cenobitic monasticism – a communal form – enforced strict discipline on its adherents, and engaged in the amassing of wealth to feed the poor. The two strands clashed in the sixteenth century, resulting in the dissolution of the skete monasteries and the imprisonment of their monks. They had been opposed to force against heretics and so were accused of harbouring heresy; they challenged the monasteries' ownership of property; they had resisted any connection with the civil power. Unfortunately, their dissolution inhibited the church from opposing the State – and some highly dictatorial rulers were in store for Russia in later years. Nevertheless, as Binns points out, the church could on occasions stand firm, as in the resistance of Philip, Metropolitan of Moscow, to Ivan IV, the Terrible, (1547–84) and his secret police, the Oprichnina.[38]

---

[37] Binns, *Orthodox Churches*, 168.
[38] Ibid., 167.

Peter the Great, Tsar from 1682 to 1725, refused to appoint a new Patriarch of Moscow on the see becoming vacant, and in 1721 published the *Spiritual Regulation* by which the church was governed by a Holy Synod appointed by the emperor. In effect, the church was now under direct State control, a department of State rather than an autonomous – let alone autocephalous – church. Priests hearing confession were obliged to disclose any information of interest to the governing authorities. There was a concomitant series of restrictions on the monasteries. This is generally held to have had an enervating effect on the Russian church. Later, Catherine II (1762–96) closed most of the remaining monastic houses and imposed further restrictions on the rest. Yet in the nineteenth century there was a remarkable revival of spiritual vigour, seen in patristic scholarship and original thinking, especially with Alexei Khomiakov (1804–60) who paved the way for a great flowering of Russian philosophical and theological thought, with Vladimir Solovyev (1853–1900), Sergei Bulgakov (1871–1944), and Pavel Florensky (1882–1943), that fed into a whole phalanx of theologians in exile. This intellectual revival was accompanied by a renewed impetus to missionary work, as we shall now consider.

Missionary expansion

The Eastern church has been notable for vigorous missionary activity. It pushed eastwards to Syria and India, west to the Germanic tribes migrating through western Europe in the fourth century, north to the Slavs in the ninth century, spearheaded by Cyril (d. 869) and Methodius (d. 885). Later the Western church capitalized on this, absorbing the Germanic tribes and destroying the Slavic mission, introducing Latin liturgy.[39]

The guiding principle of the East from the very first was to preach to the people in their own language, to reduce the language to writing, and to translate the Bible and liturgy into the vernacular at the earliest opportunity. We justly praise Luther

---

[39] Benz, *Orthodox Church*, 112.

and Tyndale for recovering this vital task in the Reformation; the Orthodox had never lost sight of it. One of the central planks of the Reformation had always been Orthodoxy's norm.[40] They saw Pentecost as reversing Babel and so baptizing the vernacular languages as the instruments of the gospel. In this, the East is in striking contrast to the medieval and even more modern Roman Catholic Church, which until fairly recently restricted the reading of Scripture to the clergy and conducted its worship in a language that few could understand.

The mission to the Slavs

The East Slavs were Christianized by the end of the eleventh century, from Novgorod in the north to beyond Kiev in the south. Here the spread of Christianity went in step with the spread of Russian domination. As Russia expanded peacefully, ultimately to Archangel in the Arctic north and beyond the Urals into Siberia, so the church advanced, led by hunters, traders and monks.[41]

A major landmark was the Tatar invasion (1222–23), making Russia a province of the Tatar Empire. A direct consequence of this huge political reverse was a widespread desire for the monastic life among the Russian population. Now the monks led the way into new territory. A whole network of monasteries sprang up all over north and north-east Russia. These became the springboard for dramatic missionary advance in the next century, to the East Karelians and Lapps, and in the following centuries to the Far East.[42]

The Tatars, or Mongols, granted the church protection under their religious laws in the code of the Great Yasa. The church and its property were preserved. The rule of the Great Yasa tolerated all religions in the Mongol Empire, allowing freedom of worship to all. Since Genghis Khan belonged to no religion he preferred none above any other. This state of affairs

---

[40] Ibid., 105.

[41] Ibid., 110–15; Ware, *Orthodox Church*, 82–95.

[42] Benz, *Orthodox Church*, 115–16.

was little changed after the Mongols adopted Islam; priests and monks of all religions were exempt from taxation and military service. During this time relations with Rome were broken off but missionary work was carried on among the Mongols themselves.[43]

Nineteenth-century missionary expansion

After Mongol rule had ended, the Russian church conducted a vigorous missionary expansion. Michael (or Makary as he is known after becoming a monk) Glucharev (1792–1849) worked tirelessly in the grim Altai plateau in Central Asia, planting churches, a school and hospital, insisting on a thorough Christianization of church and society in doing so. He baptized only after a long period of catechetical instruction, taught that baptism was but the beginning of a lifelong process of conversion, and that converts were responsible to live as Christians in the world. A particular legacy of Glucharev is the book *Thoughts on the Methods to be followed for a successful dissemination of the Faith among Mohammedans, Jews, and Pagans in the Russian Empire*. He had a deep concern for the mobilization of the whole church and nation in missions.

Under the leadership of Innokenty Venyaminov (1797–1879), one of the great missionaries of all history, Christianity was brought to Siberia, the Russian Far East, the Aleutian Islands, Japan, and Russian Alaska.[44] Venyaminov's missionary efforts are heroic in the extreme. We in the West have paid no attention to them; they took place in far-away lands outside Western jurisdiction and in climates too cold to contemplate. Venyaminov made herculean travels across the snowfields of the far north. Wherever he went he reduced the local language to writing, translating the Bible into the vernacular. Eventually Venyaminov imbued the whole Russian church with missionary

---

[43] Ibid., 119ff; Stephen Neill, *Christian Missions* (London: Penguin Books, 1964), 440–5.

[44] Benz, *Orthodox Church*, 122–5.

zeal, especially after he was made Metropolitan of Moscow late in his life, when blind from the constant glare of the sun reflected off the snowfields.

That the Russian missionary expansion had its glaring weaknesses is obvious from the historical record. Much of it was superficial and left large numbers of converts as much pagan as they were before. Too often the apparatus of state was used to coerce populations to profess the Christian faith. Frequently missionaries baptized large numbers in order to receive the approval of their bishops. The conduct of many of those admitted to the church was unchanged. However, that should not blind us to the fact that among much dross was the genuine article; a fact that is common to all missions in history.[45] Then – wham! like a portcullis slamming down in a medieval castle the doors were shut: the Bolsheviks seized power and everything was brought to a halt; or was it?

The rise of nationalism

Under Islam, due to its subordinate status, the church became increasingly tied to national groups rather than the Byzantine Empire. Later, after the fall of Constantinople, the position of the Patriarch of Constantinople became increasingly problematic. He no longer had the support of a Christian civilization, being located in alien territory. By the nineteenth century, as the Ottoman Empire weakened and nationalist movements gained ground – now closely connected with the Orthodox churches in those countries – the Patriarch was isolated even more. Dependent on the Ottoman authorities and responsible to support them, he lost considerable favour among the Greek people. He had become detached from the Greek church and from the national struggle. Generally, the church has been the focus for national aspirations under Islamic rule. Syrian Christians became more conscious of their common roots and thus ecclesiastical divisions began to be healed. Language became central in preserving national and

---

[45] Neill, *Christian Missions*, 448-9.

ecclesiastical identity, candidates for the priesthood being taught
the national language and liturgy. Lack of central leadership and
of an educated ministry actually led to greater responsibility at
the local level. Nationalism was further fostered by the collapse
of the Russian Empire when the Bolsheviks seized power and
enthroned atheism as the official state religion.[46]

The church under Communism

The period under the Communist regime in Russia was probably
the most difficult time the Orthodox Church has experienced.
Unlike the Muslims, the Communists were determined to
eradicate religion in general, and Christianity in particular.
Churches and theological seminaries were closed, the way to
professional advancement barred to Christian believers. At
various times, more overt tactics were used to achieve this end.
In the early years of Bolshevik rule in Russia a large proportion
of bishops, clergy, and monks were martyred. The level of
persecution at this time was greater than anything experienced
in the early church.[47] Ware records a moving description of
the massive sufferings under Communism, together with this
poignant and inspiring account:

> In the village there is a chapel dug deep beneath the earth, the
> entrance carefully camouflaged. When a secret priest visits the
> village, it is here that he celebrates the Liturgy and the other
> services. If the villagers for once believe themselves safe from
> police observation, the whole population gathers in the chapel,
> except for the guards who remain outside to give warning if
> strangers appear. At other times services take place in shifts...[48]

In the end all the efforts of militant communism to overthrow
the Christian church came to nothing. At the height of Stalin's
tyranny the census of 1937 asked Soviet citizens whether they

---

[46] Binns, *Orthodox Churches*, 178–85.

[47] For a detailed account of this dark period, see Ware, *Orthodox Church*, 152–79.

[48] Ware, *Orthodox Church*, 19.

believed in God. The response was so overwhelming that the authorities were forced to suppress the result, so as not to discredit their atheistic policy.[49]

Paradoxically, the enforced exile of Russian Christian leaders by the Bolsheviks led to a creative renewal of Orthodox theology in the West. Many fled to Paris, there to establish St. Sergius Institute. Nourished by the liturgy and the study of the Fathers, and open to the West, this proved the base for a considerable revival of Orthodox fortunes. Sergei Bulgakov was the first dean. A brilliantly creative theological maverick, he was never entirely acceptable in either East or West. Building on the teachings of the seminal Russian personalist, Vladimir Solovyev (1853–1900), he developed the idea of sophiology. Using the theme of *sophia* (wisdom) he built his trinitarian, Christological and soteriological teaching around the notion. Eventually, he was censured by the Moscow Patriarchate in 1937 for teaching a fourth hypostasis in the trinity. It is not difficult to see how this could be a concern.

Others who taught at St. Sergius were Georges Florovsky (1983–79) whose theology was rooted in the Fathers and who was hostile to Bulgakov's innovations. After leaving for Yugoslavia during the Second World War, he crossed the Atlantic in 1949 to St. Vladimir's Seminary and various other prestigious academic posts in the USA. Another Russian expatriate, Vladimir Lossky (1900–58), remained under the jurisdiction of the Moscow Patriarchate and did not teach at St. Sergius Institute, but proved to be perhaps the most effective at interacting with a Western audience. Away from Russia and the Russian emigrés, the Romanian theologian Dimitru Staniloae (1903–93) is also noteworthy. He spent five years of his life in a concentration camp, repeating the Jesus prayer over and over again.

In summary, the East had no Middle Ages, no Reformation, no Enlightenment against which to contend; all was quite different, for the church had already dominated the culture.

---

[49] *BDEC*, 428.

Today, volumes written by Eastern theologians or Biblical exegetes are notable for a striking lack of interest in combating rationalistic criticism; this was simply not an issue. The words of Kallistos Ware, referring to Alexis Khomiakov's observation that all Protestants are crypto-Romanists in the eyes of the Orthodox, suggests that he

> had in mind the fact that western Christians ... have a common background in the past. All alike ... have been profoundly influenced by the same events: by the Papal centralization and the Scholasticism of the Middle Ages, by the Renaissance, by the Reformation and Counter-Reformation. But behind members of the Orthodox Church ... there lies a very different background. They have known no Middle Ages (in the western sense) and have undergone no Reformations or Counter-Reformations; they have only been affected in an oblique way by the cultural and religious upheaval which transformed western Europe in the sixteenth and seventeenth centuries. Christians in the west, both Roman and Reformed, generally start by asking the same questions, although they may disagree about the answers. In Orthodoxy, however, it is not merely the answers that are different – the questions themselves are not the same as in the west.[50]

To some of these questions we now turn.

Approximate totals of Orthodox today
Autocephalous jurisdictions
Russia 100,000,000+
Romania 20,000,000+
Greece 10,000,000+
Serbia 8,000,000
Bulgaria 8,000,000

---

[50] Ibid., 9. As an instance of this vast difference, Ware cites the case of the Patriarch of Constantinople in the 1830s who had never heard of the Archbishop of Canterbury, ibid., 11.

Patriarchate of Constantinople 5,250,000 (only 2,000 in Turkey)
Antioch 3,000,000[51]
Georgia 3,000,000
Poland 1,000,000
Cyprus 600,000
Alexandria 280,000
Jerusalem 260,000
Czech Republic and Slovakia 100,000

The West
25,000,000 (estimated), of which approximately 5,000,000 are in the USA.

---

[51] Note that there are currently no fewer than five patriarchs of Antioch – representing the Syrian Orthodox, the Greek Orthodox, the Melkite Catholic, the Syrian Catholic, and the Maronite jurisdictions.

Part Two:

Theology

6

Of Prayers and Icons

Orthodoxy is more visual than Protestantism
As you enter an Orthodox church, the most prominent feature
is the iconostasis, a screen across the whole room, towards
the front, reaching a good way to the ceiling, although in
recent years — and in smaller churches — some have reverted
to the lower level of earlier times. The iconostasis divides the
sanctuary — the area behind it — from the congregation. Only
the clergy are admitted to the sanctuary; no woman may enter.
It symbolizes the spiritual, immaterial world. The nave, where
the congregation stand, is the image of the material world.
Although the iconostasis divides them, these two are in reality
parts of one whole, the meeting place of heaven and earth.
On the iconostasis itself — standing between heaven and earth
— are several levels of icons, although there are icons almost
everywhere in the church, on the ceiling and walls. Starting at
the top level of the iconostasis — if it is a full-sized church one —
and moving down are images of the Old Testament patriarchs;
the Old Testament prophets; the liturgical feasts (representing
the fulfilment of Old Testament prophecy); the *tchin* or order,
with John the Baptist and the Mother of God in prayer before

the icon of Christ on his throne, together with various angels and others, representing the result of the incarnation and the intercession of the church; and a variety of locally significant icons. There is a careful theological point to the arrangement of these icons. Before the service begins, the Orthodox obtain a candle, go up to the icons on the lower level, cross themselves, kiss their favourite icon on the ambos in front of the iconostasis and light the candle.

There are three doors in the iconostasis, the central (or royal) door only ever traversed by the clergy. These doors are closed except for certain times during the Liturgy. Through the royal door, after the eucharist is celebrated in the sanctuary, comes the priest representing the King of glory coming to feed his people with his body and blood. Sometimes the opening of this door symbolizes the opening of the gates of paradise, while it indicates at other times the entrance to the kingdom of heaven. Much of the Liturgy is inaudible to the congregation, since it takes place behind the screen in the sanctuary, to which only the clergy are admitted. For the congregation, a choir sings beautiful and intricate liturgical music.

This entire arrangement signifies the meeting of heaven and earth, with a great cloud of witnesses present, represented by the icons, pointing to the church opening out on to eternity. Apart from some seating for the elderly, there are no pews; the vast majority remain standing, for that and kneeling are considered the only generally appropriate postures in worship.[1] Priests and worshippers intermingle informally, celebrating the Liturgy together. The priest or deacon will cense the icons and the congregation, 'thus paying homage to the image of God in man and uniting in one gesture the saints represented in the icons and the congregation – the heavenly and the earthly church.'[2]

---

[1] In many churches in the West, pews are used. In the Greek Orthodox church near where I lived in America the congregation is often seated.

[2] Leonid Ouspensky and Vladimir Lossky, *The Meaning of Icons*, Trans., G.E.H. Palmer and E. Kadloubovsky (Crestwood, New York: St. Vladimir's Seminary Press, 1982), 68.

The standard Orthodox service is far longer than a Western one. Even while the congregation is silent, its members constantly perform the sign of the cross, freely, in identification with the various intercessions. The entire building – every nook and cranny, almost every square inch – is saturated with theological meaning and symbolism.[3]

Icons (from *eikon*, image) are teaching devices, windows to heaven, through which to perceive greater realities beyond; in the words of Leontius of Neapolis, 'opened books to remind us of God.'[4] They portray the saint in a two-dimensional mode made according to strict guidelines by iconographers. These iconographers are not free-wheeling artists but monks, who compose their work in an ethos of prayer and contemplation. Titus Burkhardt writes, 'The art of icons is a sacred art in the true sense of the word. It is nourished wholly in the spiritual truth to which it gives pictorial expression.' It gives 'access to a living and inexhaustible source'.[5] Novelty is anathema, faithfulness to the archetype all-important. The iconographer's concern is not to express himself but to transmit tradition and to convey the gospel teaching.[6] Indeed, the Orthodox believe that the archetype takes the initiative. Tales are told of occasions when an iconographer breaks off work, goes elsewhere, and on his return finds that the icon has finished the job itself! Recently, an icon of St. Anna, the mother of the virgin Mary, visited the Antiochene Orthodox church near my home; it was reported to have wept tears of myrrh on a number of occasions, which the bishop suggested could as much be tears of joy as of sorrow. Either way, the idea was that St. Anna was communicating with the faithful through the icon.

The Orthodox claim that the first icons date from the lifetime of Jesus. Eusebius records that not only had he seen

---

[3] On this, see *Service Book*, xxviii–lx.

[4] *PG* 94:1276a, cited by T. Ware, *The Orthodox Church* (London: Penguin Books, 1969), 40.

[5] Titus Burkhardt, 'Foreword,' in Ouspensky and Lossky, *The Meaning of Icons*, 7.

[6] Ouspensky and Lossky, *The Meaning of Icons*, 27.

a large number of portraits of Jesus and the apostles that had
been preserved to his own day but that there was a statue of
Jesus in Caesarea Philippi put up by the woman who had the
issue of blood (Matt. 9:20-3 and parallels).[7] Jewish synagogues
in the first century AD had pictures in them, while portraiture
was popular throughout the Roman Empire.

One point is clear: Nicaea II insisted that icons are not to be
worshipped. John of Damascus, in his earlier landmark treatise
in defense of icons, distinguished between *latreia* (worship)
given only to God, and *proskunēsis* (veneration) given to the
saints. He also distinguished clearly between the icon and the
one signified.

We noted the violent passions aroused by the iconoclast
controversy. Monks died under the lash in the public circus,
a leading monk was torn to pieces by a mob, the Patriarch
Constantine of Constantinople was publicly beheaded, monks
had their nostrils slit.[8] This was, and is, no peripheral matter for
the Eastern church.

The theology of icons

Nicaea II defined icons or images as any representation of Christ,
the Mother of God, or the saints and angels, or the cross 'made
of colours, pebbles, or any other material that is fit, set in the
holy churches of God, on holy utensils or vestments, on walls
or boards, in houses and in streets.' This, as Louth points out,
includes 'mosaics, frescoes, manuscript illuminations, images
woven into cloth, engraved on metal, carved in ivory or wood,
and probably also statues.'[9]

Before the controversy broke out, the Quinisext Council 692
(which met *in trullo*, a chamber), in canon 82, required Christ to

---

[7] Eusebius, *History of the Church*, 7:18, PG 20:680. See Ouspensky and Lossky, *The Meaning of Icons*, 25.

[8] L. D. Davis, *The First Seven Ecumenical Councils (325–787)* (Collegeville, Minnesota: The Liturgical Press, 1990), 301–5.

[9] A. Louth, *John Damascene: Tradition and Originality in Byzantine Theology* (Oxford: Oxford University Press, 2002), 194–5.

be pictured in human form rather than as a lamb, as had become widespread:

> In some pictures of the venerable icons, a lamb is painted to which the Precursor points his finger, which is received as a type of grace, indicating beforehand through the Law, our true Lamb, Christ our God. Embracing therefore the ancient types and shadows as symbols of the truth, and patterns given to the Church, we prefer 'grace and truth,' receiving it as the fulfilment of the Law. In order therefore that 'that which is perfect' may be delineated to the eyes of all, at least in coloured expression, we decree that the figure in human form of the Lamb who taketh away the sin of the world, Christ our God, be henceforth exhibited in images, instead of the ancient lamb, so that all may understand by means of it the depths of the humiliation of the Word of God, and that we may recall to our memory his conversation in the flesh, his passion and salutary death, and his redemption which was wrought for the whole world.[10]

The practice of making icons of Christ had, by the seventh century, a considerable pedigree. The point the Council makes is that the symbols of the Old Testament were now fulfilled, since the incarnation had occurred. Therefore the time had passed for oblique symbolic representations of Christ. The reality of the abasement of God the Word should now be shown so as to 'contemplate his divine glory in his human image'.[11]

Initially the iconoclasts insisted that icons were idolatrous and were forbidden by the second commandment. Indeed, they claimed that the loss of the eastern territories to Islam was God's judgment for idolatry; hence, the pressing need to outlaw these practices. However, this polemic should be taken with a pinch of salt for we now know that the early synagogues had pictures in them, while the early church was opposed to images of *pagan*

---

[10] NPNF2 14:401.

[11] Ouspensky and Lossky, *The Meaning of Icons,* 29.

gods – which it saw as idolatry – but not to images drawn from the Christian faith.[12]

The landmark treatise on the subject was written by John of Damascus, *On the Holy Icons*, shortly after the iconoclast controversy began.[13] John agreed that, while it is impossible to portray God in himself, it is both possible and necessary to depict him as incarnate. The Old Testament prohibition of idolatry addresses the worship of the creature rather than the creator, false gods rather than the true God. The question, according to John, revolves around two things: the making of images, and their veneration (not worship).

In Book 3 of this treatise, John asks what is the purpose of icons? What can and cannot be portrayed?[14] In pursuit of these fundamental issues, John asks a further series of questions concerning veneration (*proskunēsis*). What is veneration? What kinds of veneration are there? What objects of veneration do we find in Scripture? Are all acts of veneration by nature acts of veneration of God? He also argues that honour given to the image passes through or proceeds to the original or prototype.[15]

An image, John writes, is a likeness, pattern and impression (*homoiōma, paradeigma, ektupōma*) of the thing that is imaged. At the same time there is, however, also a dissimilarity between the image and the original since they are different things. Thus, an image of man, although it has the impress and features of the body, lacks its natural power, for it is not alive, is unable to speak or think, nor do its features change.[16]

---

[12] M. C. Murray, 'Art and the Early Church,' *JTS* 28 (1977), 304–45; P. C. Finney, *The Invisible God: The Earliest Christians on Art* (New York: Oxford University Press, 1994); both cited by Louth, *John Damascene*, 195.

[13] John of Damascus, LOGOI APOLOGHTIKOI PROS TOUS DIABALL-ONTAS TAS AGIAS EIKONAS Logoi apologetikoi pros tous diaballontas tas hagias eikonas in B. Kotter, OSB, ed., *Die Schriften Des Johannes von Damaskos: 5 Vols* (Patristische Texte und Studien; Berlin and New York: Walter de Gruyter, 1975); PG 94:1337-1360.

[14] See III:14, in Kotter, ed., *Johannes von Damaskos*, 7, 125; PG 94:1337.

[15] III:15, in Kotter, ed., *Johannes von Damaskos*, 7, 125; PG 94:1337.

[16] III:16; ibid.

However, why should there be images? Here, John argues that, since we have no appreciation of the invisible world, the image is a guide to knowledge, for it makes these things known for our help, benefit and salvation so that we can seek what is good and turn away from evil.[17] In other words, man is a physical being to whom the spiritual world is a mystery. Icons provide a window into this world, a help on the path of salvation.

John then considers various kinds of images. First, the Son of the Father is the natural and identical (*aparallaktos*) image of the invisible God – in himself he shows us the Father. John cites John 1:18, 6:46, 14:6-13, Colossians 1:15, and Hebrews 1:3 in support. In these passages Christ is said to be the image of the invisible God, to bear the exact impress of the Father's being. So too the Holy Spirit is the image of the Son (here he cites 1 Corinthians 12:13).[18] In this John draws on a theme reaching back as far as the language and imagery of Athanasius in his *Letters on the Holy Spirit to Serapion*.[19]

The second type of image is God's eternal counsel or plan (*boulē*).[20] The third image is man, the imitation or copy of God. Man's created nature is a copy (*kata mimēsin*) of God's, the uncreated. As the Mind (*nous*) and Word (*logos*) and Holy Spirit (*pneuma to hagion*) are one God, so the *nous* and *logos* and *pneuma* are one man. John references the *locus classicus*, Genesis 1:26-28, arguing that man as the image of God mirrors the holy trinity.[21] The fourth image is the creation, which dimly reflects the divine.[22]

This leads John to the important point as to what we can and cannot image.[23] We can see neither God nor angels nor souls

---

[17] III:17; Kotter, ed., *Johannes von Damaskos*, 7, 126; PG 94:1337.

[18] III:18; Kotter, ed., *Johannes von Damaskos*, 7, 126–7; PG 94:1337-1340.

[19] Athanasius, *Letters to Serapion on the Holy Spirit* (1:14, 20, 24–5, 3:1; PG 26:564-5, 576-80, 585-9, 624-8).

[20] III:19; Kotter, ed., *Johannes von Damaskos*, 7, 127; PG 94:1340.

[21] III:20; Kotter, ed., *Johannes von Damaskos*, 7, 128; PG 94:1340-1341.

[22] III:21; Kotter, ed., *Johannes von Damaskos*, 7, 128–9; PG 94:1341,

[23] III:24; Kotter, ed., *Johannes von Damaskos*, 7, 130–1; PG 94:1344.

nor demons. However, so that we would not be left completely
ignorant of God and his bodiless creation, 'in the divine
forethought so that we could see these things he put a form
upon the bodiless and formless so as to guide us by the hand
towards a partial knowledge'. For God is by nature bodiless. But,
not wanting to leave us ignorant, he gave us representations,
likenesses and images (*tupous, schēmata, eikonas*) according to the
analogy of our bodily nature.[24] What was the first icon? God
begat his only begotten Son and Logos, and made man according
to his likeness.[25] Here John points to Christ as the image of the
invisible God, and to man made *in* the image of God.[26]

As for veneration, veneration of a person (*proskunēsis
hupostaseōs*) is a sign of subordination and lowliness on the part of
the one who offers the veneration. There are many ways we can
express this veneration,[27] while John insists that we bring worship
only to God. First in terms of service (*douleia*), all creatures are
servants of a master (*despotēs*), some willingly, some unwillingly.
The godly worship God willingly, the demons unwillingly,
while others are unwilling because they are ignorant of him.[28]
For our part, we worship God because of the glory of his nature,
in thanksgiving for all the good things he has done for us, and
because without his power nothing would be made nor would
there be anything good. So we pray to be delivered from evil
and to obtain the good. Moreover, since we have sinned, we
worship God in repentance and confession.[29]

In Scripture, what things are to be venerated and in what
ways?[30] Here, John distinguishes clearly between the worship
due to God alone and the veneration of created things:

[24] III:25; Kotter, ed., *Johannes von Damaskos,* 7, 131–2; PG 94:1344-1345.

[25] III:26; Kotter, ed., *Johannes von Damaskos,* 7, 132; PG 94:1345-1348.

[26] See P. E. Hughes, *The True Image: The Origin and Destiny of Man in Christ*
(Grand Rapids, Michigan: Eerdmans, 1989).

[27] III:27; Kotter, ed., *Johannes von Damaskos,* 7, 135; PG 94:1348.

[28] III:28; Kotter, ed., *Johannes von Damaskos,* 7, 135; PG 94:1348-1349.

[29] III:29-32; Kotter, ed., *Johannes von Damaskos,* 7, 136–7; PG 94:1349-1352.

[30] III:33; Kotter, ed., *Johannes von Damaskos,* 7, 137–44; PG 94:1352-1360.

Let us worship and serve (*proskunēsōmen kai latreusōmen*) the
creator only as by nature the God to be worshipped.... On the
other hand, let us venerate (*proskunēsōmen*) also the holy *theotokos*
– not as God but as the mother of God according to the flesh....
We venerate also the saints as elect friends of God [here he cites
Romans 13:7, 'honour to whom honour is due'] ... we worship
God and venerate the saints as friends of God ... for through
the image honour rises up to the prototype.[31]

Of the two terms, *proskunēsis* refers to bowing down or
prostration. John uses it of veneration due to objects or saints.
Latreia, on the other hand, denotes hired service and in the LXX
was used exclusively of the worship due to God, and it is in this
sense that John uses it here.[32] In short, bowing down may denote
the total worship due to God alone, or it may indicate respect
– as Jacob bowing before his brother Esau.[33] The latter, respect
due to another, includes the veneration due to images. The old
covenant itself used material images made by human hands – the
cherubim in the tabernacle – which were venerated. To reject
such veneration is to run counter to the Old Testament, besides
implying that matter is evil. Moreover, in the new covenant
God has become human and united himself with matter.

Behind all this lies a conception of the cosmos as semiotic, in
which man, who straddles the material and spiritual, is enabled
to grasp invisible, spiritual reality through material signs. In
turn, this entails a significant role for the imagination. For his
part, Ouspensky argues that the truth of Christianity underlies
icons, for the image is its basic truth and 'the preaching of Christianity to the world was from the beginning carried out by the
Church through word and image.'[34] The teaching of Dionysius
the Areopagite lay behind much of what John says here.[35]

---

[31] III:41; Kotter, ed., *Johannes von Damaskos*, 7, 142; PG 94:1357.
[32] G. Lampe, ed., *A Patristic Greek Lexicon* (Oxford: Clarendon Press, 1961), 793,
1176–7.
[33] Louth, *John Damascene*, 201.
[34] Ouspensky and Lossky, *The Meaning of Icons*, 26.
[35] Louth, *John Damascene*, 217–18.

Most importantly, Gregory of Nyssa – in his opposition to the heretic Eunomius – following Psalm 19:1-6 and Romans 1:20 in pointing to the creation declaring the glory and power of God, argued that 'this is not given in articulate speech, but by the things which are seen, and it instills into our minds the knowledge of Divine power more than if speech proclaimed it with a voice.' At heart, for Gregory the visible revelation of God in creation is superior to a verbal declaration by God's voice. This is because 'we are not told that God is the creator of words, but of things made known to us by the signification of our words.' Apprehension through the senses is more readily accessible to us and so is an aid to intellectual knowledge.[36] Gregory thought that language is inherently ambiguous. Each word contains an implicit reference to its contrary. Thus, language is inappropriate to describe God, since God's existence entails no opposition. However, creation positively indicates his existence. Eunomius held to the objectivity of language; Gregory opposed it. For Gregory, sense knowledge is clear; intellectual knowledge is not.[37] The issue of icons points to deeper and far-reaching questions concerning revelation.

Issues at stake according to the Orthodox

There is clear agreement in Orthodoxy that images were prohibited as objects of worship in the Old Testament. The second commandment is unequivocal on the point. Israel was to worship Yahweh alone. However, images existed as objects of veneration in the Old Testament. Most notable were the cherubim in the tabernacle, placed over the mercy-seat and the ark of the covenant. If the second commandment prohibited all types of image, there could have been no place for the cherubim. But God actually commanded Moses to have these objects carved and placed at a point of the deepest possible significance

---

[36] Gregory of Nyssa, *Contra Eunomium*, 2, NPNF2 5:272–73.

[37] See Michel René Barnes, *The Power of God: Δύναμις in Gregory of Nyssa's Trinitarian Theology* (Washington, D.C.: The Catholic University of America Press, 2001), 250–59.

in Israel's worship, the place where the blood of atonement was offered once a year by the high priest.

Since that time the incarnation has occurred. This has changed the picture momentously. The God who is spirit and invisible has, in the Son, taken human nature, including a human body, into permanent personal union. God now has permanent, visible, human form. The incarnation not only justifies the use of icons but mandates it. To contend that it is impermissible to make images is to fly in the face of God's own actions and is – at best – to question the reality of the incarnation, without which we could not be saved. It also misses the point that Christ has led us beyond the Old Testament prohibitions. To oppose icons is to adopt a docetic theology. It is to imply that the Son's humanity is not permanently and eternally real. It also threatens to fall into the trap of Manichaeism, supposing that the spiritual and material are somehow in opposition, with the material decidedly second rate, if not downright evil. Indeed, icons are on a par with Scripture and the cross as one of the forms of God's revelation, with identical meaning; moreover, they as windows to the spiritual world demonstrate God's will for man that he be deified.[38]

The Orthodox are equally clear on the point that the icons are not objects of worship. It is too true that Nicaea II has largely been ignored by Protestants. Attention to the decree of Nicaea II would disabuse the Reformed of the idea that the Orthodox cannot distinguish what they do with icons from idolatry.

> We therefore, following the royal pathway and the divinely inspired authority of our Holy Fathers and the traditions of the Catholic Church (for, as we all know, the Holy Spirit indwells her), define with all certitude and accuracy that just as the figure of the precious and life-giving Cross, so also the venerable and holy images, as well in painting and mosaic as of other fit materials, should be set forth in the holy churches

---

[38] Ouspensky and Lossky, *The Meaning of Icons*, 30–1.

of God, and on the sacred vessels and on the vestments and
on hangings and in pictures both in house and by the wayside,
to wit, the figure of our Lord God and Saviour Jesus Christ,
of our spotless Lady, the Mother of God, of the honourable
Angels, of all the Saints and of all pious people. For by so much
more frequently as they are seen in artistic representation, by
so much more readily are men lifted up to the memory of their
prototypes, and to a longing after them; and to these should be
given due salutation and honourable reverence, not indeed that
true worship of faith which pertains alone to the divine nature;
but to these, as to the figure of the precious and life-giving
Cross and to the Book of the Gospels and to the other holy
objects, incense and lights may be offered, according to ancient
pious custom. For the honour which is paid to the image passes
on to that which this image represents, and he who reveres the
image reveres in it the object represented.[39]

After passing this decree the council made a series of acclamations: 'This is the faith of the Apostles, this is the faith of
the orthodox, this is the faith which has made firm the whole
world.' And then, denying any connection between icons and
idolatry: 'Anathema to them who presume to apply to the
venerable images the things said in Holy Scripture against idols.
Anathema to those who do not salute the holy and venerable
images. Anathema to those who call the sacred images idols....
Anathema to those who say that any other delivered us from
idols except Christ our God.'[40]

How does this argument sound from the Reformed perspective? Any reading of the Bible brings us into contact with the
existence of images. Man himself is created in the image of God
(Gen. 1:26-7). Jesus Christ, the second and last Adam, is 'the
image of the invisible God' (Col. 1:15). The world around us
declares the glory of God and displays his handiwork (Ps. 19:1-6),
notably his eternal power and deity (Rom. 1:19-20). As I will
argue there is a closer degree of commonality between the

[39] NPNF2 14:550.
[40] NPNF2 14:550-51.

Orthodox and Reformed on this matter than many have realized. There is too a significant area of misunderstanding, while at the same time, we cannot ignore the differences that remain.

There is a church in England at which, some years ago, I had the privilege of preaching quite frequently. At that church was an elderly couple, quite affluent, who used their large old house frequently for hospitality, not only opening their doors to visiting preachers like myself but also welcoming various luminaries of the international Christian world. On the grand piano in the drawing room was a large photograph of the great preacher, Dr. Martyn Lloyd-Jones, in whose church – Westminster Chapel – they had once been members. It was an icon, an image of a departed saint. Presumably these good people venerated it. It recalled to them the blessing they received from Lloyd-Jones' ministry, it conjured up the memory of his preaching and the gospel he brought to them. Through looking at the icon they would be led further to reflect on the gospel the saint had preached and thus they were led again and again to God. There is nothing intrinsically wrong with images of departed saints, nor with venerating them. If we are not to be hypocritical, we do it all the time. The significant difference between the image on the grand piano and the icon in the Orthodox Church is that the one is a photograph, technologically reproducing the features of the great preacher, while the other is the product of a unique and specialized art handed down from one generation to the next, with no room for originality or self-expression but entirely given over to a faithful reproduction of the features of the saint.

There is another difference. I very much doubt that our friends genuflected before the icon of Martyn Lloyd-Jones or kissed it – after all, they were English! This outward posture is as much a cultural expression as anything. Paul says to a variety of churches to greet one another with a holy kiss (Rom. 16:16; 1 Cor. 16:20; 2 Cor. 13:12; 1 Thess. 5:26) as does Peter (1 Pet. 5:14). Greeting living saints with a holy kiss is a Biblical recommendation, from the apostle Paul; the kissing of icons is the kissing of images of departed saints. We recall the words of the author of Hebrews that we are surrounded by a great cloud of witnesses (Heb. 12:1). Later, he declares that in church worship we have come to Mount Zion, to the spirits of just men made perfect (Heb. 12:18-25). We remember also the teaching of Revelation that when the church gathers for worship it joins the angels and the church triumphant in heaven around the throne of the living God and of the Lamb. We are not alone. The church is not a lecture room; we are gathered with saints present and past – and the angels too[41] – as we meet around the throne of God in heaven. We have access to the worship of the renewed created order, the church centrally included. We are with the saints and the angels, the apostles, prophets and martyrs – and above all with the Lamb of God once slain, now risen, and with the holy and undivided trinity.

Is there, then, any real concern with icons? There are two factors that spring to mind. First, is their placement in the context of worship, particularly as the most prominent visual element in the place the church gathers to worship God. This, to a Reformed eye, creates the likelihood of confusion. This is another difference from the icon of Lloyd-Jones; the photograph of 'the Doctor', no matter how prominently displayed, was in the drawing room, not adjacent to the pulpit. Even allowing for the Eastern teaching that icons are not objects of worship, the obvious question is whether the line between worship and veneration is as clear as the Church intends it to be. However, in conversation with the Orthodox, it is made very evident that the distinction between the worship of the trinity and the veneration of the icons is instilled from childhood. The real questions to ask here are not what the situation may appear to be in the eyes of an outsider from the Western church who has no understanding of the place and function of icons but, instead, what is the actual situation as understood by the Orthodox themselves. This is nothing less than what the Reformed would wish outsiders from another culture to consider of Reformed

---

[41] See 1 Peter 1:10-12.

worship; they should extend the same benefit to others too. That said, there is no evidence in the Bible that pictures of saints were expected to be located in the place where the church worshipped, still less was this required. This is a development additional to Scripture. It forces attention to the relationship between Scripture and tradition, to which we will devote attention in the next chapter.

Second, the point of the most crucial difference concerns icons of Christ. Here the words of *The Westminster Larger Catechism*, 109 are pertinent:

> The sins forbidden in the second commandment are, all devising, counselling, commanding, using, and any wise approving, any religious worship not instituted by God himself; tolerating a false religion; the making any representation of God, of all or of any of the three persons, either inwardly in our mind, or outwardly in any kind of image or likeness of any creature whatsoever; all worshipping of it, or God in it or by it; the making of any representation of feigned deities, and all worship of them, or service belonging to them; all superstitious devices, corrupting the worship of God, adding to it, or taking from it, whether invented or taken up of ourselves, or received by tradition from others, though under the title of antiquity, custom, devotion, good intent, or any other pretence whatsover; simony; sacrilege; all neglect, contempt, hindering, and opposing the worship and ordinances which God hath appointed.

The *Larger Catechism* opposes icons of the trinity and – by extension – of Christ, since Christ is the eternal Son incarnate. However, the proof texts given by the Westminster Assembly uniformly refer to Israel's worship of false gods by means of material objects, a context rather different from that of Orthodox iconography. Moreover, the Catechism here does not in principle reject icons of the saints, given that these are expressly not connected with worship.

According to the Orthodox, icons of Christ are not merely permitted – they are mandated by the incarnation. To oppose images of Christ is to deny the reality of the incarnation. In the incarnation the second person of the trinity took human nature, permanently and eternally, into personal union. Therefore Christ can and must be portrayed – or we have no salvation. If it is not possible to portray the incarnate Christ, his humanity is not real but only apparent – the early heresy of docetism. Is there perhaps, it may be asked, a reflection of this heresy in *WLC* 109? Have the Reformed in general ever done justice to the incarnation?

However, to make an icon of Christ is to abstract his humanity from his person (the eternal Son), and so to fall into the trap of Nestorianism, outlawed by the third ecumenical council (Ephesus, 431). The church – the Eastern church in particular, note well – has affirmed that it is the eternal Son who took humanity into union. The incarnation was not an amalgam of two natures glued together like pieces of wood. The personal identity of the incarnate Christ is the eternal Son of God. Here the Orthodox are caught on the horns of a dilemma. If, as is the case, they vehemently deny Nestorianism on the grounds that the person of Christ cannot be divided, they are compelled to argue with Meyendorff, following Theodore of Studion, that 'the very hypostasis [person] of God the Word in the flesh' appears on the image.[42] However, is this not to depict God? The answer to this apparent conundrum is that God the Word is visible *as man*. Moreover, the Orthodox maintain a distinction between the image and that which the image represents. There is both a likeness and a difference. As Ouspensky explains it, 'Inasmuch as an icon is an image, it cannot be consubstantial with the original; otherwise it would cease to be an image and would become the original.' Yet, 'although the two objects are essentially different, there exists between them a known connection, a certain participation of the one in the other.'[43]

---

[42] J. Meyendorff, *Byzantine Theology: Historical Trends and Doctrinal Themes* (New York: Fordham University Press, 1979), 158.

[43] Ouspensky and Lossky, *The Meaning of Icons,* 32.

Lossky reinforces this conclusion when he says that icons 'express things in themselves invisible, and render them really present, visible and active.' An icon 'is a material centre in which there reposes an energy, a divine force, which unites itself to human art.'[44] This is evident in the fact that the icons are held to convey not the soiled image of a fallen world but human nature transfigured with the divine beauty. The transfiguration of Christ is the counterpart to his birth to the Virgin Mary; God became man in order than man might become God, and on the holy mountain we see Christ's humanity clothed with divine glory, yet as iron is heated by fire while remaining iron so the humanity of Christ is not destroyed but glorified, for holiness is true beauty. 'Thus, the icon is not a representation of the Deity, but an indication of the participation of a given person in Divine life.'[45]

Yet, how can this great mystery be encapsulated in a painting of human design? This question is addressed perceptively by Karl Barth. He argues that this attempt is 'quite intolerable.' It is an attempt to freeze at a definite moment what in reality is in a state of dynamic movement. It is 'far too static as a supposed portrayal of the corporeality of Jesus Christ in a given moment.' More than this, what the iconographer will never be able to convey is 'the decisive thing – this vertical movement in which Jesus Christ is actual, the history in which the Son of God became the Son of Man and takes human essence and is man in this act ... alive in the relationship of his divinity to his humanity. But he obviously cannot be represented in this movement, which is decisive for his being and knowledge.' Representations of Christ can only be made, Barth continues, by abstracting his humanity from his person. The result can only be 'a catastrophe'.[46]

Here we should recall that the commandments, in forbidding certain practices, encourage or require good actions that are the

---

[44] V. Lossky, *The Mystical Theology of the Eastern Church* (London: James Clarke & Co. Ltd, 1957), 189.

[45] Ouspensky and Lossky, *The Meaning of Icons*, 35-36.

[46] K. Barth, *CD*, IV/2: 102–3.

reverse of the prohibited evils. Hence, the point of the second commandment in forbidding the making of images for worship, is not to impose some arbitrary prohibition but to insist that we are to worship God exclusively in the image he himself has provided – Jesus Christ, the image of the invisible God.

But, as we have seen, Orthodoxy does not worship God in images, so it holds. But, apparently weakening this claim, is the famous icon of the Old Testament Trinity, painted by Andrei Rublev (c. 1370–1430). This depicts the three angels who visited Abraham (Gen. 18:1-8), each angel representing one of the Trinity. How can this be consistent with the Orthodox position that icons are not to be worshipped, or that God cannot be depicted, or with the argument that it is the incarnation that justifies the practice, since neither the Father nor the Holy Spirit became incarnate?[47] To be fair, many Orthodox deny the validity of this icon.

To this the Orthodox reply that, by the incarnation, God has determined to be made visible in human form. This he freely decided and brought into effect. In doing so he legitimized the iconographer's unique task. To oppose this is to fall foul of ontological dualism, and veer to Manichaeism. These are the two positions and I suppose this issue will not be resolved for some considerable time.[48]

There is, however, one other matter to mention. There is a surprising area of agreement between the Reformed and the Orthodox. Reformed theology believes in icons too! I have already hinted at that. The whole idea of image (*eikōn*) is an obvious Biblical category – man as made in the image of God, Christ as the image of the invisible God as the second Adam. However, it stretches even beyond this. For the Reformed

---

[47] See J. Binns, *An Introduction to the Christian Orthodox Churches* (Cambridge: Cambridge University Press, 2002), 105.

[48] Note that in the Churches of the conquered territories icons are much rarer. In Syria, Egypt, Ethiopia and South India the most prominent feature in the church building is an open Bible on a raised platform. Pictures do exist but are for didactic purposes only, not for veneration. See Binns, *Orthodox Churches*, 105–6.

everything is iconic. God has imprinted evidence of his own beauty and glory throughout creation. In the words of the Psalmist 'the heavens declare the glory of God, and the sky above proclaims his handiwork. Day to day pours out speech, and night to night reveals knowledge' (Ps. 19:1-2). And again, 'O LORD, our Lord, how majestic is your name in all the earth!' (Ps. 8:9). In line with this Paul can say that 'his invisible attributes, namely, his eternal power and divine nature, have been clearly perceived, ever since the creation of the world, in the things that have been made' (Rom. 1:20). Every blade of grass, every tree and flower displays the glory of God. Every square inch belongs to Christ, the mediator of creation (Col. 1:15-17, Heb. 1:1-3). If icons are windows to draw us to God, opened books to lead us to heaven, so too is the entire order of creation – the beauty of the hills, the colours of the grass, sea and sky, the trees and plants, the changing of the seasons.[49]

Calvin, in his commentary on Genesis, emphasizes that God reveals himself in creation. Moses' intention is 'to render God, as it were, visible to us in his works.' The Lord, 'that he may invite us to the knowledge of himself, places the fabric of heaven and earth before our eyes rendering himself, in a certain manner, manifest in them.' The heavens 'are eloquent heralds of the glory of God, and ... this most beautiful order of nature silently proclaims his admirable wisdom.' He 'clothes himself, so to speak, with the image of the world ... magnificently arrayed in the incomparable vesture of the heavens and the earth.' In short, the world is 'a mirror in which we ought to behold God'.[50] There is a symmetry in God's works to which nothing can be added.[51] The divine Artificer arranged the creation in such a wonderful order that nothing more beautiful in appearance can be imagined.[52] In the *Catechism of the Church of Geneva* (1541) he foreshadows his comments on Genesis in saying that the

---

[49] Barth, *CD* II/1, 650f.

[50] J. Calvin, *Commentaries on the First Book of Moses Called Genesis,* argument.

[51] Ibid., on 1:31.

[52] J. Calvin, *Institute,* 1:14:21.

world is a kind of mirror in which we may observe God. The account here is given for our sake, to teach us that God has made nothing without a certain reason and design.[53] The Orthodox would not, of course, deny all this – in fact, they argue that it legitimizes icons.

What Calvinism did was to open the door to a thoroughly this-worldly appreciation of beauty. By eliminating art and sculpture from the place where the church gathered to worship God, it drove it out of the church and into the world. It placed the aesthetic in the context of general revelation rather than special revelation, as the witness to God in the world rather than as the focus of the worship of God in the church. The result of this was the enormous flowering of creativity in post-Reformation culture. In a context permeated by the impact of John Calvin and Reformed theology, there flourished the Dutch masters, such as Rembrandt and Van Ruysdael, and English landscapists like Constable. Increasingly, they portrayed not the supernatural realm of angels and demons, but the world around them displaying the glory and beauty of God.

The Orthodox Liturgy

If the first thing the visitor notices in an Orthodox church is the iconostasis and the profusion of icons throughout the building, the next feature attracting attention is the Liturgy. This is no casual or perfunctory matter, as tragically it has become in many evangelical churches. It is the heartbeat of the Orthodox Church.

Orthodoxy has an unchanged Liturgy. The Orthodox pride themselves on being the church of the seven councils, recipients of the apostolic faith handed down unchanged from one generation to the next. The Liturgy is central not only to worship but to theology. It is often the source of theology. Thus, there is surprisingly little variation from one Orthodox

---

[53] *Calvin: Theological Treatises* (J. Reid; Philadelphia: Westminster Press, 1954), 93–4.

jurisdiction to the next, or between the present and the past. There are two main strands of Orthodox Liturgy: the Liturgy of St Chrysostom and The Liturgy of Basil the Great. The latter is used only occasionally. While these liturgies bear the names of the two great Fathers, it has been claimed that there is no historical evidence that the various elements can be traced directly to them as the source. However, in recent years it has been established that their roots do in fact lie in the fourth century.

The Orthodox Liturgy is full of Scripture, far more than the starvation rations prevalent in evangelical churches, much more even than in *The Book of Common Prayer of the Church of England* – which has fallen into desuetude virtually everywhere except in Cathedrals. In Orthodoxy, the whole Psalter is read through once every week, and twice a week in seasons such as the Great Fast. A good example of the volume and intensity of Biblical reading in the Orthodox Liturgy is the service for Great (Good) Friday, which contains the following readings from the Gospels: John 13:31–18:1; John 18:1-28; Matthew 26:57-75; John 18:28–19:16; Matthew 27:3-32; Mark 15:16-32; Matthew 27:33-54; Luke 23:32-49; John 19:25-37; Mark 15:43-47; John 19:38-42; Matthew 27:62-66. After each of these readings comes the refrain 'Glory to thy long-suffering, O Lord.' After hymns and refrains, there follows the Imperial Hours, composed by Cyril of Alexandria. These contain a series of Biblical readings and hymns. The readings are: Psalm 5; Psalm 2; Psalm 22; Zechariah 9:10-13; Galatians 6:14-18; Matthew 27:1-56; Psalm 35; Psalm 109; Psalm 51; Isaiah 50:4-11; Romans 5:6-10; Mark 15:1-41; Psalm 54: Psalm 140; Psalm 91; Isaiah 52:13–54:1; Hebrews 2:11-18; Luke 23:32-49; Psalm 69; Psalm 70; Psalm 86; Jeremiah 11:18-23; Jeremiah 12:1-15; Hebrews 10:19-31; John 18:28–19:37. Besides this, the regular Liturgy contains 98 quotations from the Old Testament, and 114 from the New Testament.[54]

---

[54] Ware, *Orthodox Church*, 209.

This compares with the Good Friday service in *The Book of Common Prayer of the Church of England* (1662), which specifies readings from Hebrews 10:1-25 and John 19:1-37. The service of Morning Prayer in the 1662 Prayer Book has readings from both the Old and New Testaments and, in addition, an opening sentence from a range of Biblical passages, the reading or singing of the Venite (Ps. 95), and the Benedictus (Luke 1:68-80) or Jubilate Deo (Ps. 100). Evening Prayer contains, in addition to the usual lessons from the Old and the New Testaments, the Psalms of the day, of which there are on average five but in practice one is sung, the Magnificat (Luke 1:46-55) or Cantate Domino (Ps. 98), and the Nunc Dimittis (Luke 2:29-32) or Deus Misereatur (Ps. 67). In both Morning Prayer and Evening Prayer there are, read or sung, an average of five sizeable sections of the Bible.

In stark contrast is modern evangelicalism. In my own service of Morning Worship we normally have readings from the Old and New Testaments, and sing part of a Psalm. However, in many evangelical churches today it is fortunate to have anything but a cursory reading of a short passage of Scripture. At a funeral in England in 1997, I was assigned the task of reading from the Bible. I chose the great Pauline passage, 1 Corinthians 15:12-26. I was emphatically rebuffed; this was 'far too long,' I was told. No congregation in England would stand for so much of the Bible being read in one go! It could not be allowed! This – note – was in an evangelical context, a segment of the church that has usually prided itself on its commitment to Scripture. These facts make a mockery of evangelical claims.

The liturgical prayers in the Orthodox Liturgy are powerfully trinitarian and doxological. Here is a brief sample.

> When in Jordan thou wast baptized, O Lord, the worship of the Trinity was made manifest. For the voice of the Father bare witness unto thee, calling thee his beloved Son, and the Spirit, in the form of a dove, confirmed the steadfastness of that word. O Christ our God, who didst manifest thyself, and dost enlighten the world, glory to thee.[55]

Glory to the Father, and to the Son, and to the Holy Spirit.

Through the Holy Spirit unto all men come adoration, good will, wisdom, peace and blessing: For equally with the Father and the Son he hath effectual power.

Now, and ever, and unto ages of ages. Amen.[56]

Come, O ye people, let us worship the Godhead in three Persons, the Son in the Father with the Holy Spirit. For the Father before time was begat the Son, who is coeternal and is equally enthroned, and the Holy Spirit who was in the Father, and was glorified together with the Son; one Might, one Essence, one Godhead. Adoring the same let us all say: O Holy God, who by the Son didst make all things through the cooperation of the Holy Spirit: O Holy Mighty One, through whom we have known the Father, and through whom the Holy Spirit came into the world: O Holy Immortal One, the Spirit of comfort, who proceedest from the Father, and restest in the Son: O Holy Trinity, glory to thee.

Glory to the Father, and to the Son, and to the Holy Spirit, now, and ever, and unto ages of ages. Amen. O heavenly King, the Comforter, Spirit of Truth, who art in all places and fillest all things; Treasury of good things and Giver of life: Come, and take up thine abode in us, and cleanse us from every stain; and save our souls, O Good One.[57]

Glory to the Holy, Consubstantial, Life-giving and Undivided trinity, now, and ever, and unto ages of ages.[58]

The Orthodox service is long. It is not something hastily cobbled together, with an eye on the attention span of the congregation or with a view to boosting the box office records. It has been centuries – millennia – in the making. It is not a short pit

---

[55] For Epiphany, Antiphon III, Tone I: Service book, 188.

[56] The Order for the Burial of the Dead (Priests), Service Book, 398.

[57] Pentecost, At the all-night vigil, Service Book, 245, 249.

[58] Collect for Easter, *Service Book of the Holy Orthodox-Catholic Apostolic Church* (Third ed.; I. F. Hapgood; Brooklyn, New York: Syrian Antiochene Orthodox Archdiocese of New York and all North America, 1956), 226.

stop to fill the spiritual tank, interrupting the important rush of modern life; it is the meeting ground between heaven and earth, time and eternity, and so the clock is put in its proper place.

There is, then, in Orthodox worship an enormous amount from which the Reformed – and others in the Western church – can learn. However, there are two particular areas of concern: prayers addressed to 'the holy birth-giver of God', which we will consider now, and the marginalizing of the preaching of the Word of God in favour of the visual, which we will discuss in the next chapter.

Prayers to the saints

A further element that will strike the Reformed visitor to Orthodox worship are prayers to the saints, especially the (correctly named) holy birth-giver of God. Here is an ascription of praise from the Liturgy for Great Saturday:

> Let us sing the praises of Mary, Virgin, Door of heaven, Glory of all the world, sprung forth from man, who also bare the Lord; the Song of the Bodiless Powers, and the Enriching of the faithful. For she revealed herself as Heaven and the Temple of the Godhead. She destroyed the bulwarks of enmity, and ushered in peace, and threw open the kingdom. Wherefore, in that we possess this confirmation of our faith, we have a defender, even the Lord who was born of her. Be bold, therefore, be bold, ye people of God, for he, the All-Powerful, shall vanquish your foes.[59]

The following is a hymn to the Birth-giver of God, from the Easter Liturgy:

> Hail, O thou hallowed, divine abode of the Most High! For through thee, O Birth-giver of God, was joy given unto those who cry aloud to thee: Blessed art thou among women, O Lady all-undefiled! ...More honourable than the Cherubim, and beyond compare more glorious than the Seraphim, thou who

[59] Service Book, 223.

without defilement barest God the Word, true Birth-giver of God, we magnify thee.[60]

In the Divine Liturgy, the following prayer is made to Mary secretly by the priest:

O Birth-giver of God, in that thou art a well-spring of loving-kindness, vouchsafe unto us thy compassion. Look upon the people who have sinned. Manifest thy power as ever; for trusting in thee we cry aloud unto thee: Hail! as aforetime did Gabriel, Chief Captain of the Bodiless Powers.[61]

Finally, from Great Vespers, in the All-night Vigil service, comes this typical prayer to Christ that we would be granted remission of sins through the prayers of Mary:

O most merciful Master, Lord Jesus Christ our God, through the prayers of our all-undefiled Lady, the Birth-giver of God and ever-virgin Mary: and of all thy Saints: Make our prayer acceptable; grant us remission of our transgressions; hide us under the shadow of thy wings; drive far from us every foe and adversary; make our life peaceful, O Lord. Have mercy upon us and upon thy world; and save our souls: forasmuch as thou art gracious and lovest mankind.[62]

First, we must note again an area ripe for misunderstanding on the part of the Reformed. The point is that all Christians make intercession to the saints. It is characteristic of believers to ask others to pray to God on their behalf, to put in a word for them to Jesus Christ. It is extremely reassuring to do this, and it is entirely without detriment to the sovereign grace of God and the sole mediatorship of Jesus Christ. After all, have you *never* asked someone to pray for you or *never* prayed for someone else?! If not, may I urge you to do so very soon. It is part of what being a Christian is – to share one another's burdens – for God

[60] Service Book, 237.
[61] Service Book, 68.
[62] Service Book, 12.

has placed us in the church, and does not intend us to be isolated hermits cut off from the covenant community he has formed for his glory. What we do in this normal Christian practice is to request a saint to make intercession on our behalf to God through the mediation of Jesus Christ the Son. It may be for this or that matter, or for God's grace to help us in a particular situation, when undergoing an operation or facing bereavement. There is nothing wrong in this – in fact the Bible requires it! Paul requests that prayers be made for himself, for rulers, for all kinds of people (e.g., Rom. 15:30-33, Col. 4:2-4, 1 Tim. 2:1ff). So we should all make intercession to the saints on a regular basis.

This question surrounds the propriety of asking *dead* saints to make intercession for us to the Father through the Son by the Holy Spirit. It concerns whether we are able to make contact with the departed saints and if, in turn, they are able to hear us and so to pray on our behalf. Is there any Biblical evidence that supports this claim? The condition of the dead in Christ is something revealed (1 Thess. 4:13-18) not something we know from other sources. While they, as well as we, are unbreakably united with Christ, and participate in the worship of God (Rev. 4–5, Heb. 12:18ff), there is no record of contact between us and them. Neither Jesus nor Paul nor any other Biblical writer communicated with the departed. The expectation of the Christian is the resurrection at the last day, not interaction with departed saints. This is clear in 1 Thessalonians 4:13-18, where Paul could easily have reassured his readers, if this was a reality, by referring to ongoing contact with those who had fallen asleep. He did not do this. Instead, he looked forward to the time when we will be reunited, *at the return of Christ*. Moreover, Jesus' parable of the rich man and Lazarus gives no hint that the one could communicate with the other (Luke 16:19-31).

Some might suggest that the practice is forbidden by the Old Testament prohibition on making contact with the dead (Lev. 19:31, 20:6, 27; Deut. 18:9-11). However, these are two very different matters. Attempts to contact the dead in the Old Testament period were to foretell the future, and involved the

activity of evil spirits, and departure from the true and living
God by turning to pagan divinities. Often, as is clear from the
contexts in Leviticus and Deuteronomy, this was associated with
vile sacrificial rituals, including child sacrifice and magic. It was
the pagan practice of necromancy.[63] This was vastly different
from the trinitarian intercessions offered in the Orthodox
Liturgy. The object here is not to establish contact with the
departed, to use magic, or to abandon faith in the triune God,
but to engage the departed saints in intercession on our behalf
to the Father through his Son.

There are three possible pieces of supporting evidence from
the New Testament. In Revelation 6:9-11, the souls of those
slain for the Word of God are heard under the altar to call on
God to reveal how long it will be before their blood is avenged.
'O Sovereign Lord, holy and true, how long before you will
judge and avenge our blood on those who dwell on the earth?'
It is clear that they are aware of the passage of time, realize that
the consummation of the church's salvation has yet to occur,
and so call out to God in prayer for vindication. In turn, they
are told that they must wait. However, there is no inkling that
they have meaningful contact with the saints on earth. Again,
in Revelation 20:4-6 those who have been beheaded 'for the
testimony of Jesus and the Word of God' come to life and reign
with Christ for a thousand years. This difficult passage may very
possibly refer to the reign of the saints with Christ here and now,
and so it might be supposed by good and necessary consequence
that they are aware of what is happening, for they could hardly
be reigning with Christ and ignorant about that over which
they were given authority. Thirdly, there is the account of Jesus
talking with Moses and Elijah on the mount of transfiguration
(Matt. 17:1-8, Mark 9:2-8, Luke 9:28-36). However, this event

---

[63] See, *inter alia* R. Harrison, *Leviticus: An Introduction and Commentary* (Leicester:
Inter-Varsity Press, 1980), 202, 205, 207–8; J. Thompson, *Deuteronomy: An
Introduction and Commentary* (Leicester: Inter-Varsity Press, 1974), 210–12; P. C.
Craigie, *The Book of Deuteronomy* (Grand Rapids: Eerdmans, 1976), 260–1.

is a unique and proleptic glimpse of Christ in his glory. Even more to the point is the fact that Moses and Elijah are talking to *Jesus* – not to the apostles – and that the apostles did not have any communication with Elijah and Moses. Taken together, these three passages – at best – by no means demand the conclusion towards which Eastern theology would direct us. It is a barely possible reading – just. Yet such possibilities require clearer passages elsewhere to lend the proposal credence. Nor, in the absence of such corroboration, is it adequate to say with Alexander Schmemann, that the departed saints are not dead but alive in Christ. This is correct, of course, but it merely begs the question.[64]

The relationship between living and dead saints is comparable to what happens when two independent observers simultaneously look at the moon from different continents. Their gaze coincides at the moon's surface but there is no direct contact between them. So both the church militant and the church triumphant are united in the same Christ, safe in his hands, and secure in his intercession (John 17:1-26; Heb. 4:14-16; 7:25; 1 John 2:1-2), but between them there is no communication.

Prayers to the departed saints are wrong, not because there is anything intrinsically evil in asking saints to intercede for us but because there is no contact between us and dead saints and so they can neither hear our requests nor respond to them. It is neither possible, legitimate, nor desirable to make the attempt. Moreover, it is superfluous since we have a great high priest who is more than able to send us the help we need (Heb. 4:14-16). There are plenty of living saints too who can lend us a hand in the spiritual battle without having recourse to departed ones. Conversely, while the practice is in error – and it does have serious repercussions – it is not heresy, since it does not overthrow any cardinal doctrine of the faith. In other words, *if* it were true and legitimate, it would not falsify the Christian

---

[64] A. Schmemann, *Introduction to Liturgical Theology* (A. E. Moorhouse; Leighton Buzzard: Faith Press, 1996), 144.

faith. However, it diverts attention from Jesus Christ, who is the unshakeable source of assurance of salvation, and so can have a detrimental effect. This is evident in the widespread popular belief that some of the saints – Mary and the martyrs – have not merely an intercessory but also a mediatorial role.[65]

It is important to acknowledge, however, that the Roman Catholic doctrine of purgatory is generally rejected in Orthodoxy. The vast majority believe either that the faithful do not suffer between death and resurrection or that the atoning sacrifice of Jesus Christ, the Lamb of God, is sufficient to atone for all sins, and so is our only atonement and satisfaction.[66] In addition, while a good deal of attention is given to Mary, Orthodoxy does not give dogmatic significance to the traditional teaching about her. Most believe in Mary's perpetual virginity, considering the references to Jesus' 'brothers' in the Gospels to point to cousins or half-brothers, as the word can sometimes mean. On the other hand, the majority reject the idea of the immaculate conception, by which Rome claims that Mary was preserved from original sin from the moment she was conceived. Here, the difference lies largely in differing views of sin and its transmission, while additionally the East has been loathe to consider Mary in such distinction from the rest of humanity. On the question of the bodily assumption of Mary, proclaimed as dogma by the Pope in 1950, which teaches that Mary has already received her resurrection body, the Orthodox are in agreement with Rome. However, the most striking difference between Orthodoxy and Rome on all these matters is that they are not dogma in the East, but are regarded simply as theological opinions which individual believers are free to accept or reject.[67]

---

[65] D. Fairbairn, *Eastern Orthodoxy Through Western Eyes*, Louisville: Westminster John Knox Press (2002), 134–36.

[66] Ware, *Orthodox Church*, 259.

[67] Ibid., 262–64.

7

Scripture and Tradition

Scripture as part of the living tradition

It is an axiom of historic Protestantism, and of the Reformed churches in particular, that the Bible is the supreme authority in all matters of faith and conduct, the highest court of appeal in questions of controversy. Beside it, the teachings of the church are in a secondary position. They are effectively a commentary on Scripture. The Word of God written has priority and all human opinions must submit to the voice of the Holy Spirit speaking in Scripture. In the words of *The Westminster Confession of Faith*:

> The supreme judge by which all controversies of religion are to be determined, and all decrees of councils, opinions of ancient writers, doctrines of men, and private spirits, are to be examined, and in whose sentence we are to rest, can be no other but the Holy Spirit speaking in the Scriptures (I:X).

This is because

> All synods or councils, since the Apostles' times, whether general or particular, may err; and many have erred. Therefore

they are not to be made the rule of faith, or practice; but to be
used as a help in both (XXXI:IV).

In this sense, the Bible and the church are in a certain tension.
Synods and councils are necessary, their pronouncements
a help in faith and practice. The Westminster Assembly was
itself a council of divines, called by Parliament to reform the
government, worship and discipline of the church in England,
Wales and Ireland, initially to defend *The Thirty-Nine Articles
of Religion of the Church of England* against 'false aspersions and
calumnies.' Often, and wrongly, Scripture and church councils
are seen by some Protestants as in opposition to each other.
Ideally, they are in harmony. The Westminster Assembly
considered the Trinitarian and Christological pronouncements
of the first six ecumenical councils to be in harmony with the
Bible, and entertained few doubts about its own conclusions.
Yet such bodies are liable to error whereas the primary author
of Scripture is the Holy Spirit, who does not and cannot err.
Therefore, Scripture is the supreme authority, in view of who
its original author is.

In Orthodoxy, the picture is rather different. Firstly, it is
important to grasp that – for the Eastern church – tradition
means the whole teaching of the church, whether in church
councils, the Bible, official dogma, or the liturgy. As Timothy
Ware puts it, tradition has a broad, comprehensive meaning:

> to an Orthodox Christian ... it means the books of the Bible;
> it means the Creed; it means the decrees of the Ecumenical
> Councils and the writings of the Fathers; it means the Canons,
> the Service Books, the Holy Icons – in fact, the whole system
> of doctrine, Church government, worship, and art which
> Orthodoxy has articulated over the ages. The Orthodox
> Christian of today sees himself as heir and guardian to a great
> inheritance received from the past, and he believes that it is his
> duty to transmit this inheritance unimpaired to the future.[1]

---

[1] T. Ware, *The Orthodox Church* (London: Penguin Books, 1969), 204.

In the West, Scripture and tradition tend to be seen as in some way competitive. This is especially so in Protestantism, where it is common to think that the Reformation brought about a rejection of tradition in favour of Scripture alone (*sola Scriptura*). In fact, this slogan cannot be traced to the sixteenth century; it was a much later concoction. Its intention was not to suggest that only the text of the Bible was acceptable. Indeed, the Reformers produced a wide range of new catechisms and confessions. Far from distancing themselves from the past, they were keen to stress that they – not the contemporary Roman church – were in harmony with the Fathers and the ancient councils. What they taught was that the Bible is the supreme authority, and sits in judgment on the teachings of the church, not vice-versa. As Calvin expresses it, 'we cannot otherwise distinguish between councils that are contradictory and discordant, which have been many, unless we weigh them all, as I have said, in the balance of all men and angels, that is, the Word of the Lord.'[2] This followed Martin Luther's development in thought that proved decisive for all that followed.

In 1517, when Luther nailed his Ninety-five Theses to the door of the Castle Church in Wittenberg, he firmly believed in the ultimate authority of the Church, with the Pope as its head. His theses were a formal academic protest against the sale of indulgences, an invitation to open, public debate. He looked to the Pope to put matters right, believing him to be ignorant of what was going on at the local level in Germany. In that sense, the Reformation itself did not begin on 31 October 1517. This famous event was merely the first in a chain of happenings that eventually led to the changes we now call the Reformation.

Luther was immediately challenged on his naive belief that the Pope was blithely ignorant of the sale of indulgences. His interview with Cardinal Cajetan at Augsburg in October 1518 took the matter a stage further. Cajetan insisted that Luther's attack on indulgences was an attack on Papal authority. To

---

[2] Calvin, *Institute*, 4:9:9.

Luther's horror he realized that all was happening with the connivance and approval of the Papacy. Nevertheless, he would not recant and his supporters had to smuggle him out of the city by night.

Next month, he appealed for a general council of the church. In the previous century, the conciliar movement had been at its height and there has always been a tension in Rome between the hierarchical impact of the Papacy and the more collegial emphasis of the conciliarists. However, Luther still assumed the primacy of church authority. In July 1519, in debate, Eck – then a Professor at Ingolstadt – accused Luther of sharing some of the views of Jan Hus, condemned as a heretic by the Council of Constance (1414–18), and burned at the stake. This forced Luther to recognize that neither Pope nor Council would give him the backing he needed. Lacking in debating skills, he acknowledged that Hus was right in some of his views and the council wrong. It was to Scripture he must appeal. This insight was the result of a process, not a sudden flash of inspiration from the skies. The issue was now clear. The only adequate support in matters of controversy was the Bible. The Bible must judge the decisions of man, not vice-versa.

On the other hand, these matters passed the Eastern church by. For the Orthodox there has never been a conflict between the Bible and the teaching of the church. Partly, this is because the question of authority has not arisen in the way it has in the West, where Rome has an infallible Pope. The great councils simply recognized the truth, and their recognition received support from the people.[3] No one bishop has had jurisdiction beyond his own diocese. This is in stark contrast to the West, where Pope and magisterium have authority to pronounce on matters of dogma for the worldwide church, by the power they

---

[3] 'A council must be the object of discernment by the whole church, guided by the Spirit,' John Meyendorff, 'Orthodox Christianity,' in Erwin Fallbusch, Jan Milic Lochman, John Mbiti, Jaroslav Pelikan, Lukas Vischer (eds.), *The Encyclopedia of Christianity*, trans. Geoffrey W. Bromiley (Grand Rapids: Eerdmans, 2003), 3:862.

claim to have received from Christ. The laity simply accept these pronouncements.

From an early time the Eastern church considered Scripture to be part of the apostolic tradition, which had a living continuity and was wider than the Bible alone. Basil the Great wrote, 'We do not content ourselves with what was reported in Acts and in the Epistles and in the Gospels; but, both before and after reading them, we add other doctrines, received from oral teaching, and carrying much weight in the mystery.'[4] The liturgy and the writings of the Fathers were the basis for understanding the Bible.[5]

As Lossky explains, this was fostered by the indissoluble bond between theology and spirituality. The two have never been detached. Moreover, there is an identity between personal spiritual experience and the experience of the church, due to the catholicity of the Christian tradition. Tradition is not merely the aggregate of the dogmas, rites and institutions of the church. It is dynamic and living, unchanging and constant, the revelation of the Holy Spirit in the church. Dogma cannot be understood apart from spiritual experience. Doctrine and experience go together, mutually conditioning one another. Behind this, the final goal of Orthodox theology is union with God. Its focus is salvation. This stems from its Eucharistic nature – it is from the Eucharist that we learn that Christ's death was a sacrifice – and from the tradition (*paradosis*), in which Christ was handed over to us by the Father and in turn the apostles handed down the deposit of faith to the church.[6] The church is thus always the same, although its *oikonomia*

---

[4] Basil of Caesarea, *On the Holy Spirit*, 27:65.

[5] J. Meyendorff, *Byzantine Theology: Historical Trends and Doctrinal Themes* (New York: Fordham University Press, 1979), 8.

[6] See, *inter alia*, John Zizioulas, *Eucharist, Bishop, Church: The Unity of the Church in the Divine Eucharist and Bishop during the first three Centuries* (Brookline, Massachusetts: Holy Cross, 2001); and, although from a non-Orthodox source, Joseph Cardinal Ratzinger, *The Spirit of the Liturgy*, Trans. John Saward (San Francisco: Ignatius Press, 2000).

with regard to the outside world may change as society and the historical environment alter.[7]

Thus, Scripture and tradition are not opposed, nor to be juxtaposed as two separate realities. They are distinct but not separate. The incarnation of the Word and the presence of the Holy Spirit in the church are together the twofold condition of the fulness of revelation. The tradition is transmitted and received in the Holy Spirit, who is the power for expressing the truth, whether in intelligible definitions or in sensible images and symbols. Tradition is not so much revealed content but a faculty owed to the Holy Spirit for receiving the revelation. This can only be recognized in the church, for the church alone possesses the tradition.[8]

Lossky argues that this is alien to the Western church. While this tradition is the same on the incarnation, those dogmas relating to Pentecost, the Holy Spirit, grace and the church are no longer common to East and West. Moreover, because of this later division, even those things held in common are no longer approached in common. 'Henceforth a St. Basil or a St. Augustine will be differently interpreted according as they are considered within the Roman Catholic tradition or in that of the Orthodox Church.' Rather contentiously, Lossky insists that one can only recognize the authority of an ecclesiastical writer from within the tradition to which he belongs.[9]

The nature of the Bible according to Orthodoxy

The Orthodox accept that the Bible is the Word of God, a record of his will. As Stylianopoulos says, 'An Orthodox approach has to do with a comprehensive and balanced appreciation of Holy Scripture in its own nature, authority, and witness as the Word

---

[7] V. Lossky, *The Mystical Theology of the Eastern Church* (London: James Clarke & Co. Ltd, 1957), 236–7.

[8] V. Lossky, 'Tradition and Traditions,' in Leonid Ouspensky and Vladimir Lossky, *The Meaning of Icons*, Trans., G.E.H. Palmer and E. Kadloubovsky (Crestwood, New York: St. Vladimir's Seminary Press, 1982), 15-7.

[9] Lossky, *Mystical Theology*, 237–8.

of God, while at the same time being committed to standards of critical study and freedom of research.'[10] However, there is a marked difference from the Western approach to critical theological study. Firstly, much Western theology and Biblical study in the past three hundred years has come out of the worldview and methodology of the Enlightenment, with its inbuilt aversion to authority, including the authority of God. The Eastern church, in contrast, has not had to contend with an Enlightenment. Flowing from this, secondly, Western critical Biblical study has been pursued mainly in an academic environment detached from the church, with the Bible considered as simply another book. The Eastern church, however, places theology (correctly, in my judgment) in the context of the church, the believing community, since the Bible was given to the church in the first place. While literary, historical and theological aspects must all be integrated, and critical judgment cultivated, this must be rooted ecclesially, in faith, recognizing that we must share in the same reality established by Jesus and actualized by the Holy Spirit.[11] Stylianopoulos argues that the Orthodox view of Scripture is dynamic. God's revelation dealt with persons, patriarchs, prophets, priests and ultimately with Jesus Christ. Authority was not usually accorded to the Biblical books at the time they were composed but came gradually over the course of centuries. Thus behind the books of the Bible lies a dynamic history of oral tradition.[12]

The Orthodox canon

In point of detail, there are differences between the Orthodox and Protestants on the identity of the Biblical canon. For Orthodoxy, 'canon' is more than a list of books; it is the standard by which all truth is to be gauged. It is the sacred deposit that Paul urged Timothy to guard (2 Tim 1:14). Stylianopoulos argues

---

[10] T. G. Stylianopoulos, *The New Testament: An Orthodox Perspective: Volume One: Scripture, Tradition, Hermeneutics* (Brookline, Massachusetts: Holy Cross Orthodox Press, 1997), 7.

[11] Ibid., 7–13.

[12] Ibid., 17.

that the Biblical books gained the status of sacred authority only slowly.[13] In this, he supports the claim that the church defined the canon, with the result that the Bible is part of the tradition, rather than something set over it. However, is there not evidence that the New Testament books were recognized as canon much sooner than that? Peter refers to the difficulty of understanding Paul's letters, at the same time speaking of them as Scripture (2 Pet. 3:16). Paul himself cites the Gospel of Luke in tandem with a reference to the Pentateuch, to prove that overseers in the church should be paid for their work (1 Tim. 5:17). Paul also makes a strong allusion to the prophecy of Zacharias (Luke 1:79) in Romans 3:17, amidst a catena of citations from the Old Testament Scriptures. The point the Orthodox make is the historical one, that in the battle against gnosticism in the second and third centuries the apologists defended the faith by recourse to the unbroken line of bishops. Truth lay with the church. Christ handed the deposit of faith to the apostles, who in turn passed it on to the church, and in particular to the bishops of the church. Hence, the writings of Scripture cannot be disentangled from the church to which they were given and the bishops who were charged with preserving them and who were the representatives and embodiment of the church.

The main differences over the canon relate to the Old Testament and the apocryphal literature. Protestants have followed the Jewish canon, while the East has adopted the Alexandrian canon. The Protestant Old Testament is the Massoretic text (MT), the Hebrew text compiled with meticulous precision by the Massoretes, whereas the Orthodox use the Septuagint (LXX), the Greek translation of the Old Testament that Jesus and the apostles usually cite. The Orthodox believe that the Holy Spirit inspired the LXX. For example, in Isaiah 7:14 (MT) the word *almah* is used, meaning 'a young woman', whereas the LXX has the word *parthenos*, 'a virgin.' The New Testament follows the LXX in Matthew 1:23[14]

---

[13] Ibid., 18.

In turn, Protestants, following the Jewish canon, exclude the apocrypha (hidden books), although they regard them as useful for historical purposes. The Orthodox include additional historical books – 1 Esdras, Judith, Tobit, and 1–4 Maccabees – and extra segments of Esther and Daniel that are not in the Hebrew text; in Daniel these passages are the Prayer of Azariah, the Song of the Three Youths, the story of Susanna, and Bel and the Dragon. Additionally, the Orthodox have Psalm 151, Ecclesiasticus and the Wisdom of Solomon. Protestants place these in the Apocrypha.[15]

The Orthodox canon consists of 38 Old Testament books (Ezra – Nehemiah, in the LXX, is one book) plus the 10 readable books that Protestants regard as apocrypha. Often, it has been held in the East that there are 22 canonical Old Testament books, matching the number of letters in the Hebrew alphabet. To arrive at this total, some of the books were combined as single volumes. This procedure implied that the Jewish canon had a special place over the 'readable books' or 'Deutero-Canonical Books'. The Roman Catholic Church considers the Old Testament to consist of 46 books (the Letter of Jeremiah is joined to Baruch, and there are 7 deutero-canonical books included). Protestants have 39 books (with Ezra and Nehemiah separated).[16] There are also a number of Jewish books that Protestants call pseudepigrapha (falsely titled), including the Book of Jubilees, the Martyrdom of Isaiah, and the Assumption of Moses, which the Orthodox call apocrypha, and regard as of lesser authority.[17]

Moreover, the sequence of Old Testament books varies between Protestant, Roman Catholic and Orthodox Bibles. The Orthodox, together with Rome, integrate the readable books within the Old Testament, while Protestants place them in an appendix. However, there are trends in Orthodoxy

---

[14] Ware, *Orthodox Church*, 208.

[15] Stylianopoulos, *The New Testament: An Orthodox Perspective*, 24.

[16] Ibid., 24–5.

[17] Ware, *Orthodox Church*, 209.

to de-emphasise the readable books; Beckwith points out that 'the belief that only the books of the Hebrew Bible are actually inspired has gradually gained ground among the Orthodox, at the expense of the Roman view.'[18] Meyendorff writes in similar vein, when he states that the issue 'retains some fluidity in the consciousness of the Orthodox Church' and 'the books that are not included in the Hebrew canon are generally referred to as deuterocanonical. Significantly, the modern Russian Synodal translation of the OT is based on the Hebrew original.'[19]

A glance at the section 'loci citati vel alligati' at the back of the Nestle-Aland 27th edition of the Greek New Testament demonstrates that the New Testament writers were aware of the apocryphal writings – how could they fail to be? – had read them and often made allusion to them. However, there is a marked difference between awareness of a book's existence and belief that it is canonical Scripture. While modern conventions of citation did not exist in the first century, it is noticeable that the introductory formulae *legein* (it says), *graphein* (it is written), or *hoti* (a word used to introduce a reference to another source, and used frequently in the New Testament to refer to a passage of Scripture) are not used to refer to the apocryphal literature. I have yet to discover how far the Orthodox have grappled with Roger Beckwith's important work, *The Old Testament Canon of the New Testament Church*. Beckwith's massive research argues that the Hebrew Bible was accepted as canonical not at the Synod of Jamnia in AD 90 but in the mid second century BC. The theory of a wider Alexandrian canon is untenable, the inclusion of apocryphal and pseudepigraphal writings in the canon of early Christianity followed the church's breach with the synagogue, 'among those whose knowledge of the primitive Christian canon was becoming blurred.' Jesus, the apostles, and the New Testament church, endorse 'various Jewish titles for the canon,

[18] R. Beckwith, *The Old Testament Canon of the New Testament Church: And Its Background in Early Judaism* (Grand Rapids: Eerdmans, 1985), 2–3.

[19] Meyendorff, *Encyclopedia of Christianity*, 3:861.

the threefold Jewish structure, the traditional Jewish order for the books' while 'on the question of the canonicity of the Apocrypha and Pseudepigrapha the truly primitive Christian evidence is negative.'[20] If the Orthodox conception of the canonical books is to be maintained, a coherent and sustainable answer to Beckwith is imperative.

When it comes to the New Testament, Orthodoxy is no different to Protestantism. Although there was much hesitation about the book of Revelation, particularly in Syria, the Alexandrian position, in which Revelation had a place, prevailed by the sixth century.[21] In other ways, too, there is agreement. The Old Testament is an integral part of the Bible and the liturgy is filled with its language, and with direct citations. Christ and the gospel is the hermeneutical key to understanding not only the New Testament but the Old Testament as well.[22]

The Word of God and the words of man

The Orthodox agree that Bible is called 'the word of God' because it communicates the knowledge God has chosen to give through the inspired authors. It bears witness to God's thoughts and his saving action in history, it communicates God's truth and wisdom and the mystery of the living God himself. It proclaims the true God in contrast to false gods. It is principally addressed to God's people.[23]

Nevertheless, the word of God is given to us through the words of man. It is here that discussion has arisen in the West in the last two hundred years. Historical criticism has subjected the Bible to intense scrutiny, examining it from many differing angles: sources, authorship, grammatical and textual analysis, *sitz im leben*, literary genre, audience analysis and so on. All these things are appropriate, providing due recognition is given

---

[20] Beckwith, *OT Canon,* 386–405, 434–37.

[21] Stylianopoulos, *The New Testament: An Orthodox Perspective,* 25; Ware, *Orthodox Church,* 208.

[22] Stylianopoulos, *The New Testament: An Orthodox Perspective,* 27–31.

[23] Ibid., 32–5.

to the nature of holy Scripture, which has not always been the case. B.B. Warfield, in his classic defence of the inspiration and authority of the Bible, pointed to the crux of the matter: Christian discipleship requires that we believe Christ and the apostles to be reliable teachers of doctrine. There are matters of faith that underlie and should inform academic criticism. Warfield noted the massive internal Biblical evidence that Christ and the apostles equated the Bible with the words of God. The statements 'Scripture says' and 'God says' were for them identical, without in any way diminishing the humanity of the Bible. Here, Warfield had recourse to the sovereign providential work of God. If he wanted a letter like Romans to be written he prepared a Paul to write it, including all the particular details of his life, upbringing, education, environment and so on. The result is a letter like Romans, written by a man like Paul![24]

Orthodoxy has a different approach from Warfield. For Stylianopoulos, the Bible is the record of revelation rather than revelation itself. This flows from a dynamic concept of revelation and inspiration that involves a process of personal divine-human interaction.[25] It is unclear how far Stylianopoulos speaks for Orthodoxy as a whole. It will certainly take time, possibly a long time, before this is known. His arguments sound suspiciously like a neo-orthodox position, although it would be a mistake to lump the two together. The neo-orthodox operated with a Kantian dualism between the phenomenal realm, open to historical and scientific observation, and the noumenal realm, beyond such investigation. The Enlightenment passed the East by. Orthodoxy's approach to the Bible and revelation reaches back, along a different historical track, to the Fathers.

Stylianopoulos acknowledges that it is difficult to disentangle the divine and human aspects of Scripture. 'The reader must engage the biblical witness in its totality and distinguish between central claims pertaining to salvation and subsidiary matters of

---

[24] See B. B. Warfield, *The Inspiration and Authority of the Bible* (Philadelphia: Presbyterian and Reformed, 1970).

[25] Stylianopoulos, *The New Testament: An Orthodox Perspective*, 37.

history, chronology, language, and culture.' Therefore 'the concept of the Bible as the word of God pertains primarily to the saving message of Scripture and cannot be applied literally to the exact words of each biblical verse. The latter view would virtually render the Bible a kind of massive computer printout of the mind of God, a gross misconception.' It would entail 'insuperable difficulties' in view of 'the scientific inadequacies and historical discrepancies in Scripture.' Moreover, God is both revealed and hidden and cannot be identified with the text of the Bible. 'Each author must be granted one's own personality, cultural framework, conceptual understanding, literary skills, and spiritual insight as an active contributor to the divine-human interaction.' Rather, Stylianopoulos continues, Orthodox theology holds to a personal and dynamic, rather than mechanistic and verbal, concept of inspiration for 'God did not merely dictate words or propositions to passive authors.'[26] Here it is clear that Stylianopoulos has never come to grips with the Reformed view of Scripture, taught in The Westminster Confession of Faith and espoused by, *inter alia*, Warfield and J.I. Packer. As Packer says, 'this "dictation theory" is a man of straw. It is safe to say that no Protestant theologian, from the Reformation till now, has ever held it; and certainly modern Evangelicals do not hold it.' While writers in the seventeenth century spoke of Scripture as dictated by the Holy Spirit, they signified 'not the method or psychology of God's guidance of them, but simply the fact and result of it.' The way they spoke of the operation of the Spirit was of 'accommodation' – 'God completely adapted his inspiring activity to the cast of mind, outlook, temperament, interests, literary habits and stylistic idiosyncrasies of each writer.'[27]

Stylianopoulos continues by arguing that while all Scripture is God-breathed (2 Tim. 3:16) it is not equally so because of the

---

[26] Ibid., 38–40.
[27] J. I. Packer, *'Fundamentalism' and the Word of God: Some Evangelical Principles* (London: Inter-Varsity Fellowship, 1958), 79.

variability of human receptivity. Some parts of the Bible are more useful than others – Isaiah in comparison to Ecclesiastes, John over against Jude. Because of their insistence that all of Scripture is of the same authority, advocates of inerrancy among conservative Protestants are forced to artificial defensive positions, attributing absolute truth to Scripture when it belongs only to God. Rome, too, insists on infallibility but for Orthodoxy the Bible is seen as *sufficient*.[28] In line with this, those who support a 'dictational view of revelation and inspiration [*sic*]' [!] are inclined to defend traditional attributions of authorship at all costs, whereas those who hold a dynamic position – such as the Orthodox – are less anxious since they see God's hand at work over the whole process. They understand there to be a dynamic correlation between the Bible and the believing community, realizing that the Bible does not stand alone. So 'the question of authorship is important but not critical. The ultimate theological criterion of truth is the life of the Church.'[29]

Whatever the views of Stylianopoulos, the Orthodox hold firmly to the Bible as the authoritative and powerful Word of God, that sits in judgment on us, rather than vice-versa. The Bible functions powerfully in the Orthodox liturgy, precisely as the Word of God. The view of Scripture held by Jesus and the apostles – and by Orthodoxy in general – is a good deal stronger than that advanced by Stylianopoulos. Jesus affirms that 'Scripture cannot be broken' (John 10:35), Paul repeatedly equates the words of Scripture, the words of God, and the words of the human authors (Rom. 9:33, cf. Isa. 28:16; Rom. 10:19, cf. Deut. 32:21; Rom. 10:20, cf. Isa. 65:1), and both are prepared to base crucial arguments on single words (John 10:35, Gal. 3:16).

Moreover, Stylianopoulos' argument is weak when he argues that all Scripture is not equally inspired, for this is dependent on the variable degrees of human receptivity. Rather, the question

---

[28] Stylianopoulos, *The New Testament: An Orthodox Perspective*, 40–1.
[29] Ibid., 41–2.

of inspiration is a question of *origin*. It refers to Scripture being 'God-breathed', and is better called ex-spiration rather than inspiration. It is not a matter of the quality of this or that Biblical passage, of how central it is to the doctrine of salvation. Instead, it refers to the original author, the Holy Spirit who 'breathed out' Scripture. Whether human beings believe the message, or whether this or that passage is more crucial for its teaching than another, does not affect the question of whether such passages are breathed out by God.

As we have suggested, it would be a mistake to equate Stylianopoulos' position with Orthodoxy as such, which – allowing for its placement of the Bible in the tradition – is remarkably similar to the classic Reformed one. However, Stylianopoulos demonstrates that as Orthodoxy increasingly interacts with Western culture, many of its prominent spokesmen are becoming influenced by the intellectual and theological cross-currents within that culture.

The authority of Scripture

In Stylianopoulos' view, as the word of God, the Bible bears God's authority, while insofar as it is composed historically it is the word of Israel and the church and so has the communal authority of these respective traditions. Unfortunately, over the years the critical study of the Bible in university settings has separated it from the life of the church. It has led to brilliant academic achievements but also to a denigration of its authority as the word of God.[30] This has 'imperceptibly given rise to an intimidating supposition that only scholars can truly know the Bible, a notion as arrogant as it is foolish' and has bred a detached rational reading based on autonomous human reason.[31] Moreover, while historically the Bible and tradition were seen as complementary, the Protestant Reformation introduced a radical cleavage between Scripture and tradition.[32]

---

[30] Ibid., 45–6.
[31] Ibid., 68.
[32] Ibid., 47.

While there is a dynamic interplay between the Bible and the communities to which its authors belong, Stylianopoulos acknowledges the superior (but not supreme) authority of Scripture, for 'the very fact of a biblical canon clearly implies recognition of the unique authority of what is received as divine revelation and thus the superior authority of the Bible in the general tradition.' So 'it is essential therefore to acknowledge the authority of Scripture for tradition.'[33] As Thomas Hopko writes:

> Once the Bible has been constituted as the scripture of the church, it becomes its main written authority within the church and not over or apart from it. Everything in the church is judged by the Bible. Nothing in the church may contradict it. Everything in the church must be Biblical; for the church, in order to be the church, must be wholly expressive of the Bible; or, more accurately, it must be wholly faithful to and expressive of that reality to which the Bible is itself the scriptural witness.[34]

This, while putting the Bible in the centre of the church's life, is not the same as Reformed teaching. For the Orthodox, according to Hopko, the Bible is the church's *main* written authority, it is not over the church but within it, and the church must reflect the reality to which the Bible bears witness. In short, truth is one, whether in the Liturgy, the sacraments (or mysteries), the Bible, or prayer. Christ is the supreme revelation of the Father, and gave himself to us in the apostolic teaching. The Bible cannot be abstracted from this context. So, nothing is above the Bible – in Meyendorff's words, 'Scripture is considered the primary and essential Word of God'[35] – but the Bible is located within the tradition.

The Orthodox understanding of the place and context of the Bible raises some important points that can help clarify our own

---

[33] Ibid., 47–55.

[34] Cited in Stylianopoulos, *The New Testament: An Orthodox Perspective*, 55–6.

[35] John Meyendorff, in *The Encyclopedia of Christianity*, 3:861.

appreciation of the origins and authority of Scripture. It is often said by Protestants that the Biblical books imposed themselves on the church and thus the Bible preceded the church. This is held to contrast with the idea, to which Orthodoxy subscribes, that it is the church that gave us the Bible. But are either of these proposals adequate?

Surely, the obvious point is that the church was produced by the Holy Spirit, who also is the ultimate author of the Bible. The church was born through the preaching of the word. But who was it who preached the word? It was the apostles – Peter on the day of Pentecost. Who was Peter? a part of the church!

So too the Biblical books were composed by apostles and others, themselves part of the church. These books, in being recognized as canonical, were products on the human level of people who were members of the church already. In that sense, the church *did* produce the Bible. It is not the whole story, of course, but it is still part of the story. Again, to whom was the Bible given? To private individuals? To universities and scholars? Or to the church? There is a dynamic interplay here. The common Reformed notion that the Bible came into existence independently of, and prior to, the church is untenable. The human authors of Scripture were part of the church already. At the same time, the Orthodox tend to overstate their position as if the church created the Bible or approved it. What happened was that the Holy Spirit formed the church, empowered the preaching of the gospel, and inspired Scripture. In turn, the church, formed and enlightened by the Holy Spirit, recognized the Scriptures that the same Spirit had inspired through the agency of its apostles and leaders.

It points to the nub of the matter; the Holy Spirit originated *both* Scripture *and* the church – something Stylianopoulos recognizes. As he says, 'the mutual relationship between divine word, oral traditions, texts, canon, and community constitutes a seamless part of the same dynamic life of faith, a pulsating tradition which is responsive and propulsive, not merely passive and receptive.' Indeed, all these things result from the work of the Holy Spirit – 'just as there could be no Church without gospel, so also there could be no gospel without Church.'[36]

All this should not belittle the central place the Bible has in the belief and worship of Orthodoxy. Ware points out that among the various elements of tradition a unique preeminence belongs to the Bible, to the creed, to the decrees of the ecumenical councils. The Bible is the supreme expression of God's revelation to man. It is the church alone that can interpret the Bible with authority.[37] Reformed readers may be reassured by these remarks of St. Peter of Damascus (who probably lived in the eleventh or early twelfth centuries). St. Peter comments, 'there is no contradiction in Holy Scripture ... every word of Scripture is beyond reproach. The appearance of contradiction is due to our ignorance.... We should attend to them [the words of Scripture] as they are.' The person who searches for the meaning of Holy Scripture will not put forward his own opinion but will take as his teacher, not the learning of the world, but Scripture itself.[38]

How Scripture is used

Here the Orthodox have maintained the churchly context of Scripture more effectively than the West has done, Reformed Protestantism included. We noted how the Bible is dominant in the liturgy, either explicitly or in a more underlying and pervasive way. The Book of the Gospels is kept in a prominent place on the altar. The Bible is seen as a verbal icon of Christ. Contemporary conservative Protestantism could well learn from the Orthodox at this point. It is also evident in preaching, for 'preaching at its best energizes worship and makes the liturgy a more powerful experience.'[39] It forms the heart of the

---

[36] Stylianopoulos, *The New Testament: An Orthodox Perspective*, 57.

[37] Ware, *Orthodox Church*, 205–7.

[38] St. Nikodimos of the Holy Mountain, *The Philokalia* (G. Palmer; London: Faber and Faber, 1983), 3:144.

[39] Stylianopoulos, *The New Testament: An Orthodox Perspective*, 64.

catechetical, devotional, and doctrinal life of the church. We saw how Protestantism has often divorced Scripture from its intended use in the church; the study of the Bible was long ago hived off to an academic world that generally had no ecclesiastical responsibilities, with the result that the laity increasingly viewed themselves as lacking in the competence needed to understand what the Bible was saying. In the case of Orthodoxy, strong ecclesial and doctrinal anchors have largely spared them from the turmoil over critical scholarship that has engulfed the Western church.

Let us consider this further. Whereas in the West, theology is a rational activity that provides the foundation for piety but is distinct from it, the situation in the East is quite different. Here theology and piety are inseparable. In fact, theology stems from spiritual experience; it always has to be checked against the tradition and Scripture. A theologian is one who has a living experience of God, just as the goal and nature of salvation is union with God in deification (see chapter 10). Theology is not a purely intellectual activity; indeed, the intellect is simply part of the whole, just as it is only part of man. Revelation is in some sense accessible to the whole church, not the province merely of professional theologians. Again, doctrine could not develop; the experience of the saints was the same in all ages. As Meyendorff points out:

> In Jesus Christ, therefore, the fulness of Truth was revealed once and for all. To this revelation the apostolic message bears witness, through written word or oral tradition; but, in their God-given freedom, men can experience it to various degrees and in various forms. The world to which this witness is announced continually raises new challenges and new problems. The very complexity of the human being; the reluctance of the Byzantine Christian mind to reduce theology to one particular form of human appropriation – the intellectual; the character of the New Testament message, concerned not with abstract truths, but with a Person; the absence in the Byzantine Church of a permanent, infallible criterion of truth; all these elements

192 Eastern Orthodoxy: A Reformed Perspective

contributed, in Byzantium, to an understanding of Christianity as a living experience, for whose integrity and authenticity the sacramental structure of the Church is certainly responsible, but whose living content is carried on, from generation to generation, by the entire community of the Church.

These same elements also determined that the evolution of theology in the Byzantine Church could only have been a slow and organic process, requiring a tacit agreement of the entire body of the hierarchy and the faithful.[40]

This, as Meyendorff stresses, is not some static and sterile restriction to tired old formulae. The East has always, in its liturgy, looked forward to the life of the world to come (as in the prayer at the conclusion of the communion liturgy). But this is only possible if novelties inconsistent with the apostolic foundation of the faith – given once for all in Scripture and in the original gospel message of the eyewitnesses of Jesus – are avoided.[41] As such, many in the East recognize a certain kinship with evangelical Protestantism. Stylianopoulos himself thinks that Orthodox scholars will be 'wise to take cognizance as well of Evangelical scholarship with which they share significant theological ground'.[42]

The Bible and hermeneutics

Stylianopoulos expounds the place and authority of the Bible in the context of the modern hermeneutical debate in a way that should resonate with any serious Reformed scholar. He envisages the need for what he calls a dynamic conservatism anchored on four presuppositions: a high regard for the authority of Scripture, the Church, and classic Christian doctrine; the importance of prayer, worship, and the spiritual life for the study of Scripture; an honest quest for truth, based on the primary meaning of the text gained by critical historical-grammatical exegesis; and the realization that the purpose of exegesis is to il-

---

[40] Meyendorff, *Byzantine Theology*, 9–10.

[41] Ibid., 224.

[42] Stylianopoulos, *The New Testament: An Orthodox Perspective*, 76.

luminate the theological truths and ethical values of Scripture.[43] He then proceeds to a lengthy and sophisticated discussion of hermeneutics.

Scripture as part of tradition again

Binns helpfully summarizes the nature of tradition as understood in the Orthodox churches. 'It is almost true to say that the Holy Spirit, the Christian Church, and the Tradition are phrases which refer to the same reality and, in practice, mean the same. The term Orthodoxy can also be used as a description of this body of truth handed down from generation to generation within the Church. All local Orthodox Churches are conscious of their existing within the one tradition.' Tradition in this sense, Binns explains, is the communication of grace rather than some external set of authoritative rules.[44]

This is bound up with Orthodoxy's view of the church and salvation. Lossky points to the theandric nature of the church. As with Christ, in whom a created nature is inseparably united to God, so the church has a permanent operation of the Holy Spirit within it. This impersonal union with the Holy Spirit —impersonal in the sense that the church and its members are not assumed into a personal union such as occurred in the incarnation – gives to the actions of the clergy an objective character independent of particular persons or intentions. From this, the sacraments and sacred rites have two simultaneous wills or operations; the concurrence of the words of the priest and the efficacy of the Holy Spirit. The words of the very first council, at Jerusalem, epitomize this concurrence – 'it seemed good to the Holy Spirit and to us' (Acts 15:28) – and this is the pattern for all the councils of the church thereafter. Hence, tradition has a pneumatological character – it is the life of the church in the Holy Spirit. Moreover, truth can have no external criterion outside itself to which it is subject, for it is manifest in itself: it

[43] Ibid., 81.

[44] J. Binns, *An Introduction to the Christian Orthodox Churches* (Cambridge: Cambridge University Press, 2002), 61.

is given in greater or lesser degree to all members of the church. Here the Christological and pneumatological aspects are in harmony with the catholicity of the church, the task of stating dogmas belonging to the Christological aspect, grounded on the incarnation.[45] In this way, tradition is not something set against the Bible for there is a harmony and congruity to all aspects of the work of Christ and the Holy Spirit.

How then does this relate to the classic Reformed idea of Scripture and tradition? First, we must explode the myth held by many Orthodox that Reformed theology has no doctrine of the church but is purely individualistic. Central to Reformed theology is the doctrine of the covenant. This focuses on God's commitment to his people, expressed in the declaration that occurs at each stage in its historical development: 'I will be your God, you shall be my people' (Gen. 17:7-8; Jer. 11:4; 24:7; 30:22; 31:31-34; 32:38; Ezek. 34:24; 37:21-28; Rev. 21:3). Covenant theology is as far from individualism as night from day. It is expressed classically in The Westminster Confession of Faith, from chapter 7 onwards, while there is an extensive section on the church and sacraments in chapters 25–31. In the classic Reformed confessions of the sixteenth century, church and sacraments are integral. The sections on matters relating to the nature of the church, its sacraments, ministry, and rites take up a very sizeable proportion of these documents.[46] John Calvin devotes the whole of book four of his *Institute of the Christian Religion* to the doctrine of the church.

It needs to be restated forcefully that the idea of 'the right of private interpretation' is *not* a Reformed principle. This alien

---

[45] Lossky, *Mystical Theology*, 186–9.

[46] The following references are to P. Schaff, *The Creeds of Christendom* (Grand Rapids: Baker, 1966). The Heidelberg Catechism (1563), 65–85, Schaff 3:328–38; The Belgic Confession (1561), 27–35, Schaff 3:416–31; The Scots Confession (1560), 16–23, 25, Schaff 3:458–74, 476–79; The French Confession (1559), 24–38, Schaff 3:373–81; The Thirty-Nine Articles of Religion of the Church of England (1563, 1571), 8, 19–36, Schaff 3:492, 499–512; The Second Helvetic Confession (1562, 1566), 17–28, Schaff 3:868–905.

notion supposes that any individual Christian has the right, privilege, and duty to interpret the Bible as he or she sees fit. A striking example of this thinking is the case of the Particular Baptists in Nottinghamshire, who 'followed the common Particular Baptist practice of constituting themselves into a church in a solemn ceremony in which participants covenanted with one another and with God to live in church fellowship according to the will of God as they saw it.'[47] The Bible was not given by God to private persons but to the church of Jesus Christ, his Son. Hence, the celebrated first chapter of the Second Helvetic Confession roots the preaching of the word of God in the life of the church. 'Wherefore when this Word of God is now preached in the church by preachers lawfully called, we believe that the very Word of God is preached, and received of the faithful.'[48] It is preachers *lawfully called* – called by the church and preaching in the church – whose preaching is the word of God. Alongside this we should note the rigorous requirements of the Westminster Assembly's *Directory for the Publick Worship of God* and *The Form of Presbyterial Church-Government* concerning those who preach.[49] This body was called by Parliament to provide a confession of faith, and ordinances for the government of the church, and had as its task the licensing and ordaining of ministers. To categorize Reformed theology as individualistic, with no doctrine of the church, is an error of monumental proportions.

The error of equating the classic Protestant and Reformed doctrine of Scripture with the later idea of the right of private interpretation is committed repeatedly by the Orthodox in discussing Protestantism. Evidently they are best acquainted with fundamentalist and evangelical sects with their highly

---

[47] F. Harrison, 'The Nottinghamshire Baptists: Polity,' *BQ* 25 (1974), 212–31: see 217.

[48] Schaff, *Creeds*, 3:832.

[49] See *The Confession of Faith, the Larger and Shorter Catechisms with the Scripture proofs at large together with The Sum of Saving Knowledge* (Applecross, Ross-shire: The Publications Committee of the Free Presbyterian Church of Scotland, 1970), 369–93, 394–416.

individualistic and non-ecclesial slant. Stylianopoulos makes this mistake many times.[50] They need to come to terms with the fact that the Reformed faith is an ecclesial faith, as the plethora of confessions published in the century and a half after the Reformation attest. There is simply no excuse for ignoring the strong stress the Reformers had on the Fathers. The work of scholars such as A.N.S. Lane has demonstrated this irrefutably in the case of Calvin.[51] The same is true of the Westminster Assembly, the members of which were constantly referring to the Fathers in support in their discussions.[52]

It seems, for their part, that the Reformed need to realize the commitment of the Orthodox to the Bible as the word of God. Their reluctance to talk of the inerrancy of Scripture is not due to the impact of critical liberal post-Enlightenment rationalism. Rather, it is an outflow of the more dynamic notion of tradition, of which Scripture is a part, and thus of its strongly ecclesial rooting. Moreover, it could well be asked what exactly is the cash-value of the conservative Protestant doctrine of inerrancy as such, an idea that could well be held by the Jehovah's Witnesses or other sects whose connection to the historic Christian faith would be difficult to establish, and has been used by heretics as a stick with which to beat the orthodox (small 'o') down the ages.[53]

Allied to this is the false notion of the phrase *sola Scriptura* held in many Reformed circles. This is often taken to mean that the Bible is to be the only source for theology. It is almost universally claimed that it is one of the central pillars of the Reformation. However, there is no evidence of such a slogan in

---

[50] E.g., to cite but one of many instances, Stylianopoulos, *The New Testament: An Orthodox Perspective*, 55.

[51] A. N. S. Lane, *John Calvin: Student of the Church Fathers* (Grand Rapids: Baker, 1999).

[52] See my forthcoming volume, *The Theology of the Westminster Assembly* (Phillipsburg, New Jersey / Philadelphia: Presbyterian & Reformed/Craig Center for the Study of the Westminster Standards).

[53] Gregory Nazianzen, *Oration* 31:3, 21–24, *PG* 36:136–37, 156–60; Calvin, *Institute* 1:13:2–4.

the entire sixteenth century. It is probable that it did not put in an appearance until the eighteenth century at the earliest. Contrary to so much hot air, it is *not* a Reformation slogan. When it was coined it was held to affirm that the Bible is the highest court of appeal in all matters of religious controversy, *which is what the Reformers and their successors actually held*. The slogan itself, still less the reality to which it was intended to point, never meant that the Bible was the only source for theology.[54]

Moreover, the doctrine of Scripture taught in the Westminster Confession of Faith allows room for the development of doctrine in the church.

> The whole counsel of God concerning all things necessary for his own glory, man's salvation, faith and life, is either expressly set down in Scripture, or by good and necessary consequence may be deduced from Scripture ... (I:VI).

What is to be believed is *either* expressly set down in Scripture *or* by good and necessary consequence may be deduced from Scripture. This allows room for deductions, for considered theological exegesis of the Bible – and this exegesis, if it can be shown to be a legitimate development from Scripture, is part of the whole counsel of God for our salvation. It allows for extra-Biblical language to explain and defend the truth the Bible teaches.[55] Hence it is possible for a preacher in a Reformed congregation to utter from the pulpit infallible truth taught by a church council but which may not necessarily be expressly set down in the Bible. The declaration that 'Jesus Christ is the eternal Son of God, of the identical being as the Father' is absolute truth, infallible, eternally valid, more certain than the fact of the preacher who declares it; yet, it is not to be found in the Bible in precisely those terms. It is something elaborated in

---

[54] See A. Lane, 'Scripture, Tradition and Church: An Historical Survey,' *VE* 9 (1975), 37–55

[55] Hence, the words *homoousios* and *ousia* were used in the fourth-century Trinitarian controversies to defend the Biblical teaching on God against heresy.

the history of the church and recognized at the early ecumenical councils.

An Orthodox person may argue that the Reformed doctrine of Scripture has not been a safeguard against the emergence of heresy. This is sadly true. On the other hand, neither has the Orthodox view of Scripture and tradition prevented heresy – it was in the Eastern church that most of the major early heresies arose. All this shows is that a correct grasp of doctrine, in its proper context, must be wedded to prayer and faithfulness, in dependence on the grace of God.

We end with the words of Stylianopoulos. Referring to the different approaches to soteriology between Orthodox and Protestants, a theme we will consider in chapter 10, he says this:

> The burning hermeneutical point is to submit the norms themselves to critical evaluation in the light of the total witness of Scripture. The 'justification theology' focusing on the issue of faith and works is no less traditional simply because a Protestant declares it 'biblical.' Nor is the 'theosis theology' focusing on union with Christ in the Spirit unbiblical simply because an Orthodox declares it 'traditional.' An exegetical approach may well find that both the 'participatory' and 'forensic' views of salvation are part of the larger biblical witness, and that deeper appreciation of both may be achieved precisely by seeing them in positive comparative light. But the hermeneutical point is that, functionally, whether by selection or omission, Scripture and tradition play equally important roles in every faith community. The difference is that, because of their respective biases, Protestants tend to ignore the role of tradition, whereas the Orthodox tend to boast about it.[56]

---

[56] Stylianopoulos, *The New Testament: An Orthodox Perspective*, 209–10.

8

Church and Sacraments

Orthodoxy is a family of self-governing (autocephalous and autonomous) churches

The Eastern Church has never had a hierarchical structure such as Rome has had, with the church embodied in a single bishop. It has been close to the doctrine of the church expounded by Cyprian (200-58). Since Cyprian understood the passage in Matthew 16, where Jesus says he will build his church on Peter, to refer to all the apostles – not Peter alone – he wrote that all bishops sit collectively, together (*in solidum*) on the chair of Peter. In other words, Cyprian saw the text as a reference to the whole college of apostles, and thus applying in an ongoing sense to all bishops together.[1] Consequently, major differences have always existed with Rome on the position of Peter and the bishop of Rome. While Rome regards the bishops of Rome as the successors of Peter, to whom Jesus committed authority over the universal church, the East tends to interpret the rock on which the church is built (Matt 16:18) as Peter's confession of faith.

---

[1] See Cyprian, 'On the Unity of the Church,' 4–6, in *ANF* 5:422-3.

Furthermore, the East is markedly different from the West. The juridical emphasis of the West is almost totally absent. The question of authority does not arise in the same way. The Western church has been heavily marked by legal concerns stemming from Rome's position in the ancient world. Not so the East – the great ecumenical councils, all based in the East, did not meet to impose authoritative decisions on the whole church, but rather to confess the faith. Tradition in the East is a living dynamic process, of which Scripture, the Fathers, and the liturgy are an integral part. The councils simply recognized the truth, and the people received it. The validity of the decisions was effected in their universal recognition. Thus the assembled bishops confess the faith of the apostles, and their confession depends on being recognized by the entire church.[2] The Council of Florence (1439), at which agreement was effectively imposed by Rome on the Greeks due to the imminence of attack from the Turks, has never been accepted in the East, since it did not accord with the historic faith of the Church. Most of the Eastern bishops revoked their agreement on their return home.

The East acknowledges a *parity of bishops*. No one bishop has greater authority than any other – indeed, no member of the church has greater authority than any other. However, the bishoprics in the most prominent dioceses are accorded a higher respect. There are five – *the Pentarchy*: Jerusalem, Antioch, Alexandria, Rome and Constantinople – but their position is one of respect rather than power. They are *primus inter pares*. Not only are these bishops no higher than any others but bishops in general are not over the people. Thus each main Orthodox communion is *autocephalous*; no other jurisdiction can claim

---

[2] See the helpful discussion by Ware; T. Ware, *The Orthodox Church* (London: Penguin Books, 1969), 23, 254-8. He points to the mutual relation between the bishop and his flock, infallibility as belonging to the whole Church, not the episcopate alone, and the need for truth to be lived. 'At a true Ecumenical Council the bishops recognize what the truth is and proclaim it; this proclamation is then verified by the assent of the whole Christian people, an assent which is not, as a rule, expressed formally and explicitly, but *lived*' (Ware, 257).

authority over it. It is a collection of local churches without a higher centre that claims overall jurisdiction.

Problems of a different kind arose in the nineteenth century and beyond. Due to their success in permeating society, so closely were the autocephalous churches related to the nations to which they belonged that some restricted communion to those nationalities alone. This was known as *phyletism*, and was condemned as heresy by the Council of Constantinople in 1872.

There is no figure in Orthodoxy with the authority of the Pope

We noted that authority in the juridical sense is not something that even occurs in the East, in stark contrast to the Western church. The ecumenical councils simply recognized the truth, for tradition is a dynamic living thing. The assembled bishops confessed the truth and the church recognized what they confessed. So, the holy Synod at Nicaea II cried out in response to its decree

> So we all believe, we are all so minded, we all give our consent and have signed. This is the faith of the Apostles, this is the faith of the orthodox, this is the faith which hath made firm the whole world. Believing in one God, to be celebrated in Trinity, we salute the honourable images! ... For we follow the most ancient legislation of the Catholic Church. We keep the laws of the Fathers.[3]

In the Cyprianic model of the church, with parity of bishops, to be in the church is to be in communion with the bishop. Thus, the local church is the heart of Orthodoxy. The claims of the Papacy are abhorrent to the East.[4] It follows that the Orthodox

[3] H. R. Percival, *The Seven Ecumenical Councils of the Undivided Church: Their Canons and Dogmatic Decrees* (A Select Library of Nicene and Post-Nicene Fathers of the Christian Church: second series; Edinburgh: T.&T. Clark, 1997 reprint), 550–1.

[4] See O. Clément, *You Are Peter: An Orthodox Theologian's Reflection on the Exercise of Papal Primacy* (New York: New City Press, 2003).

churches are highly flexible, in comparison to Rome, capable of adapting quickly to changes around them. This is even more so, due to the fact that law does not have the prominent place that it has in the West.

Orthodoxy and Rome
Christ and the church
At this point we will summarize briefly the development of Papal power in the Roman church, so as to see exactly how Orthodoxy differs from it. According to *Lumen Gentium*, issued at the time of Vatican II, the 'light of Christ shines out visibly from the church'. The church has no other light than Christ. We do not believe *in* the church – so as not to confuse God with his works.[5] The church, in Christ, is like a sacrament – a sign and instrument of communion with God and of unity among all men. It is therefore the sacrament of the unity of the human race – in the church this unity has already begun. As a sacrament the church is Christ's instrument for the salvation of all. This is in line with Rome's teaching that the church is the continuation of the incarnation. Moreover, the church is centred in Rome under the leadership of Peter and his successors. Hence, in *Lumen Gentium* 8:2:

> The sole church of Christ is that which our Saviour, after his resurrection, entrusted to Peter's pastoral care, commissioning him and the other apostles to extend and rule it ... this church, constituted and organized as a society in the present world, subsists in the Catholic Church, which is governed by the successor of Peter and by the bishops in communion with him.

Furthermore, Vatican II's decree on ecumenism states:

> For it is through Christ's Catholic Church alone ... that the fulness of the means of salvation can be obtained. It was to the apostolic college alone, of which Peter is the head, that we

---

[5] *Catechism of the Catholic Church* (London: Geoffrey Chapman, 1994), 172, para 748.

believe that our Lord entrusted all the blessings of the New Covenant, in order to establish on earth the one Body of Christ into which all those should be fully incorporated who belong in any way to the People of God.[6]

What about churches that have broken away from Rome? For the later rifts, both sides were to blame. However, those born into those communities cannot be charged with the sin of separation.

The Catholic Church accepts them with respect and affection as brothers ... all those who have been justified by faith in baptism are incorporated into Christ. They have a right to be called Christians and with good reason are accepted as brothers in the Lord by the children of the Catholic Church.

Many elements of sanctification and truth are found outside the visible confines of the Catholic Church – the written word of God, the life of grace, faith, hope, and love.[7] Christ uses these churches as means of salvation, whose power derives from the fulness of grace and truth that Christ has entrusted to the Catholic Church. Thus, any validity attaching to either Orthodoxy or to the churches of the Reformation is due to their sharing in the fulness of grace and truth that Christ has given to the church of Rome!

The problem of Roman primacy

The pre-eminence of Rome emerged gradually. The church there was prominent as early as the first century due to the city's geopolitical importance; already hints of this can be discerned in Romans 1:8. Both Peter and Paul were martyred there in the 60s; so they are for ever present, presiding in the church of Rome. Peter is unique, since his office cannot be repeated; he was one of the apostles who lived with Jesus and saw him

---

[6] *Unitatis Redintegratio,* 3:5.

[7] *Unitatis Redintegratio,* 3:1–2; *Lumen Gentium,* 15.

at his resurrection. All this is independent of the later claims to universal jurisdiction.

Rome bases its claims on its reading of the New Testament. In particular, Matthew 16:18 features prominently. Jesus' statement that he will build his church on Peter is understood to refer to Peter himself and those who succeeded him as bishop of Rome. This includes three contentious elements.

First is the idea that it is to Peter in distinction from all other apostles that Jesus speaks these words. Second, there is the assumption that Peter was bishop of Rome; there is no mention of Rome in the text, nor in connection with Peter anywhere else in the New Testament, nor is there any credible historical evidence that Peter was ever bishop of Rome. Third, there is the assumption – dependent on the validity of both preceding ones – that all subsequent bishops of Rome are included in the ultimate reach of Jesus' statement.

In addition to the passage in Matthew, there is also Jesus' promise to Peter in Luke 22:32 that, when he had repented, he was to strengthen his brothers – understood to refer to his future pastoral role over the whole church. Further, in John 21:15-17, Jesus is said to give to Peter the responsibility of feeding his sheep, again seen as entailing universal pastoral oversight. Olivier Clément points out that all these passages are situated in a resurrection or eucharistic context – according to the early church the eucharist is the basis for the connection of the local church with all the churches.

This view that Jesus refers in Matthew 16 to the person of Peter was first argued by Popes in the early third century and gained ground in the next two hundred years.[8] At first Rome claimed no authority over other churches but only a pastoral role. However, by the fourth century it granted the right of appeal

---

[8] On the history of the papacy, see Geoffrey Barraclough, *The Medieval Papacy* (New York: W.W. Norton Company, 1979); Bernhard Schimmelpfennig, *The Papacy*, trans., James Sievert (New York: Columbia University Press, 1992); Walter Ullmann, *The Growth of Papal Government in the Middle Ages: A Study in the Ideological Relation of Clerical to Lay Power* (London: Methuen, 19703).

from bishops in Western Europe, setting itself up as a court of appeal from churches in Africa and the East, where Rome was one of the pentarchy. By the time of Leo the Great (440–61), the primacy of Rome was complete. The Bishop of Rome represents the perpetual presence of Peter, and so is the head of the entire church. The Pope is thereby juridically identical with Peter. But Leo never intervened except to defend the truth of the gospel, nor did he believe he had the right to intervene as bishop of each individual church. Later, Gregory the Great (590–604) saw the primacy of Rome as a primacy of help and counsel. At this time many of the Popes were exemplary pastors and led the church both theologically and in missionary enterprise.

The East, for its part, saw the primacy of Rome as a primacy of honour due to the position and prestige of Rome itself (since the centres of the Eastern church were based on their political prominence). It did not accept that Rome had any jurisdiction over all other churches. Nestorius was condemned by the Council of Ephesus (431) on the basis of the letters of Cyril of Alexandria, without recourse to Rome. Rome ratified the decision, making it ecumenical, but the decree itself did not require Roman approval. The Council of Chalcedon (451) saw itself as complete in itself – it simply received the Tome of Pope Leo. Constantinople II (553) affirmed that the truth could be recognized by a council as such. If a Pope opposes an ecumenical council he cuts himself off from the church. Constantinople III (680–81) anathematized former Pope Honorius. In fact, from the fourth to the ninth centuries Clément acknowledges a creative tension between Popes and councils.

The extension of Papal powers was based on forged documents. *The Donation of Constantine* alleged that Emperor Constantine acknowledged Pope Sylvester's right to rule the Western Empire after he had cured Constantine of leprosy. Constantine then withdrew to a new city since he felt himself unworthy to live in the same city as the Pope. It was not realized to be an eighth-century forgery until Lorenzo Valla's research during the Renaissance, when he established the science of textual criticism, convincing even the then Pope. *The Pseudo-Isidorian Decretals*, mid-ninth-century forgeries, were frequently used from the ninth to the eleventh centuries to undergird the Papal claims of Gregory VII (Hildebrand) (c. 1023–85: Pope from 1073–84), who introduced a series of reforms enormously enlarging Papal power. The Pope could now theoretically depose or transfer bishops, and ordain clergy whenever he wished. His decisions could not be overruled but he himself could overrule decisions by all others. He had the power to depose emperors,[9] and was the sole legislative authority.

In the fourteenth and fifteenth centuries there was a reaction against Papal supremacy. The Papacy left Rome and based itself at Avignon, in the south of France, from 1309 to 1377, the period known as the Babylonian Captivity. Shortly after the Pope returned to Rome in 1377, a rival Pope was elected at Avignon, creating dual Popes from 1378 to 1413, a time known as the Great Schism. At one point, a compromise Pope was elected but he was rejected by the supporters of the other two, creating the even more bizarre spectacle of three Popes simultaneously! This chaos led to the rise of the Conciliar Movement. The Papacy was now at its lowest ebb. The Council of Constance decreed in 1415 that the council holds directly from Christ the power before which all others – Emperors and Popes – must bow. This was the council that condemned and burnt Hus.[10] The Council of Basle (1431–49) made the Pope its agent; here the movement over-reached itself and fizzled out, although there has been a continued tension thereafter between Papal power and the conciliar tendency. This tension is seen at the point where in

---

[9] It was in Gregory VII's pontificate that the Investiture Controversy occurred. This arose over lay investiture, the right of civil rulers to make ecclesiastical appointments. Gregory deposed the German king Henry IV in 1075, and excommunicated him in 1076; at Canossa in 1077 he received Henry as a submissive penitent but did not reinstate him. After civil war in Germany he excommunicated Henry a second time. But the tables were turned in 1080 when Henry encouraged the election of a rival Pope, Clement III, and then in 1084 deposed Gregory and had him sent into exile.

[10] For technical reasons this is not a recognized conciliar decree.

1870 Vatican I acknowledged that the Pope speaking *ex cathedra* was infallible. The tension between the Papacy and conciliarism is clear in that the dogma of papal infallibility could only be proclaimed in a council! Clément cites the comment that the Pope needed a council to pronounce infallibly that he never needed it!

So there has always been a tension in the Roman church between the hierarchical tendency – the ultramontane view, with the Pope supreme – and the conciliar tendency, seen in the conciliar movement of the fifteenth century, the earlier erosion of papal power in the fourteenth century, and in modern times with Vatican II. This is exemplified in the relative prominence of two metaphors: the body of Christ – which entails a head, the Pope – and the people of God, which points to collegiality. With Vatican II the latter became more prominent but with Pope John Paul II the pendulum swung back towards the Papacy and the magisterium. The death of John Paul II, and the probable short pontificate of Benedict XVI, may bring these tensions out into the open again.

The Papacy now claims jurisdiction over the entire Christian church: hence *Roman* – Catholic. This claim flows from the apostolicity of the church. Jesus is the Father's emissary. He appointed apostles as witnesses of his resurrection and united them to his own mission. This function is unique. But there is a permanent aspect to it, for Christ promised to be with them to the end of time. Therefore the apostles appointed successors. As the office transmitted to Peter alone as the first of the apostles was transmitted to his successors, so also the office the other apostles received of shepherding the church is exercised without interruption by the order of bishops. Thus the bishops have by divine appointment taken the place of the apostles and whoever listens to them listens to Christ.[11]

This centralized hierarchy the Eastern church denies. All bishops are equal, and there is no central authority over them.

---

[11] *Catechism*, 200, sect. 860–2.

All church members are equal, and conciliar decisions must have the support of the people to attest their validity – which is why the Councils of Lyons (1274) and Florence (1439) failed to achieve acceptance. This is clearly different from the position of Rome. There, the mission of the Magisterium[12] is linked to the definitive nature of the covenant established by God with his people in Christ; its task is to preserve God's people from deviations and defections and to guarantee them the objective possibility of professing the true faith without error. 'To fulfil this service, Christ endowed the Church's shepherds with the charism of infallibility in matters of faith and morals.' The exercise of this charism takes many forms. The Roman pontiff enjoys infallibility in virtue of his office when as supreme pastor and teacher of all the faithful he proclaims by a definitive act a doctrine pertaining to faith and morals. The infallibility promised to the church is present in the body of bishops when, together with Peter's successor, they exercise the supreme Magisterium, above all in an ecumenical council.[13] For Orthodoxy, there is no such concept of infallibility residing in one man or in one group of men. In council, the assembled bishops simply recognize the apostolic faith, but this recognition cannot be imposed on the rest of the church, as if it came from a higher authority. It must receive recognition; it is possible for the bishops to be wrong. Moreover, the local churches are either autocephalous or autonomous. An autocephalous church has full authority over its own affairs.[14] Usually these are based on national units. Autonomous churches are independent in the conduct of their internal affairs but require the approval of another church for the appointment of their chief hierarch, and on occasions in other matters.

---

[12] Ibid., 206, sect. 890.

[13] Ibid., 206–7, sect. 891.

[14] This does not negate the right of any bishop, priest, or layperson to bring a charge against a bishop in another jurisdiction.

The sacraments

In Orthodoxy, the sacraments are called mysteries. This is due, as Ware indicates, to the point Chrysostom made: 'because what we believe is not the same as what we see, but we believe one thing and see another.'[15] As Ware puts it: 'This double character, at once outward and inward, is the distinctive feature of a sacrament.... At baptism the Christian undergoes an outward washing in water, and he is at the same time cleansed inwardly from his sins; at the Eucharist he receives what appears from the visible point of view to be bread and wine, but in reality he eats the Body and Blood of Christ.' In the sacraments Christ takes material things and makes them a vehicle for the Spirit. So the sacraments look backward to the incarnation, when Christ took material flesh and made it a vehicle for the Spirit, and they look forward to and anticipate the *apokatastasis* and the final redemption of matter at the last day.[16] Meyendorff makes the point that the sacraments enable us to participate in the divine life, which is the natural state of humanity. They are therefore not isolated acts in themselves.[17]

The Orthodox usually talk of seven sacraments: baptism, chrismation (the counterpart of confirmation in the West), the eucharist, repentance (or confession), holy orders, matrimony, and the anointing of the sick. However, unlike Rome, there is no absolute dogmatic significance to the number seven. Before the seventeenth century there was much flexibility about the number of the sacraments. John of Damascus spoke of two, Dionysius the Areopagite of six.[18] It was only in the seventeenth century, when the impact of the West was at its height, that seven gained wide acceptance, more as a convenience for teaching, popular because of the supposed mystical value of the number. Even for those who accept seven sacraments, not all are considered

---

[15] Chrysostom, 'Homilies on 1 Corinthians,' *PG* 61:55. Homily on 1 Corinthians 7:1.

[16] Ware, *Orthodox Church*, 281.

[17] J. Meyendorff, *Byzantine Theology: Historical Trends and Doctrinal Themes* (New York: Fordham University Press, 1979), 191.

[18] Ware, *Orthodox Church*, 282.

equal in value; for instance, the eucharist is at the heart of the church in a way the anointing of the sick is not. Baptism and the eucharist have special significance that sets them apart as 'pre-eminent among the mysteries'. In fact Gregory Palamas thought there were only two sacraments – baptism and the eucharist – 'on these two our whole salvation is rooted.' On the other hand, that the number seven does have significance in Orthodoxy is clear from the Syrian Antiochene-Orthodox forms for receiving converts from other churches. Converts from Lutheranism and the Reformed churches are required to renounce their former denial of the sacramental identity of marriage, orders, anointing of the sick, confession, and chrismation.[19]

Moreover there are a vast range of quasi-sacramental blessings and rites in Orthodoxy from which the sacraments proper cannot be isolated – 'blessings of corn, wine, and oil; of fruits, fields, and homes; of any object or element. These lesser blessings or services are often very practical and prosaic: there are prayers for blessing a car or a railway engine, or for clearing a place of vermin.'[20] A common misconception of Orthodoxy by the West is that it is in practice saturated by mysticism. However, as Every noted in 1947, 'The popular religion of Eastern Europe is liturgical and ritualistic, but not wholly otherworldly. A religion that continues to propogate new forms for cursing caterpillars and for removing dead rats from the bottoms of wells can hardly be dismissed as pure mysticism.'[21]

Every sacred rite begins with a doxology, such as 'Blessed is the kingdom of the Father, and of the Son, and of the Holy Spirit.' In this the worshippers lay themselves and all their interests aside and glorify the Lord for his own sake. They proceed to give thanks for his goodness and love for mankind, counting their own wickedness as the backcloth of his generosity and liberality. Moreover, the doxology demonstrates that

---

[19] *Service Book*, 456-7.

[20] Ware, *Orthodox Church*, 283.

[21] G. Every, *The Byzantine Patriarchate* (London: SPCK, 1947), 198.

'from the very beginning the Trinity must shine forth and be proclaimed'.[22]

Moreover, the intensely personal nature of the sacraments is evident when the priest names the individual when giving communion. He says, 'The servant of God [name] partakes of the holy, precious Body and Blood of Our Lord,' while at the anointing of the sick he says, 'O Father, heal Thy servant [name] from his sickness both of body and soul.'[23]

Baptism

In Orthodoxy, baptism, chrismation, and communion are closely linked. The one baptized – infant or adult – is immediately anointed (chrismated) and then receives his or her first communion. For Orthodoxy there are two things essential to baptism – the invocation of the triune name and threefold immersion in water. As Ware says,

> The priest says: 'The servant of God [name] is baptized into the name of the Father, Amen. And of the Son, Amen. And of the Holy Spirit, Amen.' As the name of each person of the Trinity is mentioned, the priest immerses the child in the font, either plunging it entirely under the water, or at any rate pouring water over the whole of its body. If the person to be baptized is so ill that immersion would endanger his life, then it is sufficient to pour water over his forehead; but otherwise immersion must not be omitted.[24]

The Greeks, who should be best able to judge the meaning of Greek words, are greatly distressed that the West has largely abandoned the practice of the early church in using immersion. If there is no immersion the correspondence between outward sign and the reality is broken. Sacramental symbolism requires

---

[22] N. Cabasilas, *A Commentary on the Divine Liturgy* (J. Hussey; London: SPCK, 1960), 43–4.

[23] Ware, *Orthodox Church*, 283.

[24] Ibid., 284.

that the candidate be immersed in the water, buried in the waters of baptism, to rise out of them again.

Baptism must normally be administered by a bishop or a priest, although in an emergency a deacon or any Christian can do it. Through baptism we receive full forgiveness of sins, original and actual. We become members of the body of Christ. Thus we are baptized into union with Christ, to die his death and to rise again in his resurrection.[25] Chrismation follows immediately, together with communion.

Chrismation

In chrismation, various parts of the baptizand's body are anointed with the chrism: forehead, eyes, nostrils, mouth, ears, chest, hands, feet. As the priest marks each he says, 'The seal of the gift of the Holy Spirit.' The baptizand receives the gift of the Spirit, becomes a full member of the body of Christ and is enabled to share in the prophetic ministry, and the royal priesthood of Christ.[26] The chrism must first have been blessed by a bishop who is thus involved indirectly in the chrismation. In the West, the Orthodox bishop is the one who actually confirms. Converts from other Christian bodies (Rome, Protestantism) are normally received simply by chrismation, as are repenting apostates.

Eucharist

The Orthodox hold that the bread and wine are changed into the body and blood of Christ but, unlike Rome, make no attempt to explain what they consider to be a mystery; still less do they use Aristotelian philosophical terminology to describe it. Most Orthodox writers insist that other terms than transubstantiation could equally be used to explain the mystery and that the term itself has no dogmatic significance of its own. Only God can understand what happens. The point is that the bread and the wine are changed into the body and blood of Christ through the Holy Spirit. Beyond this, it is claimed, we cannot go. As

[25] N. Cabasilas, *Life in Christ* (M. Lisney; London: Janus, 1995), 23.
[26] See also Cabasilas, *Life in Christ*, 32–3.

Nicholas Cabasilas puts it, 'The essential act in the celebration of the holy mysteries is the transformation of the elements into the Divine Body and Blood.'[27]

The bread that is to be changed into the body of Christ is separated from the rest of the loaves by the priest, who places it on the holy paten and consecrates it to God. Then he carries it to the altar and there offers it up in sacrifice. It is still only bread. The priest then marks the bread with the symbols of Christ's passion. He then, holding the bread, recites the words of institution, and refers to the events of Christ's sufferings, which are far more necessary than miracles.[28] When the congregation is ready to proceed to the eucharist, the catechumens are dismissed with prayer, since the uninitiated have no part in this mystery.[29] Then the priest departs, carrying the offerings head high, and goes to the altar, surrounded by candles and incense. He places the offerings on the altar, asking the congregation to pray that his intentions may be appropriate.[30] The consecration occurs when the priest recites the words of Jesus expressing the mystery. When this happens 'the sacrifice is complete; the splendid Victim, the Divine oblation, slain for the salvation of the world, lies upon the altar. For it is no longer the bread, which until now has represented the Lord's body ... it is the true Victim, the most holy Body of the Lord, which really suffered ... was crucified and slain.... In like manner the vine has become the blood which flowed from that Body.'[31] How can we believe this? Cabasilas points to the words of institution. The Lord's words accomplish this mystery, through the medium of the priest, his invocation and prayer.[32] Yet he also warns that if anyone adores the bread and wine and prays to them as such he has been led into error.[33]

---

[27] Cabasilas, *Liturgy*, 25.
[28] Ibid., 34–6.
[29] Ibid., 63.
[30] Ibid., 66.
[31] Ibid., 70.
[32] Ibid., 72.
[33] Ibid., 66.

In short, the sanctification of the mysteries is the task of the priest, not relying on human strength but the power of God, for the Holy Spirit who made Christ incarnate of the Blessed Virgin Mary now transforms the gifts of bread and wine into that same body and blood. 'We are assured of the result, not by reason of man who prays, but by reason of God who hears: not because man has made a supplication, but because the truth has promised to grant it.'[34] In the consecration, the priest prays to the Son rather than the Father, to teach us that he has this power because of the divine power he shares with the Father.[35]

The Orthodox, therefore, understand there to be a sacrifice. Christ offers himself – both priest and victim. We offer to the whole trinity, not just to the Father. It is also a propitiatory sacrifice offered on behalf of all – the living and the dead.[36] According to Cabasilas, it is a true sacrifice, not merely symbolic: it is the body of Christ that is offered, not merely bread. Since Christ's sacrifice was once only, it is not the offering of the bloody immolation of the Lamb but the bread is transformed into the sacrificed Lamb. Sacrifice is a figure for the whole mystery of Christ's redemptive work.[37] It is not a new sacrifice nor a repetition of the sacrifice of Calvary – rather, the events of Christ's sacrifice are made present.[38]

Everything done in the entire service represents the work of redemption. Before the preparation of the offerings the events of the scheme of redemption before the death of Christ are symbolized, while after the psalms the period that follows comes into view.[39] The laity receive both kinds – together in a spoon.[40] A little warm water is poured into the wine, to symbolize the descent of the Holy Spirit on the church.[41] To sum up, the food

---

[34] Ibid., 73.
[35] Ibid., 79.
[36] Ware, *Orthodox Church*, 293.
[37] Cabasilas, *Liturgy*, 52.
[38] Ware, *Orthodox Church*, 293–4.
[39] Cabasilas, *Liturgy*, 27.
[40] Ware, *Orthodox Church*, 294.
[41] Cabasilas, *Liturgy*, 90.

in the eucharist undergoes a change, becoming assimilated to
the person who eats it. It eventually becomes human blood. On
the other hand, in the Eucharist, the Bread of Life alters the
one who eats it, changing and transforming him into himself.[42]
Thus, the Eucharist sanctifies the faithful, turning us towards
God and obtaining pardon of our sins.[43]

What happens before the eucharist is also important. The
Orthodox are responsible to have confessed their sins and sought
reconciliation with their brethren beforehand. They attend
Vespers the evening before, and say the appropriate prayers,
which extend to around 90 pages in the prayer book. Fasting
from food and from sexual relations is required the night before
and in the morning of Divine Liturgy. The Orthodox come to
the eucharist to meet their God and King, and to do so prepare
themselves as if they are about to die.

Repentance

In confession, post-baptismal sins are forgiven. A person will go
to confession from an early age, as young as six or seven. The
priest will pronounce absolution and will give spiritual advice.
Often confession takes place in front of the iconostasis, although
it may occur behind a screen, but generally in the presence of
a gospel book or cross. Wherever the location, strict confiden-
tiality is required of the priest. Both priest and penitent stand,
not directly facing each other but both face a cross and an icon
of Christ, identifying the priest as an adviser not a mediator.

Holy Orders

There are three orders in the church – bishop, priest and deacon. In addition there are two minor orders: sub-deacon and
reader. Only a bishop has power to ordain. There must be at
least three bishops in attendance at a consecration of a bishop,
owing to episcopal collegiality. The congregation is required
to acknowledge ordinations by exclaiming at the appropriate

[42] Cabasilas, *Life in Christ*, 46.
[43] Cabasilas, *Liturgy*, 26.

time, 'He is worthy!' There are separate orders of married and unmarried priests. No unmarried priest is permitted to marry after ordination, and most of these will be monks. No married priest is permitted to remarry if his wife dies. Bishops are taken exclusively from the ranks of monks.[44] A widowed priest can become a bishop if he has become a monk before consecration. Parish priests are almost invariably married. Deacons, unlike in Rome, are a distinct office, rather than simply a staging post on the way to higher things.

Patriarchs are the heads of autocephalous churches. Metropolitan and archbishop are titles used differently in Greek and Russian churches. In the Greek church, archbishops preside over a province while metropolitan is used for every diocesan bishop. The reverse is true in the Russian church: the metropolitan is in charge of a province, while archbishop is a title used for bishops of distinction. Archimandrite is now used for priest-monks of outstanding distinction, where once it applied to heads of a range of monasteries. Arch-priest is used for distinguished non-monastic priests, while archdeacon is applied to distinguished monastic deacons.

Marriage

Married persons require a special gift from the Holy Spirit, given in the sacrament of marriage. This takes place in the service of crowning, which follows the exchange of vows and rings in the service of betrothal. On the heads of the bride and groom the priest in the Russian church places crowns of silver or gold; or of vegetation, in the Greek church. These crowns signify the gift of the Holy Spirit, and are regarded as crowns of both joy and martyrdom, since marriage entails self-sacrifice.

Apart from this, the Orthodox view of marriage is strikingly similar to the Reformed. Divorce, while discouraged, and remarriage are both permissible. It is recognized that Jesus allowed for divorce in the case of adultery. Orthodox canon

---

[44] Ware, *Orthodox Church*, 298.

law forbids remarriage for a fourth time. For a remarriage to take place in a church, and thus be sacramental in the full sense, a church divorce must be given in addition to the civil one.[45]

Anointing of the Sick

This sacrament is based on James 5:13-17, where James instructs the sick to call the elders of the church to pray over him or her and anoint them with oil. In Orthodoxy, this serves a twofold purpose: the healing of the body and the forgiveness of sins. It can be given to any who are sick, regardless of whether the sickness is life-threatening. Whether the sick person recovers or not, the sacrament heals – for the sickness is banished either by healing or death. In all these things, Christ is the mediator through whom God has given us all good things. 'He unites us to himself, and makes us each ... sharers though him in those graces which are his own.'[46]

The ministry of the Word

Here is one of the major differences between Orthodoxy and the Reformed churches. There are, of course, others, as our brief summary of Eastern sacramental theology has made clear. While differing from Rome, Orthodoxy shares a more objective view of the sacraments than the Reformed – although we should be clear that Reformed sacramental theology cannot be identified with evangelicalism's purely symbolic virtual non-sacramentalism.[47] According to Reformed theology, God's own nature is linguistic; there is continuous and eternal communication in the Godhead between the Father, the Son and the Holy Spirit. Jesus introduces us to this in his own communication with the Father (John 17:1-5, 24). The Son is called the

---

[45] Ware, *Orthodox Church*, 301–2.

[46] Cabasilas, *Liturgy*, 100.

[47] See my short, popular-level book, *The Lord's Supper: Eternal Word in Broken Bread* (Phillipsburg, New Jersey: Presbyterian & Reformed, 2001), as well as the classic Reformed confessions: e.g. The Westminster Confession of Faith, 27–29.

Word (John 1:1ff). For us, God's creatures – made in his image – language and understanding are inseparable; we understand through language. Moreover, God has ordained that the gospel be communicated verbally (Rom 10:13ff; 1 Cor 1:18ff.).

The New Testament is clear that the Holy Spirit accompanies the preaching of the Word (1 Thess. 1:5; 2:13; 1 Cor. 2:1-5). This is not surprising since the original author of Scripture is the Holy Spirit and the primary ministry of the Spirit is to testify of Christ, which is also the primary focus of preaching. Christ and the Spirit are in close conjunction after Jesus' resurrection (2 Cor. 3:11-18). From all this, the preaching of the word of God is the equivalent of Christ preaching. In Romans 10:14, Paul says concerning unbelieving Israel, 'how shall they believe him whom they have not heard?' (my translation). As Cranfield argues, the subjective genitive is preferable here, Paul referring to Christ being heard in the preaching of his appointed emissaries. Again, in Ephesians 2:17, he states that 'he [Christ] came and preached peace to you who were far off and peace to you who were near', meaning that both Jews and Gentiles heard Christ preach peace. Yet Christ never visited Ephesus! Paul evidently refers to his own preaching – for it was he who planted the church there – as the equivalent of Christ himself preaching. Similarly, Jesus looks forward to the day when the dead will hear the voice of the Son of God and be granted life (John 5:25ff), something distinct from the resurrection, to which he refers in verses 28 and 29, and fulfilled in the preaching of the gospel.

So not only at the start of the Christian life (1 Cor 1:21), but continuously thereafter (2 Tim 4:1ff), preaching is the principal means the Holy Spirit uses to establish and build up Christ's church; not only in bringing people to saving faith but also in sanctification. This can be seen by even a cursory glance at church history. When education and culture reached its lowest ebb after the collapse of the Roman empire, between 500–1000 AD, so too did the quality of preaching and church life. Conversely, the recovery of the gospel at the time of the Reformation was associated with an outburst of powerful biblical preaching. It follows that the sermon is the high point of church worship. The *Second Helvetic Confession*, 1, states the Reformed conviction most clearly. In its famous marginal reference it reads 'the preaching of the Word of God is the Word of God'.[48]

While, as we saw in chapter 6, Orthodoxy is more visual than auditory, nevertheless there are homilies in the liturgy of the Eastern Churches. Indeed, some of the greatest preachers in church history have been from the Eastern Church. Chrysostom is widely regarded as the greatest of all. Many of his sermons are available in translation. We referred in chapter 4 to Basil the Great's famous sermons on Genesis 1. Gregory Nazianzen's profoundly influential theological output comes to us in the form of orations. His oratorical ability was seen in his speech resigning the Patriarchate of Constantinople, which was greeted with a standing ovation by his hearers, who were by no means uniformly sympathetic to him. However, Orthodoxy gives nowhere near the same prominence to the sermon as do the Reformed. The priest addresses the congregation like a father talking to his family, rather than as a herald declaiming to an audience or an evangelist urging unbelievers to repentance, and the main focus is either visual or — when auditory — liturgical.

In summary, Orthodoxy is more visual, the Reformed Church more auditory. For Orthodoxy, the Eucharist is the centre of worship; while the sermon is a series of reflections on the Word, the Eucharist is the Word itself. For the classic Reformed confessions, Christ is present in both Word and sacrament, the one directed to our ears, the other to our eyes. In keeping with this, Orthodoxy has not confronted the great hermeneutical revolution begun by Calvin. The backdrop in Calvin's case was the medieval Western church, which also had a strong visual focus. The path of salvation led to the beatific vision, when the saint would be granted a vision of God. Knowledge of God was cast in a dominantly visual form. However, the beatific vision was

---

[48] See P. Schaff, *The Creeds of Christendom* (Grand Rapids: Baker, 1966), 3:237–8, 831–2.

not possible in this life. Therefore, the Christian could not have direct intuitive knowledge of God. This posed a huge problem for assurance of salvation. The way Calvin resolved this question was to recast the knowledge of God in *auditive* terms rather than visual ones. For Calvin, God reveals himself *in his Word* by the Holy Spirit. In the Word read and proclaimed, God addresses us personally. We cannot see him but we can hear him. Moreover, he is as he says he is – his self-revelation is true and reliable. The Holy Spirit, who is himself fully God and the whole God, accompanies the preached Word and grants us, through faith, direct auditive intuitive knowledge of God. This resolves the problem of the knowledge of God and simultaneously enables us to have assurance of salvation through the direct work of God the Holy Spirit.[49] The East, through historical circumstance, has never dealt with this question. If, as, and when the Orthodox do face it, there should be a revival of preaching to empower the liturgy still further. In conclusion, the Reformed must consider the focus of Orthodoxy to be a serious problem: Paul, in his final charge to Timothy and his successors, makes clear that the chief task of the Christian ministry is to preach the Word (2 Tim. 4:1).

---

[49] See T. F. Torrance, 'Intuitive and Abstractive Knowledge: From Duns Scotus to John Calvin,' *De Doctrina Ioannis Duns Scoti: Acta Congressus Scotistici Internationalis Oxonii et Edimburgi 11–17 Sept. 1966 Celebrati* (Romae: Curae Commissionis Scotisticae, 1968), 4:291–305; T. Torrance, *The Hermeneutics of John Calvin* (Edinburgh: Scottish Academic Press, 1988).

9

The Trinity[1]

Differences between the East and the West

The East and West have two significantly different concepts of the trinity. This comes to expression in the controversy over the *filioque* clause that the West added to the Niceno-Constantinopolitan creed (C).

The Western Church

The West, ever since Augustine, has consistently started its consideration of the trinity from the one divine essence, or being, of God. Augustine, in his treatise *De Trinitate*, produced a series of illustrations from creation to show how the persons of the trinity could be revealed separately, yet work together indivisibly. He sought these in the human mind, with – *inter alia* – its distinctions of memory, understanding and will. As he says, 'I have discovered ... three things, which are exhibited

---

[1] This chapter is an adaptation of chapter 10 of my book, *The Holy Trinity: in Scripture, History, Theology, and Worship* (Phillipsburg, New Jersey: Presbyterian & Reformed, 2004), in which the question is explored in much greater detail. Sections of that chapter are reproduced here with permission.

separately, whose operation is inseparable.'[2] He had struggled with this question since shortly after his conversion. In each case Augustine sees the trinity reflected in three aspects of a single human mind. His assumption is that the one being of God is self-evident but the trinitarian persons are problematic.

This has been the consistent emphasis of the West ever since Augustine. If anything, the tendency became more entrenched. Augustine himself aimed to follow in the footsteps of the great Cappadocians who had helped to resolve the fourth-century trinitarian controversy. His successors, however, moved further in the direction he pointed them. As a result, the one being of God took precedence over the three persons. The upshot was that God's being tends to be impersonal, for it is considered prior to the persons. In turn, the three persons are problematic, the subjects of lengthy discussion and proofs. Moreover, Thomas Aquinas (1225–74) defined the persons as simply mutual relations within the one essence. So strong was Aquinas' doctrine of God's simplicity (his oneness) that it seems to many scholars that he could scarcely hold to a clear doctrine of the trinity.[3] The persons seem, in Aquinas' thought, to be less than personal.

Moreover, Augustine considered the Holy Spirit to be the bond of love between the Father and the Son. This is supported by one of his trinitarian illustrations, where he refers to a lover, the one loved, and the love between them; the lover and the loved are clearly persons, but love is a quality not a person. So the question arises as to whether, for Augustine, the Holy Spirit is a person and – if so – whether he is subordinate.[4] This emphasis, acute in Augustine's trinitarian analogies, has been

---

[2] Augustine, *Letter 169*, NPNF 1:541, PL 33:740f.

[3] C. Hughes, *On a Complex Theory of a Simple God: An Investigation in Aquinas' Philosophical Theology* (Ithaca: Cornell University Press, 1989), 187-239; R. Letham, *The Holy Trinity*, 235-7. But see Richard A. Muller, *Post-Reformation Reformed Dogmatics: The Rise and Development of Reformed Orthodoxy, ca. 1520 to c. 1725: Volume 4: The Triunity of God* (Grand Rapids: Baker, 2003), 44-9, who provides strong countervailing evidence.

[4] Letham, *The Holy Trinity*, 184–200.

passed down in the Western tradition ever since. Indeed, if the Spirit is understood in this way it may be asked whether he is properly considered to be a person in his own right?

A tendency towards modalism – by blurring the distinctions between the three persons – is therefore endemic in Western trinitarianism, even in more recent theology. Following this, the trinity has been increasingly divorced from the life and worship of the Western church. For the overwhelming majority of Western Christians it is hardly an exaggeration to say that it is considered more a mathematical conundrum than a vital matter of everyday faith and worship. The most common expressions used to refer to the deity are 'God' or 'the Lord'. These could equally be used by an orthodox Jew. There is nothing explicitly trinitarian about them. A random sample of Western Christians, asked what the trinity means to them, would invariably respond with blank stares. The hymnology of the Western church is sadly lacking in clearly trinitarian compositions. Even some of the best known hymns are defective in this way: 'My God, how wonderful thou art,' 'Great is thy faithfulness' (at best binitarian), 'Praise my soul, the King of heaven,' and so on. A recent chorus, trying hard to be trinitarian, falls into heresy in the attempt, with a refrain which runs 'Thank you, O our Father, for giving us your Son, and *leaving your Spirit* till the work on earth is done [my italics].'

The Eastern Church

The trinity is more central to the life and worship of the church than in the West, as Orthodox service books make transparently clear. As Ware says, 'Orthodoxy believes most passionately that the doctrine of the Holy Trinity is not a piece of "high theology" reserved for the professional scholar, but something that has a living, *practical* importance for every Christian.'[5]

The East, for its part, has consistently focused on the three persons. In the Bible and in Christian faith the Son and the Holy

---

[5] T. Ware, *The Orthodox Church* (London: Penguin Books, 1969), 216.

Spirit are encountered as divine agents of salvation. Consequently, God is at once one and three, as Gregory Nazi-anzen so graphically portrayed it. This is strikingly clear in Orthodox liturgies, some samples of which we included in chapter 6.

The monarchy of the Father is a key factor. The Father, rather than the divine essence, is the origin or cause of the divine nature in the Son and the Spirit. Thus the Father begets the Son and the Holy Spirit proceeds from the Father. However, the West asks, how far has the relation between the Son and the Spirit been clarified? To many Westerners it seems to follow from opposition to the *filioque*, with the stress on the Spirit's procession from the Father and *not* the Son, that there is a distancing of the work of Christ from the work of the Holy Spirit. As Gerald Bray has argued, this has a far-ranging effect on Orthodoxy's view of salvation. It involves a pneumatocentric rather than a Christocentric piety and so renders the evangelical and Reformed view of the Christian faith – in which the person and work of Christ is central – impossible.[6] We shall consider this criticism later.

The *Filioque* Controversy

We referred to this, the largest single cause of division between East and West, in chapter 5. We shall now examine this matter in more detail. It belies recent attempts to paper over the cracks by claiming that there has been no real divergence between the East and West on the trinity. A millennium or more of church history cannot be ignored or swept under the carpet.[7]

The Niceno-Constantinopolitan creed (C) states that the Holy Spirit 'proceeds from the Father.' There is no mention of his proceeding from the Son as well. However, in Spain due to the threat of a continued Arianism, in localized liturgies an addition crept in – *a patre filioque* – 'from the Father *and the*

---

[6] G. Bray, 'The Filioque Clause in History and Theology,' *TB* 34 (1983), 139-44.

[7] See Lewis Ayres, *Nicaea and its Legacy: An Approach to Fourth-Century Trinitarian Theology* (New York: Oxford University Press, 2004).

Son.' This addition spread and was adopted by local councils, particularly the Council of Toledo (589),[8] was accepted by the French church in the late eighth century, but was not inserted into the Creed by Rome until 1014 under Pope Benedict VIII. The fourth Lateran Council of 1215 mentioned it and the Council of Lyons in 1274 proclaimed it as dogma.

The East objects to this development on ecclesiastical grounds. Such a change (more a development, since C did not deny the *filioque* but simply did not comment as it was not an issue) should require an ecumenical council akin to Nicaea, Constantinople and Chalcedon, it maintains. As Stylianopoulos puts it, 'Can a clause deriving from one theological tradition simply be inserted in a creed deriving from another theological tradition without council?'[9] *The East also objects on theological grounds.* We shall examine the reasons for this in a moment. Since East and West understand the trinity differently, on Eastern premises this Western development appears to undermine heretically the church's teaching on the trinity.

To appreciate the significance of this question and not to dismiss it as sterile one must, as Dietrich Ritschl observes, 'let one's thought sink into the classical trinitarian modes of argumentation.'[10] Stylianopoulos comments: 'at stake was not

[8] But see R. Haugh, *Photius and the Carolingians: The Trinitarian Controversy* (Belmont, Massachussetts: Norland, 1975), 160–1, who questions this explanation and argues that it 'first entered the Ecumenical Creed in the Latin West by a simple method of transposition and not by any willful act of interpolation in conscious violation of the Ecumenical decrees.' Sergei Bulgakov rightly argues that the phrase was unnecessary, for Arianism could have been rebutted quite readily without it; 'pour rejeter l'arianisme et reconnaître l'équi-divinité et la consubstantialité du Fils au Père, on n'a nul besoin de cette surérogation' (S. N. Bulgakov, *Le Paraclet* [C. Andronikof; Paris: Aubier, 1946], 125).

[9] T. Stylianopoulos and S. Mark Heim, eds, *Spirit of Truth: Ecumenical Perspectives on the Holy Spirit. Communion on Faith and Order, NCCCUSA October 24–25, 1985 – Brookline, Massachusetts* (Brookline, Massachusetts: Holy Cross Orthodox Press, 1986), 32.

[10] D. Ritschl, 'Historical Development and the Implications of the Filioque Controversy,' *Spirit of God, Spirit of Christ* (L. Vischer; London and Geneva, 1981), 46.

an abstract question but the truth of Christian salvation.'[11] In
Pelikan's terms, the Greek Fathers and the early councils did
not construct a science of divine ontology but one of divine
revelation.[12] The key question is whether the clause is consistent
with Scripture and C.

Biblical teaching on the procession of the Holy Spirit

In the *locus classicus*, John 15:26, Jesus says he will send the
Paraclete (a reference to Pentecost, the historical sending),
who in turn *proceeds from (ekporeuetai)* the Father, denoting
a continuous procession. Much modern New Testament scholarship argues that the procession here refers to economic activity
only – the relations between the Father, the Son and the Holy
Spirit in human history – and not at all to eternal antecedent
realities in God himself. Robert L. Reymond thinks referring
this to immanent realities in God is to go beyond the bounds
of Scripture. De Margerie rightly calls this restriction to the
temporal mission 'a simplistic exegesis that lacks a theological
background'.[13] It effectively undermines the reality and
truthfulness of God's revelation by positing the idea that what
God does economically does not necessarily reveal who he is.

The Spirit proceeds from the Father. The question in
dispute, however, concerns whether this procession is from
the Son also. Jesus refers to the Father's sending the Spirit at
Pentecost, in response to his request, or in his name (John 14:16,
26). However, Jesus also says he himself will send the Spirit at
Pentecost (John 16:7), and later he breathes on the disciples and
says, 'Receive the Holy Spirit' (John 20:22). So he shares with

---

[11] T. Stylianopoulos, 'The Biblical Background of the Article on the Holy Spirit
in the Constantinopolitan Creed,' *Études Theologiques: Le IIe Concile Oecuménique
Chambésy-Genève: Centre Orthodoxe Du Patriarcat Oecuménique* (1982), 171.

[12] J. Pelikan, *The Christian Tradition 2: The Spirit of Eastern Christendom* (Chicago:
University of Chicago Press, 1974), 33.

[13] R. L. Reymond, *A New Systematic Theology of the Christian Faith* (New York:
Nelson, 1998), 331f; B. de Margerie S.J., *The Christian Trinity in History* (E. J.
Fortman S.J.; Petersham, Massachusetts: St. Bede's Publications, 1982), 169.

the Father in the sending of the Spirit. Moreover, he says he and the Father are one (John 10:30). So it may be asked whether the Son does not also share with the Father in spirating the Spirit in that eternal manner to which John 15:26 refers?

Overall, the Bible paints a complex picture of the relations of the Spirit to the Father and the Son. The Holy Spirit hears the Father, receives from the Father, takes from the Son and makes what he receives known to the church, proceeds from the Father, is sent by the Father in the name of the Son, is sent by the Son from the Father, rests on the Son, speaks of the Son, and glorifies the Son. The relation between the Spirit and the Son is not one-directional but mutual and reciprocal. The Spirit plays an instrumental role in the coming of Christ and in his resurrection. The Spirit is active throughout the earthly life of the incarnate Son. So while Christ sends the Spirit he himself lives in union with the Spirit and – as far as his incarnate existence is concerned – in dependence on the Spirit.[14] The Spirit is called the Spirit of God, referring to the Father, but he is also the Spirit of Christ, the Spirit of God's Son, and the Spirit of the Lord.

The trinity according to the Eastern church

The dominant influences in Eastern trinitarianism, the Cappadocians and John of Damascus, stress the Father as the source of the personal subsistence of the Son and the Holy Spirit. The Father is the guarantor of unity in the Godhead, the sole principle, source, and cause of the Son and the Spirit. Thus the Holy Spirit proceeds from the Father. Gregory Nazianzen corrected this emphasis with his teaching that the monarchy is the whole trinity, not the Father alone, but this primary stress remains.

The trinity according to the Western church

Augustine has exerted an overpowering influence up to the present day. He makes the divine essence, not the person of the

---

[14] John 16:7, 13-15; 15:26; 14:26; cf Mark 1:10; Luke 3:22; Luke 1:34-35; Matthew 1:18-20; Luke 4:1,14; Romans 1:3-4; 8:11.

Father, the foundation for his doctrine of the trinity. Western theology has followed by starting from the one essence. The continued threat of Arianism in the West, particularly in Spain, led the church to lay extra stress on the consubstantiality of the Father and the Son. The *filioque* is intended to undergird this – the Holy Spirit's procession from the Father *and the Son* serves in Western eyes to safeguard the identity of being of the Son and the Father. In turn, following Augustine's psychological analogy, the Spirit is seen as the bond of union between the Father and the Son.[15]

The Western church according to Photius

Photius, Patriarch of Constantinople (858–67, 880–86), confused the situation further.[16] He insists that the Holy Spirit proceeds from the Father *alone*, the Son having no part to play, although he did not require this to be accepted by Rome. His intent is not to deny the intimate relations between the Son and the Spirit but to make very clear that the Father alone causes the existence of the Son and the Spirit. In turn, Photius attributes to the Western church the arrangement whereby the Holy Spirit proceeds from the Father and the Son as from two separate principles. He regards this as heresy since two separate principles in the trinity would destroy the unity of God.[17]

The origin of the Western view in Augustine

However, Photius' understanding of Western trinitarianism had been explicitly repudiated by Augustine four hundred and fifty years earlier:

---

[15] See L. Vischer, ed., *Spirit of God, Spirit of Christ: Ecumenical Reflections on the Filioque Controversy* (London: SPCK, 1981), 12–16, for a clear and incisive evaluation of these differences.

[16] Photius, *On the Mystagogy of the Holy Spirit*, PG 102:280–391.

[17] See Aristeides Papadakis, *Crisis in Byzantium: The Filioque Controversy in the Patriarchate of Gregory II of Cyprus (1283–1289)* (Crestwood, New York: St. Vladimir's Seminary Press, 1997), 113–7, for an evaluation of the weaknesses of Photius' argument. The whole book is an exposition of the contribution of Gregory II; see especially 201–8.

> ...yet there is good reason why in this trinity we call none
> Word of God but the Son, none Gift of God but the Holy
> Spirit, none of whom the Word is begotten and from whom
> the Holy Spirit originally (*principaliter*) proceeds, but God the
> Father. I add the word 'originally', because we learn that the
> Holy Spirit proceeds also from the Son. But this is part of
> what is given by the Father to the Son, not as already existing
> without it, but given to him as all that the Father gives to his
> only-begotten Word, in the act of begetting. He is begotten in
> such a manner that the common gift proceeds from him also,
> and the Holy Spirit is Spirit of both.[18]

For Augustine, the Holy Spirit proceeds from the Father and the
Son *as one principle of origination*. The Father is the sole principle
of deity, the Son is begotten by the Father, and *from their common
love proceeds, as a single principle*, the Holy Spirit *a patre filioque*.[19]
The Holy Spirit thus proceeds firstly from the Father and by the
Father's gift at no temporal interval from both in common.[20]
Photius rejects this also, for reasons we will mention later. As
Ritschl suggests, Augustine's beginning with the trinity rather
than with the Father, as the Cappadocians had done, together
with his stress on the divine simplicity, makes the *filioque* almost
inevitable.[21]

The Western view according the Eastern apologists

Despite Photius, overall Eastern objections to the *filioque* are not
that it implies two separate sources for the Holy Spirit; as we saw,
Augustine taught that the Spirit proceeds from the Father and
the Son as from a single source. Nor is it that the clause might
subordinate the Holy Spirit to the Son, another point of issue
for Photius, since the Western affirmations of consubstantiality
offset that possibility. The main concern is that the *filioque*
compromises the monarchy of the Father by positing that not

---

[18] Augustine, *De Trinitate*, 15:26:47.
[19] Ibid., 15:17:27.
[20] Ibid., 15:26:47.
[21] Ritschl, 'Filioque Controversy,' 60–1.

only the Father but also the Son is a source, origin or cause of the Holy Spirit. The Greek Fathers held that the Holy Spirit is the treasure and the Son is the treasurer – the Son receives and manifests the Spirit but he does not cause its existence as such, since only the Father is the source or origin or cause of both the Son and the Holy Spirit through ineffably different but united acts.

Another related problem in Eastern eyes is that the clause confuses the Father and the Son. The Father is not the Son. This is evident in that the Father begets the Son, while the Son is begotten by the Father. Thus, the relation between the Spirit and the Father differs from the relation between the Spirit and the Son. Since the Son and the Father are not the same, their respective relations to the Holy Spirit cannot be the same either. Therefore to talk of the Spirit proceeding from the Father *and* the Son without differentiation is to confuse the two. This is underlined by Augustine's teaching that the Spirit proceeds from both as from a common source. By avoiding the suggestion that there are two separate sources of the Spirit (which would divide the trinity), the West confuses the distinctiveness of both the Father and the Son. According to the East, all three persons are one God by consubstantial union and mutual indwelling but are never to be confused in their personal distinctiveness (as in the modalistic heresy).

What can we say to this? With respect to the monarchy, the West has never intended to compromise the monarchy of the Father and has consistently affirmed it. So much is evident, *inter alia*, in Aquinas[22] and Calvin,[23] to name but two. The monarchy is not a point in dispute, although it has come to expression in

---

[22] Aquinas, *ST* Pt. 1a, Q.33, art. 1–2, where he argues that the Father is the *principium*, signifying not the cause but the origin of the Son and the Holy Spirit. This, he says, does not imply superiority and inferiority, dependence or subordination.

[23] Calvin, *Institute*, 1:13:18, 24, 25; *Le catechisme de l'eglise de Geneve,* in *OS* 2:76–77, *CO* 6:13–14; his draft for the French Confession, in *OS* 2:312; and *Expositio Impietatis Valentini Gentilis*, in *CO* 9:369.

differing ways in East and West. The *filioque* was never directed against this. Stylianopoulos agrees but adds 'the *que* (and) of the *filioque* does not seem to relinquish the "monarchy" of the Father in the Augustinian context but unintentionally does relinquish it in the Cappadocian context.'[24] However, the claim that the *filioque* confuses the Father and the Son is, I submit, of greater weight. One other objection can be dismissed quickly as far-fetched. According to some Eastern apologetes, the *filioque* led in the West to ecclesiasticism, authoritarianism and the dogma of the Pope.[25]

Joseph Farrell goes a step further and accuses Augustine of working out 'a synthesis of the Orthodox faith and Neoplatonism'. Plotinus had posited a supreme being, the One, characterized by absolute simplicity (with no internal distinctions or particulars). In virtue of this simplicity, the One's existence, nature, activity, and will are identical. Augustine saw common ground between the Christian doctrine of God and the NeoPlatonic idea of divine simplicity. In doing so he made the one essence of God primary. With no internal distinctions, great problems arose as to how to conceive of, and defend, the doctrine of the trinity. Moreover, since the essence had priority over the persons, the overwhelming tendency for Augustine, and the West thereafter, was to an impersonal view of God. Assuming absolute divine simplicity, the persons can only be relations in the one divine essence – less than attributes.[26] Following this, Western theologians have almost uniformly considered the trinity only after long examination of the existence, nature, and attributes of God, with the result that the trinity has been reduced to a virtual irrelevance in the daily life of the Western church. Farrell makes many other criticisms of Western trinitarianism, some telling, others possibly overdone,

[24] T. Stylianopoulos, eds, *Spirit of Truth*, 50.

[25] Ware, *Orthodox Church*, 222–3.

[26] Joseph P. Farrell, 'Introduction,' *Saint Photios: The Mystagogy of the Holy Spirit* (Brookline, Massachusetts: Holy Cross Orthodox Press, 1987), 20–29.

but it is undeniable that there are crippling weaknesses in the
Western doctrine of God.

The Eastern view according to Western apologists

As we mentioned, according to the West, the Eastern repudiation
of the *filioque* leaves no clear relation between the Son and the
Holy Spirit. This is in odd contrast to the patristic teaching
of *perichoresis*, whereby the persons of the trinity indwell and
interpenetrate one another. The West holds that this exhibits
subordinationist tendencies from as far back as Origen, for in the
East the Son and the Holy Spirit are commonly said to receive
their deity from the Father and so both seem to be derivative. In
contrast, the *filioque* affirms the intimate relation between the Son
and the Spirit. This, the West claims, has led to a gulf in the East
between theology and piety. Speculative theology, grounded
on the Logos, has been separated from worship, mediated by
the Holy Spirit. Thus Eastern piety, so Western observers like
Bavinck claim, is unduly dominated by mysticism.[27]

Neither of these two arguments bears much scrutiny. In the
first place, let us examine the claim that the East, by rejecting
the *filioque*, holds apart the Son and the Holy Spirit. This is
simply wrong. Throughout, the Eastern church has accepted
terminology such as 'from the Father through the Son' as a valid
expression of the intent of C. It maintains a mediating role for
the Son in the procession of the Spirit, while insisting that the
Father is the sole source, cause or origin. Again, the East argues
the Holy Spirit rests on the Son (as at Jesus' baptism) and is
received by him, and in turn is sent by the Son.[28] In saying that
the Spirit proceeds from the Father, the East presupposes the
relation existing in the trinity between the Father and the Son,
for the Father is the Father of the Son, the Son is eternally in and
with the Father, and the Father is never apart from the Son.[29] For

---

[27] H. Bavinck, *The Doctrine of God* (Edinburgh: Banner of Truth, rpr, 1977), 313–7.

[28] W. Pannenberg, *Systematic Theology* (G. W. Bromiley; Grand Rapids: Eerdmans, 1991), 1:317–9.

Western theologians to make this claim ignores the Cappadocian teaching on mutual indwelling, first taught by Gregory of Nyssa. This is a crowning affirmation of the close relations of the Son and the Holy Spirit. Besides, C minus the *filioque* clause (the original version of C) is not silent on the relation of the Holy Spirit and the Son, for the Spirit is worshiped and glorified together with the Father and the Son, and is the author and giver of life together with the Father and the Son, 'by whom [the Father] made the worlds.' In short, the East consistently affirms that the Son participates in the Holy Spirit's procession from the Father both immanently and economically.

On the second point, one of the most famous elements of Eastern piety, the Jesus prayer, is thoroughly Christocentric – 'Lord Jesus Christ, Son of God, have mercy on me a sinner' can hardly be more evangelical or Christological in tone. That the East has no monopoly on unbridled mysticism is evident by the Toronto blessing and other similar phenomena, which are distinctly Western in effect. This claim is, in short, akin to the Eastern argument about a supposed connection between the *filioque* and the papacy. There are reductionist dangers in attributing all perceived ills to a single cause.

A third objection, however, carries much greater weight. Following John of Damascus, and especially Gregory Palamas (1296–1359), the East considers the essence of God to be unknowable, only God's energies or operations being revealed, the things around him ('all that we can affirm concerning God does not shew forth God's nature, but only the qualities of his nature').[30] This dichotomy, as a sympathetic critic like T.F. Torrance argues, 'implies that to know God in the Spirit

[29] See the references to Athanasius below. Jürgen Moltmann's proposal that the Spirit proceeds 'from the Father of the Son' assumes a consensus would form in the East in support; see his volume, *The Trinity and the Kingdom: The Doctrine of God* (London: SCM, 1991), 185–7.

[30] John of Damascus, *The Orthodox Faith*, 1:4. For a lucid explanation of this distinction, see Vladimir Lossky, *The Mystical Theology of the Eastern Church* (Crestwood, New York: St. Vladimir's Seminary Press, 1998), 67–90.

... is not to know God in his divine Being – to know God is only to know the things that relate to his Nature as manifested through a penumbra of his uncreated energies or rays.' This drives a wedge between the inner life of God and his saving activity in history, ruling out any real access to knowing God in himself. This is not to take 'the key Nicene concept of identity of being or *homoousion* seriously'.[31] It also departs from earlier Greek patristic thought, although there is definite evidence that the idea was afoot in the fourth-century crisis that we know God not as he is in himself but in terms of his working (*energeia*) in the world.[32] The questions to be addressed to these developments are whether, firstly, a yawning chasm has not been opened between the economic trinity and the immanent trinity, and secondly whether there is not here a tendency towards a quaternity – the unknowable divine essence plus the three revealed persons. Along these lines, Fairbairn suggests that the distinction tends to create 'a crisis of confidence in God's character. If we insist that we can know nothing of God's inner life ... then can we really be confident that God's outer life is consistent with his inner life?' He asks whether the constant refrain in the Orthodox liturgy – 'Lord, have mercy' – epitomizes a lack of confidence in God's mercy, a belief that he is distant, aloof, and unpredictable.[33]

---

[31] T. F. Torrance, *The Christian Doctrine of God: One Being, Three Persons* (Edinburgh: T.&T. Clark, 1996), 187.

[32] Athanasius, *On the Decrees of the Synod of Nicaea*, 22. See also Dorothea Wendebourg, 'From the Cappadocian Fathers to Gregory Palamas: The Defeat of Trinitarian Theology *StPatr* 17 (1982):194–8, who argues that the Palamite development is not merely a departure from classic Trinitarianism but actually destroys it. However, Michel René Barnes, *The Power of God: Δύναμις in Gregory of Nyssa's Trinitarian Theology* (Washington, D.C.: The Catholic University of America Press, 2001), produces strong evidence that the concept of power was crucial in the fourth-century trinitarian debates and that this is noticeable in Gregory, who argued – against Eunomius – that God has a natural productive capacity by which he generates a Son with the same nature, and creates a universe with a different nature. Gregory used the term *energeia* rather than *dunamis* to denote the operations of God. Hence, the idea of God's energies was present in the crisis.

[33] Donald Fairbairn, *Eastern Orthodoxy through Western Eyes* (Louisville: Westminster John Knox Press, 2002), 115–6.

The early Eastern view

According to Basil the Great true religion teaches us to think of the Son together with the Father.[34] The good things that come from God reach us 'through the Son'.[35] The Son's will is in indissoluble union with the Father's.[36] Thus, the Holy Spirit is in all things inseparable from the Father and the Son.[37] Moreover

> the way of the knowledge of God lies from one Spirit through the one Son to the one Father, and conversely the natural goodness and the inherent holiness and the royal dignity extend from the Father through the only-begotten to the Spirit.[38]

Hence, the Spirit shares in the works of the Father and the Son.[39] In short, the Father is the sole principle of deity. From the Father the Holy Spirit proceeds through the Son. The deity communicates itself from the Father through the Son to the Holy Spirit.

John of Damascus, in his *De Orthodoxa Fide*, teaches that the Spirit of God is 'the companion of the Word and the revealer of His energy ... proceeding from the Father and resting in the Word, and shewing forth the Word, neither capable of disjunction from God in Whom it exists, and the Word Whose companion it is ... being in subsistence the likeness of the Word.'[40] Never at any time was the Father lacking in the Word, nor the Word in the Spirit. The Holy Spirit proceeds from the Father and rests in the Son, is communicated through the Son, is inseparable and indivisible from the Father and the Son, possessing all the qualities the Father and the Son possess, except that of not being begotten or born. Both the Son and the Spirit have their being from the Father. The three are in each other,

---

[34] Basil of Caesarea, *On the Holy Spirit*, 14.

[35] Ibid., 19.

[36] Ibid., 20.

[37] Ibid., 37.

[38] Ibid., 47.

[39] Ibid., 53.

[40] John of Damascus, *The Orthodox Faith*, 1:7.

having the same essence and dwelling in each other, being the same in will, energy, power, authority, and movement. They cleave to each other and have their being in each other, without coalescence or commingling. The Son and the Spirit, therefore, do not stand apart. It is like three suns cleaving to each other without separation and giving out light mingled and conjoined into one. The Spirit is manifested and imparted to us through the Son.[41]

De Margerie points out that Photius ignores all this, and he cites Bulgakov, who commented, 'It is stupefying that the very learned patriarch, who knew the Greek Fathers much better than many of his predecessors and contemporaries, did not know that the patristic doctrine of the procession of the Holy Spirit ... differed radically from his own.'[42]

Problems of East and West

(1) Western theology has often said that the East exhibits a tendency toward tritheism by starting with the Father rather than the one divine essence. There is little evidence for this. The monarchy of the Father (or of the whole trinity in the case of Gregory Nazianzen), consubstantiality, and perichoresis are the preservatives. Moreover, the East has been able to hold to the integrity of the three persons and thus to a fully personal doctrine of God in a way that has often eluded the West.

(2) On the other hand, the Eastern split between God's essence and his energies is a reality, developed by Gregory Palamas from earlier work by Pseudo-Dionysius and John of Damascus, and hints in the Cappadocians, and feeding into contemporary Orthodox theology. What this means is that we are unable to know God in his essence, for he is beyond the dialectic of being and non-being. Instead, we know his energies, his powers at work in the world. Thus, the Eastern doctrine, as it developed, made a distinction between the immanent and economic trinities,

---

[41] Ibid., 1:8.
[42] de Margerie S.J., *Christian Trinity*, 166; Bulgakov, *Le Paraclet*, 102.

between God in himself and God as he has revealed himself. This threatens our knowledge of God with a profound agnosticism. It also defies rational discourse. We can say nothing about who God is. The acme of the Christian life is mystical contemplation rather than *fides quaerens intellectum*.[43] Originally mooted in contrast to the heretic Eunomius, who held that the human mind can have exact knowledge of God's essence, it developed from a legitimate assertion of the incomprehensibility of God (that God infinitely transcends our capacities) – which does not rule out his revealing who he is to us in a way that we *can* grasp – to an axiom that he is unknowable in himself. As Barth says, 'it goes beyond revelation to achieve a very different picture of God "antecedently in Himself."'[44] It also makes no sense – since if we cannot know God as he is, there is no way of knowing whether his energies truly reflect who he is. Behind this lies the idea in Gregory of Nyssa that language is inherently ambiguous and so is less than fully satisfactory as a vehicle of disclosure for God. In contrast, he states, the visible evidence of God's operations in creation is more reliable.[45] The consequence of this is a different view of God, and different views of revelation, of the sufficiency of Scripture, and of worship.

In this way, Eastern apologists can say that references to the Son sending the Spirit apply only to the energies, to the purely economic. Jürgen Moltmann answers this with great clarity when he says we can speak of only one trinity and of its economy of salvation and so 'the divine Trinity cannot appear in the economy of salvation as something other than it is in itself. Therefore one cannot posit temporal trinitarian relations within the economy of salvation which are not grounded in the primal trinitarian relations.' Thus, Moltmann continues, this relation

---

[43] For a fuller exposition and criticism of this approach, see Letham, *The Holy Trinity*, 237–51, 338–48. In contrast, Athanasius had insisted that in Christ we do not deal with something surrounding God's essence, for when we say 'Father' we denote the essence of God himself; Athanasius, *On the Decrees*, 22: PG 25:453–56.

[44] K. Barth, *CD* I/1, 480.

[45] Gregory of Nyssa, *Against Eunomius*, 2 in NPNF2 5:272–3.

between the Son and the Holy Spirit cannot be restricted to the temporal sending. If this were so, there would be a contradiction in God. This cannot be, for God remains true to himself. He is faithful and trustworthy. What holds true in his revelation is true in his being.[46]

(3) In the West, the danger of modalism is very real, evident in all Western theology down to Barth and Rahner. If we start with the divine unity, expressed in the idea of absolute divine simplicity, the persons become problematic as real, personal, permanent, irreducible, and eternal ontological distinctions. Colin Gunton has argued forcibly that the Augustinian model has bred atheism and agnosticism.[47] Indeed, most Western Christians are practical modalists. Certainly, the trinity is little more than an arithmetical conundrum to Western Christianity.

(4) The *filioque* clause is misleading for two possible reasons. First, if in the Augustinian sense (the way the West has consistently understood it) the Spirit proceeds from the Father and the Son *as a single source,* the distinction of the Father and the Son is blurred. The Son is not the same as the Father – he is begotten, and the Father is not. The Son is forever the Son, and the Father is forever the Father. Thus, the Son does not have the identical relation to the Holy Spirit that the Father has. The doctrine of the procession of the Holy Spirit must take this distinction into account. Second, there appears *some* evidence of a *tendency* to the subordination of the Holy Spirit if the *filioque* is needed to support the consubstantiality of the Son. If the deity of the Son requires him to be the spirating source of the Holy Spirit, where does that leave the Spirit, who is the source of no other hypostasis? The argument for the *filioque* comes with a price, a subtle undermining of the trinity. In this connection, is not a basic principle of trinitarian theology flouted by the

---

[46] J. Moltmann, 'Theological Proposals Towards the Resolution of the Filioque Controversy,' *Spirit of God, Spirit of Christ: Ecumenical Reflections on the Filioque Controversy* (ed. L. Vischer; London: SPCK, 1981), 165–6.

[47] C. Gunton, 'Augustine, the Trinity, and the Theological Crisis of the West,' *SJT* 43 (1990), 33–58.

West? The attributes of the divine nature are shared by all three persons while the divine properties are held by one person. Here a property (spiration) is shared by two persons while the third is excluded.[48]

From all this it is clear that both the Western and Eastern lines of approach have serious weaknesses. These are highlighted when both are exposed to dialogue with the other as has been the case in recent decades, something that has never seriously happened before. As a result, the question is now arising as to whether there is some way to transcend this great divide, to preserve the best intentions of both sides while avoiding their damaging weaknesses?[49]

Towards a resolution of the problems of East and West

Where do we go from here? It is clear that we need simultaneously to preserve both the unity and identity of the one indivisible being of God and, at the same time, the irreducible differences between the three persons. Here Gregory Nazianzen is brilliantly helpful. In the passage in which Calvin found vast delight he says:

> This I give you to share, and to defend all your life, the one Godhead and power, found in the three in unity, and comprising the three separately; not unequal, in substances or natures, neither increased nor diminished by superiorities or inferiorities; in every respect equal, in every respect the same; just as the beauty and the greatness of the heavens is one; the infinite conjunction of three infinite ones, each God when considered in himself; as the Father, so the Son; as the Son so the Holy Spirit; the three one God when contemplated together; each God because consubstantial; one God because of the *monarchia*. No sooner do I conceive of the one than

---

[48] Photius argues that 'everything not said about the whole, omnipotent, consubstantial, and supersubstantial Trinity is said about one of the three persons. The procession of the Spirit is not said to be common to the three, consequently it must belong to one of the three' (Photius, *Holy Spirit*, 36).

[49] For proposals on how to move towards a resolution of this problem, see Letham, *The Holy Trinity*, 213–20.

> I am illumined by the splendour of the three; no sooner do
> I distinguish them than I am carried back to the one. When
> I think of any one of the three I think of him as the whole, and
> my eyes are filled, and the greater part of what I am thinking
> escapes me. I cannot grasp the greatness of that one so as to
> attribute a greater greatness to the rest. When I contemplate
> the three together, I see but one torch, and cannot divide or
> measure out the undivided light.[50]

Gregory oscillates back and forth from the one to the three. When
he considers the one he is illumined by the splendor of the three.
When he distinguishes them he is carried back to the one. Gregory
points to the danger of building our doctrine of the trinity on
either the one being of God in isolation, *or* on the three persons
(or any one of them) in isolation. These dangers are demonstrated
thoroughly in the subsequent history of the church.

Gregory's hermeneutic, as he expresses it in this passage, is
strikingly modern. Physicists working at the atomic level oscillate in thought between waves and particles. The reason for this
is that on the atomic level matter has both a wave-character
and a particle-character, the so-called 'wave/particle duality of
matter'. Thus, an electron acts both like a particle and a wave,
as also does light. As a result it is not possible to measure both
the speed and position of such particles. The most famous, and
perplexing, aspect of the wave character of particles is seen in
the double slit experiment. When an electron is fired at a metal
target with two small slits in it, suitably spaced, it appears that
the electron goes through both slits, and produces an interference
pattern just like a light wave does on the opposite side of the
target. Thus at a fundamental level – because of the wave character of particles – it is impossible, no matter how many observers
there may be, to determine both the position and velocity of an
atomic scale particle. Thus, to do physics at the atomic level it is
necessary to oscillate in thought between waves and particles.[51]

---

[50] Gregory Nazianzen, *Oration on Holy Baptism* 40, 41.
[51] I am indebted to Dr. John Dishman, formerly of Bell Laboratories, for this
information.

A parallel to this is the field of gestalt psychology, from which we learn that as we gain a grasp of the whole we tend to lose connection with the parts, while if we focus on the parts we lose our grasp of the whole.

Another way of putting it is to think of what happens when you focus your gaze on a particular object. Try doing it. Notice that when you look intently at this or that, the rest of your field of vision becomes blurred and indistinct. Then if you look away from the object of your former gaze and attend to the background, which now comes into clear focus, your former object of attention becomes a blur.

In this connection, the limitations of logic are apparent. James Loder and the late W. Jim Niedhardt have pointed out in what T.F. Torrance in the foreword calls 'an altogether remarkable book with unusually fresh creative thinking' that, while logic is of value in everyday life or in 'trivialities' as they call them, when we approach the boundaries of the universe it breaks down. They point to a wide range of areas where creation is not reducible to neat laws of thought. Among other things, physics, mathematics, psychology, and human development all yield this feature.[52] They illustrate the point with Escher's famous line drawings, including his *Möbius Strip II (Red Ants)* (woodcut, 1963). This is based on the 'strange loop' discovered by the grandfather of the psychoneurologist Paul J. Möbius. The Möbius band, through a 180° twist, has only one side and one edge although two are evident in any cross-sectional view. Escher's work shows ants crawling along the surface of a two-sided Möbius band. As the eye follows the ants around the band the two sides are disclosed to be only one side.[53] If a reductionist elevation of logic is impermissible in dealing with matters of creation, how much less is it to be followed in relation to the holy trinity? T.F. Torrance insists that the proper course in seeking to know is to submit our minds to the object of

---

[52] J. E. Loder, *The Knight's Move: The Relational Logic of the Spirit in Theology and Science* (Colorado Springs: Helmers & Howard, 1992).

[53] Ibid., 36–43.

knowledge so as to allow it to disclose itself on its own terms. It follows that in science knowledge is to be based on the reality of what is. Logical deductions from premises are good within certain parameters but, if absolutized, can prevent us knowing. In theology, this means we must faithfully submit ourselves to God's revelation and allow our thoughts to proceed from the basis of who he discloses himself to be, recognizing at the same time that he infinitely transcends the capacities of our minds.

10

Salvation: Justification, Deification and Synergism

There are also significant differences of content and emphasis between the Eastern and Western churches in their respective understandings of salvation. Broadly speaking, Orthodoxy views Christianity as mainly personal and mystical – centered in union with God – in contrast to the West's focus on the legal. Hence, since Athanasius the focus in the East's view of salvation is deification (union with God) rather than the West's stress on atonement for sin and, since the Reformation, justification. This does not mean that the East says nothing on the atonement or justification, any more than the West has entirely ignored what the East calls deification. It simply states that East and West (both Rome and Protestantism) have been looking in different directions.

Man and sin
The first chapter of Genesis states that man was created in the image of God. The West has debated extensively this pregnant phrase. Much hinges on how it is taken. In Reformed theology it has been common to distinguish between the image of God in

the broader sense, applicable to all people (1 Cor. 11:7, Jas. 3:9), and the image of God in the narrow sense, renewed in Christ and so affecting Christian believers only (Eph. 4:24, Col. 3:10). For its part, Orthodoxy makes a distinction between the image of God and the likeness of God. The image is what distinguishes man from the other creatures. It consists of free will, reason, and a sense of moral responsibility. It also connects man to God since, being in his image, we can have communion with him. Man is God's chief icon – man in his totality as a psychosomatic unity, not simply his reason, as the West has often taught. If we experience communion with God we can then acquire the likeness of God, which is deification. This is received in degrees and depends on our own moral choices. It underlies the Ortho-dox insistence that each person is in the image of God, and is a reason why in Orthodox worship the priest incenses not only the icons but all the worshippers.

There is a significant difference here from the Augustinian and Reformed doctrine of man. Whereas Reformed theology teaches that man was created in a state of uprightness from which he fell, the Orthodox teach that he was created in a state of innocence with the potential for moral perfection, which he was to achieve by his own efforts, assisted by God's grace. This is a more dynamic view of man. It is also a synergistic position, in which human effort co-operates with God's grace.

Correspondingly, there are highly important differences in the way the Reformed and the Orthodox view the fall and sin. Reformed theology teaches that, through the sin of Adam, all people incurred objective moral guilt before God. Moreover, all inherit a corrupted nature – corrupt in every faculty of our being. The consequence is that man, by himself, is unable to respond to the grace of God offered in the gospel. He is 'dead in trespasses and sins' (Eph. 2:1). In order to be saved, the Holy Spirit – in connection with the preaching of the gospel – must give him a new heart and mind to respond to Christ. Saving faith is a gift of God. The Spirit moves within us, regenerating us; we respond in faith.

Arminianism

For the Orthodox, this process entails co-operation between the Holy Spirit and the free will of man. Where the Reformed faith is monergistic, the Orthodox are synergistic. Both God and man are active in achieving full fellowship, although divine grace plays by far the greater part. The point is that man also plays a part; the effects of sin are not so far-reaching as to prevent him responding to God in faith, although he needs some help to do this. The famous sentence in Revelation 3:20 is held to teach that God knocks at the door but it is up to man to open it. This, the Reformed will reply, ignores the fact that the letter is addressed to a church, to believers, reproving them for their sin and calling them to repentance; it is not referring to the call of the gospel to unbelievers.

This synergism goes back to the Fathers. Chrysostom notably argued that God forces no one to be saved. Of course, there are very good Biblical grounds for agreeing with a statement like that; no one enters the kingdom of heaven against their will, apart from a free decision on their part. The problem is that the question is misplaced. According to Reformed theology, no one comes to Christ against their will, but *the Spirit makes us willing* by changing the disposition and intention of the heart so that we trust Christ gladly and willingly. This area represents a significant misunderstanding by the Orthodox of the Augustinian–Reformed teaching.

A corollary is that the Orthodox teaching on sin differs from the Reformed. It is correct in asserting that Adam disobeyed the will of God, with the result that disease and death entered the world, a new form of existence coming into effect. This new scenario, it maintains, affects all Adam's descendants, due to the unity of the human race. Its impact is not only in the physical realm but also in the spiritual as well, so that it is thereafter difficult to do what pleases God and very easy to sin. However, 'Orthodoxy, holding as it does a less exalted idea of man's state before he fell, is also less severe than the west in its view of the consequences of the fall.'[1] Adam fell, not from perfection, but from a state of undeveloped simplicity. The results are less grave than the West maintains. While his mind was darkened and he was cut off from God, Adam was not rendered incapable of God's grace. He was not, the Orthodox insist, depraved in every faculty of his being. He has never been deprived of his freedom. The image of God has been distorted but not destroyed.

Moreover, the East rejects the Western doctrine of original sin. All people inherit the corrupt nature received from Adam but there is no inheritance of Adam's guilt. Guilt arises only from actual sins which individuals commit. Participation in the guilt of Adam's sin (Rom. 5:12ff) is by imitation, not imputation. While the Orthodox agree that sin has introduced a barrier between man and God, they have a more optimistic attitude to fallen man's capabilities. As a consequence, the main thrust of Orthodox soteriology is the conquest of death by Christ's resurrection rather than atonement for sin at the cross. Indeed, as far back as Athanasius this has been the stronger theme and it is sometimes hard to discover what doctrine of atonement actually is held, other than the *Christus victor* motif. In line with this, the strong focus has been on Christ by his incarnation sharing our humanity and healing it from within, bringing this to its apex by his conquest of death. In tandem, the Holy Spirit deifies man through his coming at Pentecost. The lines of thought since Athanasius have run in different directions from in the West, and it is worth recalling that R.P.C. Hanson writes of Athanasius as holding a doctrine of salvation akin to a sacred blood transfusion.[2]

The East is also reluctant to see sin specifically as a transgression of the law of God. As Panayiotis Nellas puts it, it will be impossible for the authentic evangelical and patristic gospel 'to be heard by any reasonable modern person at all when it [contemporary Christian theology] presents sin as disobedience to a set of external rules.' This has been the case in the West, he maintains, through Augustine, and so has

---

[1] T. Ware, *The Orthodox Church* (London: Penguin Books, 1969), 228.

[2] R. Hanson, *The Search for the Christian Doctrine of God: The Arian Controversy 318–381* (Edinburgh: T.&T. Clark, 1988), 450–1.

trapped Christ, and by extension the Christian life and the realities of the Church, the sacraments, faith and the rest, within the bounds defined by sin. Christ in this perspective is not so much the creator and recapitulator of all things, the Alpha and Omega as Scripture says, but simply the redeemer from sin. The Christian life is regarded not so much as the realization of Adam's original destiny, as a dynamic transformation of man and the world and as union with God, but as a simple escape from sin. The sacraments are not realizations here and now of the kingdom of God and manifestations of it, but mere religious duties and means of acquiring grace.... The boundaries are thus narrowed in an asphyxiating manner. The Church forgets her ontological bond with the world. And the world, seeing that its positive aspects are not appreciated within the Church, feels a sense of alienation and breaks off relations with it.'[3]

This points us to Chul Won Suh's discussion of what he calls 'elevation-line theology', akin to what Nellas describes and the East in general teaches, in which Christ became incarnate in order to bring man to a position greater than he had had before, and 'restitution-line theology,' which focuses on Christ as the redeemer from sin, simply restoring man to a position he had forfeited. I have discussed the ramifications of these positions elsewhere, arguing that both are eminently Biblical and that a unity of creation and redemption should clearly be maintained.[4]

This should not be taken to imply that the Orthodox think of sin but lightly. In some ways, they take it more seriously than conservative Protestants. This is especially true in the liturgy. The Great Canon of St. Andrew of Crete (c. 660–740), sung or read at Matins on the Thursday morning of the fifth week of Lent, contains 260 stanzas punctuated by the refrain 'Have

---

[3] P. Nellas, *Deification in Christ: Orthodox Perspectives on the Nature of the Human Person* (N. Russell; Crestwood, New York: St Vladimir's Seminary Press, 1987), 94–5.

[4] Chul Won Suh, *The Creation Mediatorship of Jesus Christ* (Amsterdam: Rodopi, 1982); R. Letham, *The Work of Christ* (Leicester: Inter-Varsity Press, 1993), 203–6.

mercy upon me, O God, have mercy upon me.' It involves the whole person in an extended exercise of penitence and prayer. 'Come, wretched soul, with thy flesh to the Creator of all. Make confession to Him, and abstain henceforth from thy past brutishness; and offer to God tears of repentance.' With its address to the holy trinity – 'To Thee I raise the great thrice-holy hymn that is sung on high' – it leads the congregation to Christ – 'Christ became man, calling to repentance thieves and harlots. Repent, my soul: the door of the Kingdom is already open, and pharisees and publicans and adulterers pass through it before thee, changing their life.' Its confessions are clear; 'I have sinned, I have offended, I have set aside thy commandments; for in sins have I progressed and to my sores I have added wounds.... For this I am condemned in my misery, for this I am convicted by the verdict of my own conscience.' Many other such utterances could be cited. Where in conservative Protestantism today is there such brutally honest recollection and confession of sins? Thankfully, the liturgy does not stop there – it leads to Christ, with statements like 'Thou art the Good Shepherd; seek me, the lamb that has strayed, and do not forget me ... Make me a nurseling in the pasture of Thine own flock.... Thou art my sweet Jesus, Thou art my Creator; in Thee shall I be justified.'[5]

A position on sin and the fall has ramifications for the whole of theology, especially the atonement and justification. The disease points to the needed remedy. It is the purpose of this chapter to explore the further differences that exist here between the Orthodox and the Reformed. Afterwards, in the next chapter, we shall ask how far these different views of man, sin and salvation are complementary and how far they are incompatible.

Justification

In the service for the public reception of converts from non-Orthodox churches, a series of questions is addressed to the

---

[5] See the discussion of this liturgy in Nellas, *Deification in Christ*, 163-96.

candidates, among which are those calling upon them publicly to renounce teachings distinctive of their former communion. Hence, converts from Rome are required to renounce, *inter alia*, the universal claims of the Pope and the *filioque* clause. From those who are abandoning Lutheran and Reformed churches there are a further series of doctrines the converts are required to renounce; their former churches' denials of transubstantiation, five of the sacraments, veneration of the saints and prayers for the dead. The *filioque* clause again features, although not – for obvious reasons – the claims of Rome! However, in neither case is there a question on justification by faith. The Reformed are required to repudiate a merely symbolic view of the eucharist (one identified more with Zwingli than Calvin), and also a doctrine of predestination that can only be described as a caricature – more of that later – but there is nothing on justification, nor is there such a requirement of converts from Lutheran churches. Evidently, the doctrine of justification by faith is not perceived as a barrier: the Eastern church has certainly made no pronouncements on it.[6]

Let us remind ourselves of the classic Protestant doctrine of justification by faith alone, better expressed in the words of Tony Lane as 'justification only by faith'. This important doctrine asserts that man, by nature a sinner, guilty before God and destined for eternal condemnation, is given a right status, forgiven and absolved from all sin, on the exclusive ground of the righteousness of Jesus Christ – on our behalf suffering the penalty of the law of God which we had broken, and obeying that law throughout his life. Moreover, just as he took our place and bore our sins, we receive his righteousness, reckoned or imputed to us. This occurs only through faith, since our righteousness is only in Christ. While good works flow from faith, as a stream of water flows from a spring, these contribute nothing to justification as such. They are its consequence, not its cause. Rome misunderstood and opposed this, believing the Protestant doc-

---

[6] *Service Book*, 456–57.

trine encouraged a lack of concern for obedience to Christ by good works; the phrase 'faith alone' seemed in Rome's eyes to undermine the need for sanctification. For Rome, justification encompassed sanctification, the two being inseparable and virtually indistinguishable. This, to Protestants, erodes and undermines the gospel. Lane's phrase best summarizes and captures the intent of the Protestant and Reformed doctrine. The point here is that this controversy has not impinged on the Orthodox.

Because of that, it would be a mistake for the Reformed to identify the East with Rome at this point. For example, the famous Jesus prayer of the hesychasts, 'Lord Jesus Christ, Son of God, have mercy on me a sinner' – perhaps the single most common Orthodox prayer – encapsulates in popular piety all that justification only by faith entails. Can you find a prayer that makes the point so pithily? Even the General Confession of *The Book of Common Prayer of the Church of England*, majestic and sublime as it is, takes much more space to express and bemoan 'our manifold sins and wickedness'. This simple prayer acknowledges Jesus Christ to be the Son of God, expresses the Biblical truth that we are sinners in need of mercy, and calls on Christ to grant that mercy. It is intensely personal. It puts justification into popular piety, without expressing the doctrine in the formal and juridical terms to which Western Christianity is accustomed.

Again, St Symeon the New Theologian (949–1022), in his treatise 'On faith' writes, 'Brethren and fathers, it is good that we make God's mercy known to all and speak to those close to us of the compassion and inexpressible bounty he has shown us. For as you know I neither fasted, nor kept vigils, nor slept on bare ground, but – to borrow the Psalmists' words – "I humbled myself" and, in short, "the Lord saved me." Or to put it even more briefly, I did no more than believe and the Lord accepted me (cf. Ps. 116:6, 10; 27:10 LXX).'[7] In the same context, he goes on to affirm that this faith is a gift of God. Moreover, he says, through repentance the filth of our foul actions is washed away and we participate in the Holy Spirit through faith.[8] Here are sentiments that highlight the sheer grace of God and the undeserved mercy he grants those who repent.

St. Mark the Ascetic (of whose life little is known) wrote a treatise, 'On those who think they are made righteous by works: 226 texts.'[9] In it he comments that 'The kingdom of heaven is not a reward for works, but a gift of grace,' citing Luke 17:10, the parable of the unworthy servants. He stresses that a faithful servant is one who obeys Christ's commandments and that true knowledge is established by works. However, 'some without fulfilling the commandments think that they possess true faith. Others fulfil the commandments and then expect the kingdom as a reward due to them. Both are mistaken.' In fact, Christ through his own word redeems him who is dead in sin and there are some who teach that we cannot do good unless we actively receive the grace of the Holy Spirit.[10]

Indeed, Thomas C. Oden presents many examples to support his contention that 'key textual evidences from Origen, John Chrysostom, and Theodoret of Cyrrhus show that leading eastern patristic writers anticipated standard classic Reformation teaching on justification.' Theodoret writes that 'all we bring to grace is our faith. But even in this faith, divine grace itself has become our enabler,' and 'even when we had come to believe, [God] did not require of us purity of life, but approving mere faith, God bestowed on us forgiveness of sins.'[11] Both Chrysostom and Cyril of Alexandria affirm that we are not justified by works but by grace.[12] Chrysostom insists that faith trusts the person of Christ alone.[13] At the very least, Oden claims to establish that 'there are in patristic texts clear anticipations of the Reformers' teaching of justification'.[14]

---

[7] St. Nikodimos of the Holy Mountain, *The Philokalia* (G. Palmer; London: Faber and Faber, 1983), 4:16.

[8] Ibid., 4:40.

[9] Ibid., 1:125–46.

[10] Ibid., 1:125–32.

[11] T. C. Oden, *The Justification Reader* (Grand Rapids: Eerdmans, 2002), 44.

[12] Ibid., 61, 108, 111–3.

[13] Ibid., 131.

[14] Ibid., 49. See, *inter alia*, Chrysostom, Homily IV on Ephesians (on Eph. 2:8-9), in *NPNF1*, 13:67–8.

Justification by faith is not an item that poses an insuperable barrier between Orthodoxy and the Reformed. Differences that exist result as much from the widely different historical experience through which the two have passed. Moreover, there are expressions on the popular level and sentiments by prominent saints that point to a closer convergence here than many have considered.

Atonement

Throughout history, the interest of the Eastern church has been more with the incarnation and resurrection of Christ than his atoning death. Back in the fourth century, Athanasius had a truncated view of the atonement. For him, the decisive fulcrum is the incarnation. Christ assumed our nature so that we, by grace, might be united to God. As a result the cross has diminished significance. R.P.C. Hanson likens his theory of salvation to a sacred blood transfusion that almost does away with a doctrine of the atonement.[15] Athanasius lacks reasons why Christ should have died. For him, corruption consists in fallenness rather than sin.[16] This interest in salvation through the incarnation culminating in deification and resurrection has thereafter been the focus of the East, in self-conscious aloofness from a more legal or juridical approach.

When it comes to what the East actually understands by the atonement, Ware points to a significant difference from the West:

> Where Orthodoxy sees chiefly Christ the Victor, the late medieval and post-medieval west sees chiefly Christ the Victim. While Orthodoxy interprets the Crucifixion primarily as an act of triumphant victory over the powers of evil, the west – particularly since the time of Anselm of Canterbury (?1033-1109) – has tended rather to think of the Cross in penal and juridical terms, as an act of satisfaction or substitution designed to propitiate the wrath of an angry Father.[17]

---

[15] Hanson, *Search*, 450–1.

[16] See my book, *The Holy Trinity: In Scripture, History, Theology, and Worship* (Phillipsburg, New Jersey: Presbyterian & Reformed, 2004), chapter 6.

[17] Ware, *Orthodox Church*, 234.

However, Ware agrees that these are not absolute contrasts, nor incompatible ones. Both East and West share these perspectives; the difference is the degree to which they are emphasized. In support of this, it is striking that Nicholas Cabasilas has a doctrine of the atonement strikingly similar to Anselm.[18] Sin, he states, is a gross insult to God. A person who wants to make amends must not only repay the debt he owes but also add some compensation for the wrong done to the besmirched honour of the injured party. No one could do this simply by offering his own righteousness. Christ alone was able to offer to the Father the honour due him by his life, and with his death to plead on our behalf with regard to the insult. This was due to his leading a life free from sin, since he kept the laws of God in every detail. He cites John 3:16 in support. Thus, the body of Christ sacrificed on the cross is the only remedy for sin, and his blood is the only means of pardon for sin.[19] In a pithy aphorism, Cabasilas puts it this way: 'For since we cannot go up and share his position, he came down to us and shared our condition.'[20] Moreover, it is recognized in the West – including in Reformed circles – that the Christus Victor motif is a Biblical and thus integral aspect of the atonement. I have discussed this in detail elsewhere.[21]

Deification

For the East, there are two great moments in the triune God's work of salvation – the incarnation and Pentecost. In the incarnation the Son unites to himself a human nature conceived by the Holy Spirit in the womb of the virgin Mary. At Pentecost, the Holy Spirit pervades countless human persons.

The work of the Son and the Holy Spirit are entirely complementary. The purpose of the incarnation and the events that followed was that mankind would be indwelt and deified by the Holy Spirit. There is in the East, therefore, less a Christocentric

---

[18] On Anselm, see Letham, *The Work of Christ*, 163–6.

[19] N. Cabasilas, *Life in Christ* (M. Lisney; London: Janus, 1995), 38–41.

[20] Ibid., 43.

[21] See Letham, *The Work of Christ*, 149–55, 161–3.

and more a pneumatocentric soteriology. That explains the importance the East attaches to the *filioque* controversy. As Vladimir Lossky comments, the spiritual tradition of the Eastern church is focused on the acquisition of the Holy Spirit.[22] In both church liturgy and private prayer the Holy Spirit is regularly invoked. The summation of salvation is to become like God through the communion of the Holy Spirit. This is known as deification or *theosis* and its importance reaches back to Athanasius and the Cappadocians, particularly Basil. This is how St. Symeon the New Theologian sees it: 'He [Christ] has shared in what is ours so as to make us participants of what is his. For the Son of God became the Son of Man in order to make us human beings sons of God, raising us up by grace to what he is by nature, giving us a new birth in the Holy Spirit and leading us directly into the kingdom of heaven.'[23]

At this point let us stand aside and ask a question many Protestants would want to address: how Biblical is this teaching? It sounds alarming to many when we read Athanasius saying that Christ became man that we might become God. Can this be supported from the Bible or on the basis of sound doctrine?

First, the theological foundations of this teaching are rooted in Scripture and the historic doctrine of the church. First and foremost, God is one being, three persons: three persons, one being. The indivisible trinity consists of three irreducibly distinct persons. Their distinctness or difference is in no way whatsoever erased, obliterated, or eroded by the union. But the union is real, eternal, and indivisible. The three are one identical being.

Following this, God the Son became incarnate. He assumed into personal union a human nature, conceived in the womb of the virgin Mary. This human nature is not merely contiguous

---

[22] V. Lossky, *The Mystical Theology of the Eastern Church* (London: James Clarke & Co. Ltd, 1957), 196.

[23] St. Nikodimos of the Holy Mountain, *The Philokalia*, 4:48. Parts of the section that follows are taken or adapted from my book, *The Holy Trinity* (Phillipsburg: Presbyterian & Reformed, 2004) with permission.

with his deity, as the Nestorian heresy held, for that would not be incarnation but merely indwelling. Such an indwelling could not save us. God would not then have come *as man*, and so man would not have been brought into union with God. In contrast, the incarnation is an unbreakable *union* between God the Son and the assumed human nature – *without division, without separation*, as the Council of Chalcedon stated in 451. Moreover, this union continues for ever. On the other hand, neither the deity nor the humanity lose their distinctness in the union – Chalcedon was careful to balance the above pair of descriptors with another, *without confusion, without mixture* – for Christ is not an amalgam. His deity and humanity are not like ingredients in an ontological soup which blend into a third substance. Hence, just as the three persons of the trinity remain eternally distinct in the one being of God, so the deity and humanity of Christ are forever deity and humanity while united without possibility of severance in his one person. This means that our humanity is forever united to God in personal union!

In turn, when it comes to our own salvation, we – all believers without exception – are united to Jesus Christ. This is the foundation of the entire outworking of salvation. I have written elsewhere about how foundational is union with Christ.[24] It is central to Paul's theology, as is clear in Ephesians 1:3-14, where every single aspect of salvation is received 'in Christ' or 'in him'. The *Westminster Larger Catechism* takes this position too, in Questions 65–90, where it fits the whole *ordo salutis* under the umbrella of 'union and communion with Christ in grace and glory'. This union has substitutionary and representative dimensions to it, for Christ acted on our behalf in his life and ministry, his death, resurrection and ascension. Since God is just, there are legal aspects that undergird the atoning death of Christ. However, union with Christ is far wider than the legal or representative. For example, we are united with him in our sanctification. This is evident from passages like Romans 6:1ff.

---

[24] Letham, *The Work of Christ*.

In union with him we are adopted as God's children, given to share by grace in the relation with the Father he has by nature, so that we now call on God as 'our Father'. So union with Christ has filial dimensions to it, and this brings us at once into the sphere of personal relations. Moreover, since the Son's relation with the Father is one of indivisible union, our relation with him – and consequently with the Father – is one of indivisible union too. Paul writes that we are one flesh with Christ, 'members of his body' (Eph. 5:29-33). John records Jesus' prayer to the Father requesting that his people demonstrate visibly before the world a unity grounded on the union he has with the Father (John 17:21-24). It follows from our comments above that this union no more deprives us of our humanity than does the assumption of human nature by the Son negate the reality of the humanity he assumed. It erodes our personal distinctiveness no more than the indivisibility of the holy trinity erases the distinctiveness of the three persons. These unions preserve the diversity, as we saw in the last chapter.

The Christ with whom we are in union is of the same – the identical – being as God. Strictly speaking, we are united to his humanity – but his humanity is inseparable from his deity due to the hypostatic union – so union with his humanity is union with his person. Moreover, since the person of Christ is that of the eternal Son,[25] we are united to God. Once again, this does not mean any blurring of the creator–creature distinction, any more than the assumption of humanity by the Son in the incarnation does. His humanity remains humanity (without confusion, without mixture). So we remain human, creatures. As Hughes comments, what is meant 'is not the obliteration of the ontological distinction between Creator and creature but

---

[25] This was affirmed as dogma by the Second Council of Constantinople (553). See A. Grillmeier, *Christ in Christian Tradition: Volume Two: From the Council of Chalcedon (451) to Gregory the Great (590–604). Part Two: The Church of Constantinople in the Sixth Century* (J. Cawte; London: Mowbray, 1995), 438–62; H. M. Relton, *A Study in Christology: The Problem of the Relation of the Two Natures in the Person of Christ* (London: SPCK, 1917).

the establishment at last of intimate and uninterrupted personal communion between them.'[26]

A number of Biblical passages point to this. Probably the first that springs to most minds is 2 Peter 1:3-4. There Peter says:

> His divine power has granted to us all things that pertain to life and godliness, through the knowledge of him who called us to his own glory and excellence, by which he has granted to us his precious and very great promises, so that through them you may become partakers of the divine nature ...

Through his precious and very great promises we become sharers of the divine nature (*theias koinōnoi phuseōs*) – this Peter presents as the goal of our calling by God. He has called us 'to his own glory'. Our destiny as Christians is to share the glory of God. It recalls Paul's comment that 'all have sinned and fall short of the glory of God' (Rom. 3:23). Our proper place is to share God's glory, by sin we fell short and failed to participate in his glory, but in and through Christ we are restored to the glory of God as our ultimate destiny. Glory is what belongs distinctively and peculiarly to God. We are called to partake of what God is. This is more than mere fellowship. Fellowship entails intimate interaction but no participation in the nature of the one with whom such interaction takes place. Peter's language means that this goes far beyond external relations. There is an actual participation in the divine nature.

John, in John 14:16ff, records Jesus' teaching that the Holy Spirit, on his coming at Pentecost, 'will remain with you and shall be in you.' In the presence of the Spirit, the *Paraklētos*, Jesus himself was to be present (John 14:16-17). He then declares that with those who love him and keep his word, 'my Father will love him and we shall come to him and take up our residence with him' (John 14:23). The word *mone* means 'a place where one

---

[26] P. E. Hughes, *The True Image: The Origin and Destiny of Man in Christ* (Grand Rapids, Michigan: Eerdmans, 1989), 286.

may remain or dwell'[27] and conveys the idea of permanence.[28] The coming of the Holy Spirit is, in effect, the coming of the entire trinity. The Father, the Son, and the Holy Spirit take up residence with the one who loves Jesus. This residence is permanent – the three remain with the faithful. It is of the greatest possible intimacy – the three indwell the one who loves Jesus. The faithful thus have a relation with the trinity that is far, far closer than they enjoy with other human beings, no matter what the relationship they may have with them. This goes beyond fellowship to communion (or participation), and is strictly a union, a joining together that is unbreakable.

Further, in 1 John 3:1-2, John writes:

> See what kind of love the Father has given to us, that we should be called children of God; and so we are.... Beloved, we are God's children now, and what we will be has not yet appeared; but we know that when he appears we will be like him, because we shall see him as he is.

The Father's love is such that we now share the relation to him that his Son has. We are now the children of God in Christ. Moreover, at his return, we will be transformed so as to be like Christ the Son. We shall see him in his glory. We shall share his glory. We will be in union with him.

Paul describes the Christian life as lived 'in Christ' from beginning to end. This is clear in Ephesians 1, where the whole panorama of salvation from eternal election via redemption by the blood of Christ to our future inheritance is received in union with Christ. In 2 Corinthians 3:18 he writes of believers being transformed from one degree of glory to another by the Spirit of the Lord. This surpasses the experience of Moses, whose face glowed after communing with Yahweh at Mount Sinai (2 Cor. 3:6-11).

---

[27] LN, 1:732.
[28] Cf., LS, 2:1143.

We refer to these few passages but the whole tenor of Scripture points to it. God has made us for this. He created us in Christ, the image of the invisible God. Following our sin, and the Son's redemptive work, we are being remade in the image of Christ. The trinity created us with a capacity to live *in him*, as creatures in and with our creator. The incarnation proves it. If it were not so and could not be so, then Jesus Christ – God and man – could not be one person, for the difference between creator and creature would be so great that incarnation would not be possible. But now our humanity in Jesus Christ is in full and personal union with God, and so in union with Christ we are brought into union with God.

There are two decisive moments in this great and over-whelming sweep of God's purpose for us. First, in the incarnation the Son takes into personal union a single human nature, while, secondly, the Holy Spirit comes at Pentecost and indwells or pervades myriads of human persons. There are clear differences here that reflect the differences between the persons of the trinity. The Son unites a *single* human *nature*, while with the Spirit *countless* human *persons* are involved. With the Son there is a *personal union*, whereas the Spirit *pervades* or *indwells* us.

The Spirit, at Jesus' baptism, rested on him and led him in his subsequent faith, obedience and ministry. In union with him, we are united with the Spirit who rests on him. The idea of indwelling denotes permanence, for he comes to remain in us for ever. However, the word could connote a certain incompleteness, like in the case of a liquid poured into a bucket, the bucket itself remaining unaffected since the liquid merely fills the empty spaces. Pervasion, on the other hand, complements the image of indwelling by pointing to the idea of saturation, of thoroughness. Once more, this does not take away or diminish our humanity. After all, Jesus is fully and perfectly man – the most truly *human* man – and as such he is the Christ (the anointed One) on whom the Spirit rests, directing him throughout the course of his life and ministry. Rather, pervasion by the Holy Spirit *establishes* our humanity.[29] He makes us what we ought to be. He frees us from the grip of a sinful, fallen nature and renews us to be like Christ. This is what it means to be human.[30] Well does Staniloae comment when he affirms that only the holy trinity assures our existence as persons, and that it is only because God is triune that salvation can occur.[31] Salvation not only reveals that God is triune but it also proceeds from that reality.

In Cabasilas' words, as Christ flows into us and is blended with us so he changes us and turns us to himself.[32] As Panayiotis Nellas comments, 'The essence of the spiritual life is represented clearly by St. Paul's statement, "It is no longer I who live but Christ who lives in me" (Gal. 2:20), provided that we take this statement in a literal sense.' In fact, 'the true nature of man consists in his being like God, or more precisely in his being like Christ and centered on Him.'[33] In this, man's nature assumes the form of the deified humanity of Christ. This does not take place through the destruction of human characteristics but through their transformation.[34]

This is not pantheism, a breakdown of the creator–creature distinction. It is not understood to mean union with the essence of God, but with his energies. Nor is it some form of mixture of the divine and human, as advocated by some eastern religions. Rather, our humanity is not only preserved but enhanced. As Christ's humanity was not absorbed in the incarnation but retained its distinct integrity, so the Christian remains human.

---

[29] This pervasion is somewhat akin to marriage, where the two become one flesh. Marriage unites a man and a woman but it does not diminish either one or eliminate their proper characteristics.

[30] Incidentally, this is why naturalistic evolution is incompatible with the Christian faith, for man is made to be in union with God – in Christ and permeated by the Holy Spirit. This, not a particular exegesis of a single word in Genesis 1, utterly demarcates Christianity from evolutionism.

[31] D. Staniloae, *The Experience of God: Orthodox Dogmatic Theology Vol 1: Revelation and Knowledge of the Triune God* (I. Ionita; Brookline, Massachusetts: Holy Cross Orthodox Press, 1994), 276, 248.

[32] Cabasilas, *Life in Christ*, 44.

[33] Nellas, *Deification in Christ*, 120.

[34] Ibid., 122–3.

He becomes God, not by nature but by grace. Thus even our bodies are temples of the Holy Spirit (1 Cor. 6:19).

In Cabasilas' words, union with Christ 'is closer than any other union which man can possibly imagine and does not lend itself to any exact comparisons.' This is why, he says, Scripture does not confine itself to one illustration but provides a wide range of examples; a house and its occupants, wedlock, limbs and the head. Indeed, it is not even possible to form an accurate picture should we take all these metaphors together. For example, the limbs of Christ are joined more firmly to him than to their own bodies, for the martyrs laid down their head and limbs with exultation and could not be separated from Christ even so far as to be out of earshot of his voice. In short, this union is closer than what joins a man to himself.[35] Again, the children of God are closer to Christ than to their own parents. Separated from our parents, we survive; separated from Christ, we would die.[36] Cabasilas urges constant meditation on Christ as a result of this, and has an extended series of meditations on the Beatitudes from a Christological perspective.[37]

This is a microcosm of the redemption of the whole created order. Christ, in his incarnation, took into union a centrally important part of this order. As icons depict the transformation of creation, so at the parousia the whole creation will be transformed and suffused with the glory of God. However, at the heart of all this is the redemption of the church and its own transformation in union with God. This does not mean that there is any possibility of sinless perfection in this life. Instead, it must be seen in tandem with the continued necessity of repentance and in conjunction with obedience to the commandments of God, participation in the life of the Church, love to others and care for the poor. Contrary to popular notions, it can no more conflict with justification than can sanctification and

---

[35] Cabasilas, *Life in Christ*, 5-6.
[36] Ibid., 48–9.
[37] Ibid., 93–105.

glorification, for it is the Eastern church's way of understanding the latter two doctrines. Rather, the two foci represent differing concentrations for East and West. As much as anything, historical circumstance has fostered this. There is a legal dimension to our salvation – God is righteous and salvation is in accordance with his law – and there is also a transformational dimension.[38]

In this connection, it is important to recognize the enormous concentration in the East, in life and word, on the Christian life, seen especially in ascetic literature. The multi-volume work, *The Philokalia*, is a classic source. It is a compilation of writings, drawn from various saints and ascetics throughout history, on prayer, spiritual warfare, and the whole process of deification. For example, St. Isaiah the Solitary (d. 491?) calls the reader to self-examination, to wage war against the world, the flesh and the devil. Evagrius the Solitary (345/6–399) advises the solitary that he must 'abstain from women, and not beget a son or daughter .. he must be a soldier of Christ, detached from material things, free from cares and not involved in any trade or commerce.' He should keep to a sparse and plain diet and pay little regard to clothes, other than what is necessary for the needs of the body. He should not hanker after fine food.[39] The main demons we face are arranged into three groups, charged with inciting to gluttony, avarice and pride respectively. Other demons follow behind, attacking those wounded by the advance party. Hatred of demons contributes greatly to salvation and promotes our growth in holiness.[40] John Cassian (c. 360–c. 435), influential in the West especially with the Benedictines, wrote against the eight vices (gluttony, unchastity, avarice, anger, dejection, listlessness, self-esteem and pride).[41] St Mark the Ascetic wrote a treatise

---

[38] For further reading on deification, see A. Williams, *The Ground of Union: Deification in Aquinas and Palamas* (New York: Oxford University Press, 1999); C. Mosser, 'The Greatest Possible Blessing: Calvin and Deification,' *SJT* 55 (2002), 36-57; E. Bartos, *Deification in Eastern Orthodox Theology: An Evaluation and Critique of the Theology of Dumitru Staniloae* (Carlisle: Paternoster, 1999).

[39] St. Nikodimos of the Holy Mountain, *The Philokalia*, 1:31–5.

[40] Ibid., 1:38–44.

on the spiritual law in 200 texts, a collection of proverbs and aphorisms on the spiritual life.[42]

Particularly noteworthy is St Symeon the New Theologian. We saw how close his thought is to the Protestant doctrine of justification. Remarkably, he foreshadows the doctrine of assurance in the Westminster Confession of Faith. 'The grace of the Holy Spirit is given as a pledge to souls that are betrothed to Christ; and just as without a pledge a woman cannot be sure that her union with her man will take place, so the soul will have no firm assurance that it will be joined for all eternity with its Lord and God, or be united with him mystically and inexpressibly, or enjoy His inapproachable beauty, unless it receives the pledge of His grace and consciously possesses Him within itself.'[43] Hence, a 'firm assurance' of eternal salvation is possible, and this comes through the Holy Spirit. This is contrary to the teaching of Rome, which denies the possibility in this life of such assurance, apart from special revelation or the authority of the church, and is much closer to Protestantism.

What better way to end this section than with the words of Theodore Stylianopoulos?:

> 'The burning hermeneutical point is to submit the norms themselves to critical evaluation in the light of total witness of Scripture. The 'justification theology' focusing on the issue of faith and works is no less traditional simply because a Protestant declares it 'biblical'. Nor is the 'theosis theology' focusing on union with Christ in the Spirit unbiblical simply because an Orthodox declares it 'traditional.' An exegetical approach may well find that both the 'participatory' and 'forensic' views of salvation are part of the larger biblical witness, and that deeper appreciation of both may be achieved precisely by seeing them in positive comparative light.'[44]

---

[41] Ibid., 1:73–93.

[42] Ibid., 1:110–24.

[43] Ibid., 4:40.

[44] T. G. Stylianopoulos, *The New Testament: An Orthodox Perspective: Volume One: Scripture, Tradition, Hermeneutics* (Brookline, Massachusetts: Holy Cross Orthodox Press, 1997), 209–10.

Predestination

Here is a major sticking point between Orthodoxy and the Reformed. Converts to Orthodoxy from Reformed Churches are required, before chrismation, to renounce the doctrine of predestination taught by those churches. This became a source of contention during the ministry of Cyril Lucaris, Patriarch of Constantinople from 1623 to his death in 1638. Lucaris had earlier been sent to Poland to counter the Roman Catholic proselytism there. He came into contact with Protestants, especially of Reformed persuasion. He wrote his *Confession* in 1629, clearly a Calvinist document.[45] Often regarded as among the most brilliant occupants of the patriarchate of Constantinople, his time in office, despite his immense popularity, was bedevilled by political intrigue and plotting. Eventually, he was murdered by Turkish emissaries, his body dumped in the Bosphorus but eventually recovered and given a martyr's burial. Shortly after his demise, the Reformed doctrine of predestination was condemned. However, the doctrine to be renounced is unrecognizable as the Reformed doctrine! It is a caricature that bears hardly any resemblance.

> *Bishop:* Dost thou renounce the false doctrine, that the predestination of men to their salvation, or their rejection, is not in accordance with the Divine foreknowledge of the faith and good works of the former, or of the unbelief and evil deeds of the latter; but in accordance with some arbitrary destiny, by reason of which faith and virtue are robbed of their merit, and God is held accountable for the perdition of sinners?[46]

This question is spurious for at least two main reasons. First, it understands the Reformed doctrine of predestination as arbitrary. This betrays a culpable lack of understanding of what the Reformed churches have taught. The triune God, who works

---

[45] A translation is supplied by G. A. Hadjiantoniou, *Protestant Patriarch: The Life of Cyril Lukaris (1572–1638) Patriarch of Constantinople* (Richmond, Virginia: John Knox Press, 1961), 141–5.

[46] *Service Book*, 457.

all things together according to the counsel of his will, is just, good and faithful. His decrees are not arbitrary or capricious but wise, right, and good. Moreover, his absolute sovereignty is fully compatible with human freedom, since he made man in his own image. God's sovereignty and human responsibility stand together. They are complementary, not competitive. The Bible teaches both. We cannot restrict either side so as to produce a neat solution of our own. For that reason, secondly, God is not responsible for human sin nor for the ultimate perdition of the impenitent. As *The Westminster Confession of Faith* puts it, the reprobate are condemned *for their sins*. While eternal election is a decree of sheer grace, made in Christ, undeserved by the recipients, eternal reprobation is grounded in divine justice and takes human sin fully into account.

Synergism

Here is another crucial division between Orthodoxy and the Reformed, to my mind the single most significant point of difference. In some ways, this is a wider division than between the Reformed and Rome, for the Reformed doctrine of predestination is built on the teachings of Augustine, Thomas Aquinas, Bonaventure and others. Although there has been a Calvinist Patriarch of Constantinople and never a Calvinist Pope, yet Reformed doctrine owes a debt to the major contributions of its Western antecedents in the medieval period and earlier.

This synergistic view of salvation goes right back to the Fathers. In his *Homilies on Romans*, Chrysostom argues that grace is given to those who exercise their free will. Referring to Daniel and the escape from the fiery furnace [*sic*], 'But that, you will say, was wholly of grace. Yes, because the acts of free-will led the way thereto. So that if we be willing to train ourselves to a like character, even now the grace is at hand.' In the same homily, speaking on Romans 2:16, he says, 'God made man independent, so as to be able to choose virtue and to avoid vice. And be not surprised that he proves this point, not once or twice,

Eastern Orthodoxy: A Reformed Perspective

but several, times.'[47] In his *Homilies on Hebrews* he comments, 'What then? Does nothing depend on God? All indeed depends on God, but not so that our free-will is hindered. "If then it depend on God," (one says), "why does he blame us?" On this account I said, "so that our free-will is not hindered." It depends then on us, and on him. For we must first choose the good; and then he leads us to his own. He does not anticipate our choice, lest our free-will should be outraged. But when we have chosen, then great is the assistance he brings to us.' Again, 'For it is ours to choose and to wish; but God's to complete and to bring to an end. Since therefore the greater part is of him, he says all is of him, speaking according to the custom of men.'[48]

So too John of Damascus adopts a similar synergistic and voluntaristic theology. In *De Orthodoxa Fide*, he connects free will with reason: God knows all things in advance but he does not predetermine them.[49] 'For he knows beforehand those things that are in our power, but he does not predetermine them.'[50] We have it in our power either to abide in virtue and follow God, who calls us into ways of virtue, or to stray from paths of virtue ... and to follow the devil.[51]

This pattern – first human free will, then divine grace – is the reverse of Augustinianism. Augustine held that God's grace precedes and enables our response. This follows the fact that, as Paul says, the natural man is 'dead in trespasses and sins' (Eph. 2:1). A dead man can do nothing to bring himself to life; he needs a resurrection. This is the work of the Holy Spirit. Given new life, we believe and obey by the continued help of the Holy Spirit. For the East, fallen man is diseased but not dead. Sin has harmed him but not killed him. Therefore there

---

[47] Chrysostom, 'Homily III on The Epistle to the Romans,' *NPNF1*, 11:355-56, 365. See also Homily VIII on Philippians (on Phil. 2:12ff), in NPNF1, 13:220; Homily IX on Thessalonians (on 1 Thess. 5:6-8) in NPNF1, 13:362.

[48] Homily XII on Hebrews (Heb. 7:8), in NPNF1, 14:425.

[49] John of Damascus, *On the Orthodox Faith*, 2:25-30, in NPNF2, 9:2:39–44; and ibid., 3:14, in NPNF2, 9:2:58–59.

[50] Ibid., 2:30, NPNF2 9:2:42.

[51] Ibid., 9:2:43.

are things he can do to make himself better. The cure follows from the diagnosis. In the eyes of the Reformed, the Orthodox diagnosis is inadequate, less than Biblical, and wrong. It fails to do justice to the plight of man, and so it attributes less to the power of God. It is not sufficiently realistic.

At this point, many Eastern apologists accuse the Reformed of an implicit monotheletism. According to the Orthodox understanding of the Reformed doctrine of predestination and the sovereignty of grace, it seems that the human will is over-ridden by the actions of God. Irresistible grace, to the Eastern mind, implies that the Holy Spirit rides rough-shod over the mind of man, who contributes nothing. This is redolent of monotheletism, in which it was heretically held that Christ had only one will, and thus no distinctively human will. As the eclipse of the human will in Christ was – correctly – deemed heresy, since it undermined his humanity, so the Reformed claim that God is sovereign in bringing people to faith undermines our humanity heretically, so it is held.

This argument rests on a considerable misunderstanding. Reformed theology asserts *both* the sovereign action of God in our salvation *and* full human responsibility and free agency. Saving faith is an action in which we engage, 'receiving and resting on Christ alone for justification, sanctification and eternal life,' in the words of *The Westminster Confession of Faith* 14:2. The point is that the Holy Spirit changes our hearts, our inner being, replacing a heart of stone by a heart of flesh (Ezek. 36:26), so that whereas we were innately hostile to Christ and the gospel we become willing, ready and able to serve him. This was something taught by Fathers such as Theodoret of Cyrrhus, who asserted that every good work was made possible by the help of God, and by Chrysostom, who states that 'faith's workings themselves are a gift of God' for God has not forbidden works 'but forbidden us to be justified by works. No one, Paul says, is justified by works, precisely in order that the grace and benevolence of God may become apparent!'[52] These Orthodox apologists have

---

[52] Chrysostom, 'Homily IV on Ephesians (on Eph. 2:8-9),' *op. cit.* Oden, *Justification*, 110–1.

confused Reformed theology with fatalism, a rigid determinism exemplified by Islam, with which so many in the East have been confronted. In Islam, before the absolute will of Allah, man must simply submit (*islam*). Reformed doctrine is light years apart from that. First, the God we worship is tri-personal, three persons in indivisible and loving communion, whereas the deity of Islam is a unitary monad. Consequently, love is central to the trinity, whereas power and will are foremost in the Islamic view of Allah. It follows, that the Christian, Biblical, and Reformed doctrine of predestination is one that respects the integrity of the human person, whereas in Islam it is hard to see how personhood can even be conceived, since if love is not central persons cannot be.

Part Three:

Comparative Evaluation

11

Areas of Agreement,
Misunderstanding, and Disagreement

We will now pull together the various strands from the previous chapters and ask how the Eastern church appears from the perspective of Reformed Christianity, what the two have in common, what are the areas of agreement, how the Reformed can learn from the Orthodox, what misunderstandings exist on both sides and, finally, what matters divide them and are genuine areas of disagreement.

Positive dimensions

First, we will ask in what areas can the Eastern church teach the Reformed and so in what ways can Reformed theology learn through cross-fertilization and gain a richer understanding of the gospel of Jesus Christ? It is a mark of Christian maturity to be able to learn from those with whom we disagree on this or that. In view of the long divorce between East and West, an openness to the East may well benefit and revitalize the Reformed churches.

The trinity

In the East the doctrine of the trinity has remained a vital part of belief and worship, in contrast to the West, where for the vast majority it is little more than an arcane mathematical riddle, of no real consequence for daily living. Eastern liturgies are full of trinitarian prayers, hymns and doxologies. Elsewhere I have referred to the sad lack of appreciation of the trinity by Western Christians in general. This is all the more tragic in view of the fact that this is the God we worship and serve.[1]

Many of the most familiar Protestant hymns are less than trinitarian. 'Praise my soul, the King of heaven,' 'My God, how wonderful thou art,' 'Praise to the Lord, the Almighty, the King of salvation,' 'Immortal, invisible, God only wise,' even 'Great is thy faithfulness,' are all basically monotheistic, no more. 'How great thou art' is at best binitarian. The same applies to the recent spate of choruses, which generally show a scant understanding of classic Christian theology. If a random selection of Western Christians were asked what the trinity meant to them, the chances are overwhelming that the questioner would receive a blank response. What a contrast the Byzantine liturgy provides! The trinity saturates the prayers and acclamations. Right at the heart of Eastern piety – and thus Eastern theology – is a clear and articulated realization that the God we worship is triune. It is a truism that God is central to the Christian faith and that he is the object of faith. But which God do we trust? What is God like? The Biblical and Christian answer is that he is an indivisible trinity of co-equal persons: the Father, the Son, and the Holy Spirit. Moreover, Paul describes our relationship with God in trinitarian terms: 'through [Christ] we ... have access by one Spirit to the Father' (Eph. 2:18).[2] Prayer, one of the most basic of Christian activities, is saturated in a trinitarian ethos; the Christian life is lived in communion with the holy trinity. The worship and life of the Reformed church could be revitalized through recognizing that it has much to learn from Orthodoxy at this crucial point.

---

[1] R. Letham, *The Holy Trinity: In Scripture, History, Theology, and Worship* (Phillipsburg, New Jersey: Presbyterian & Reformed, 2004), 407–24.

[2] See Letham, *The Holy Trinity*, 80–1, 414–5.

Union with Christ and God

Due to the relative absence of analytic forms of thought, the East has maintained a focus on the key unions of the Christian faith – the union of the three persons in God, the union of deity and humanity in Christ, the union of Christ and the church, the union of the Holy Spirit with – or in – the saints. The Western thirteenth-century Bishop of Lincoln, Robert Grosseteste drew attention to these, in saying

> there seem to be grouped together the following unities or unions: the union by which the incarnate Word is the one Christ, one Christ in his person, God and man; the union by which Christ is one in nature with the church through the human nature he took on; and the union by which the church is reunited with him by a condign taking up, in the sacrament of the Eucharist.... These three unions seem to be grouped together in the One which is called the whole Christ. Of this One the apostle says, to the Ephesians [*sic*]: 'For you are all one in Christ Jesus', or, as the Greek text has it: 'You are all one person in Christ Jesus.' That One of which it says: 'That they also may be one in us' seems moreover, to add to the foregoing considerations that the Son, as Word, is one in substance with the Father, and hence with the Holy Spirit.... It adds also the unity of our conformity in the highest kind with the Blessed Trinity, through our reason. To this conformity and Deiformity we are led by the mediator, Christ, God and man, with whom we form one Christ.

Grosseteste goes on to say that 'there is an orderly descent, through the unity of the Trinity and through the incarnate Word, through his body which is the church, to our being one, in a deiform way [or 'one in God-form with the Trinity,' as another possible reading goes].'[3] Grosseteste has put his finger on the pulse of the Christian faith. These unions are the very

---

[3] *Robert Grosseteste: On the Six Days of Creation: A Translation of the Hexaëmeron by C.F.J. Martin* (Auctores Britannici Medii Aevi; Oxford University Press for the British Academy, 1996), 47–8.

heartbeat of what God is and all that he has done for us and our salvation in Christ.

In turn, this focus has encouraged a more vital connection in the East between theology and piety. This is contrary to the argument of Herman Bavinck, who thought that the East's opposition to the *filioque* was symptomatic of a split between theology and piety. By denying that the Spirit proceeds from the Son as well as the Father, he argued that the East cut adrift doctrine and ideas from life, emotion, and mysticism.[4] In common with other Westerners at the time, Bavinck knew little of the Eastern church or he would never have made this claim. He was dependent on Adolf von Harnack for this mistaken notion.[5] We will discuss this matter further later in the chapter.

In contrast, the West has always been strongly biased towards the juridical. Early on, the central position of Rome, with its highly developed administrative and legal system, encouraged the prominence of law. As a consequence, Western theology has revolved around the doctrines of the atonement and justification, issues in which the East has shown far less interest. There is nothing wrong with this juridical focus: the Bible has plenty of forensic categories. God is just and salvation is in accordance with his justice. As Paul writes the main question in our salvation was that '[God] might be just and the justifier of the one who has faith in Jesus' (Rom. 3:26). Law is right at the heart of biblical revelation: it is one of the three main parts of the Old Testament, it characterizes the Mosaic covenant, and its continued role, such as it is, dominates Paul's discussion in Romans.

However, the East, with its participatory stress, centering in deification, has preserved something the West has neglected. The theme of union with Christ is prominent in the Gospel of John, Romans, and throughout the New Testament. I have

---

[4] H. Bavinck, *The Doctrine of God* (Edinburgh: Banner of Truth, rpr, 1977), 317.

[5] H. Bavinck, *Reformed Dogmatics* (trans. J. Bolt, J. Vriend; Grand Rapids: Baker, 2004), 2:317–8.

written about this elsewhere.[6] Indeed, it is impossible to understand the gospel aright apart from this vital category. Paul considers that our whole salvation is in union with Christ (e.g., Eph. 1:3-14).

The West needs to take this participatory dimension into account just as the East should give clearer and more extensive thought to the doctrine of the atonement and justification. As we described in the previous chapter, the atonement and justification refer to the start of the Christian life, while union with Christ embraces all aspects but is fully realized in the consummation of salvation following the return of Christ.

Freedom from concerns raised by the Enlightenment

Eastern theology – due to the absence of a critical Enlightenment, and the resultant liberalism that has affected the West – has a refreshing lack of preoccupation with unbelieving critical attacks. Frequently, one can pick up a book by an Orthodox theologian and plunge straight in to substantive theological discussion, integrally related to prayer, worship and discipleship. In the West, in the last three hundred years, there has been a pressing need to answer the critics, resulting in a preoccupation with the defence of the faith against critical attack. This has often diverted attention from consideration of what salvation actually is. It has also bred a detached, purely academic approach to the gospel divorced from the life and needs of the church.

The situation of the East is particularly evident in the firm belief of the Orthodox in the return of Christ, heaven and hell. These topics have been sidelined in the West due to possible embarrassment at the likelihood of sceptical mockery. The absence of theological liberalism has freed the Eastern church to proclaim the faith undeterred by the problems Western Christians have encountered. Many of the Orthodox have suffered, whether at the hands of Islam or Communism, but they have not lost their nerve. This points to a strong element

---

[6] R. Letham, *The Work of Christ* (Leicester: Inter-Varsity Press, 1993), 75–87.

of commonality between the Reformed and Evangelicals in general, and the Orthodox. One caveat needs to be sounded. As Orthodoxy has spread into Western countries in recent decades it has encountered the problems of Western civilization and so has been forced to respond to the challenges the Western church has already faced. It remains to be seen what effect, if any, this may have.

Unity of theology and piety

The strong impact of asceticism and monasticism in the East has led to an emphasis on contemplation. The knowledge of God is received and cultivated in prayer and meditation, aided by the Holy Spirit. This contemplative approach is wedded to discipleship; it entails doing battle against the forces of darkness without and within. Eastern theologians, even if teaching in an academic setting, have worked in the context of the church, never divorcing themselves from the piety and disciplined obedience that the Christian faith requires. One of the classic expressions of this is the collection of Greek ascetic texts, the *Philokalia*, dating from the fourth to the fifteenth centuries, translated into English by Kallistos Ware and others.[7]

On the other hand, in the West since the Enlightenment the theological enterprise has generally been hived off to academic institutions with no connection to the church. The study of theology and the Bible has been centred in universities. The high priests of Western Christianity, especially of evangelicalism, have been scholars. By virtue of their setting in a secular environment, the Bible and Christian theology have been approached in a manner unsuited to their own intrinsic nature. God gave the Scriptures to the church. The Bible is the church's book. While its humanity justifies its being studied according to all the academic tools available, when the essential ecclesial base that God intended for it has been abandoned in the course

---

[7] St. Nikodimos of the Holy Mountain, *The Philokalia* (G. Palmer; London: Faber and Faber, 1983), 4 vols.

of such study, it should be of little surprise if the results are not noticeably conducive to faith and discipleship.

This contrast is still more evident in the churchly focus of the East, with the liturgy a central – if not *the* central – source for theological thought. There has been a profound integration between liturgy and doctrine, inevitable in any context but expressly recognized here. Here the unity of today's church with its historic roots, with the Fathers, and so with the apostles, is particularly clear. In contrast, Protestantism – the Reformed church included – increasingly displays a free-wheeling liturgical anarchy that bespeaks and foreshadows doctrinal confusion of the highest order.

Areas of agreement

We began the book by discussing the seven ecumenical councils, since these demonstrate the extensive agreement between the Orthodox and the Reformed. The classic church doctrines of the trinity and the person of Christ were hatched in controversies in the East and it was the Eastern church that resolved them. These are the foundational doctrines of the Christian faith. The Reformed churches, Protestantism in general, Rome and the entire Western church are all indebted to the East. There still are disagreements on the *filioque*, indicating differing approaches to the trinity. The West has often missed the vital post-Chalcedonian developments at Constantinople II and Constantinople III and so suffered from a neglect of the important refinements of Chalcedon. However, the agreement here is substantial and considerable.

With various differences of emphasis, the Orthodox and the Reformed are in general agreement on the authority of the Bible, sin and the fall (although the East does not accept the Augustinian doctrine of original sin, nor see sin in connection with the law), Christ's death and resurrection (although in the East the atonement is regarded more in terms of *Christus victor*), and the gift of the Holy Spirit. We already noted the Orthodox commitment to the return of Christ, the final judgment, heaven and hell.

On a matter at the heart of the gospel – justification by faith – there is also a real concursus. Although the East has never had to deal with justification as a matter of controversy, and so has never made an official pronouncement on it, there is an underlying consensus. Not only occasional comments by the Fathers that talk of salvation as a gift of God's grace, and faith as a gift of God, but also the prevalence of the famous Jesus prayer attest to the East's rejection of the idea that our works can contribute to our salvation. The Orthodox insist that good works are indispensable to the Christian life; this they affirm in tandem with the Reformed. But both agree that on the day of judgment we will be unable to point to our works as a reason to enter heaven. We also recognized that the Eastern doctrine of deification has various echoes and counterparts in the West and is no more incompatible with justification by faith than are the Reformed doctrines of sanctification and glorification.

Additionally, the Eastern doctrine of the church resonates with many Reformed concerns. Cyprian's stress on the unity of the church, together with the parity of bishops, and of all church members underlies the Orthodox opposition to the claims of Rome. This is a model of the church very close to the post-Reformation Anglican one – and the Church of England was widely recognized as a Reformed church.

Areas of misunderstanding
Areas where the Reformed view of Orthodoxy needs to be adjusted
There is a clear need for the Reformed to develop a more nuanced understanding of Orthodoxy so as more accurately to represent what the Orthodox believe and do. There is nothing more futile than to engage in polemics against a straw man. All that achieves is to buttress prejudice, antagonize those who are criticized, and dismay others. It undermines the credibility of the polemicist.

In the previous chapters we noted the main areas where this adjustment of outlook is needed. The Orthodox, in using icons, are not engaging in idolatry. This Nicaea II emphatically denied, hurling anathemas at those who suggested it. To accuse the Orthodox of this is to ignore the language that John of Damascus and Nicaea II used to distinguish between respect and honour on the one hand, and worship – owed to the indivisible trinity alone – on the other. As Reformed, we may and do oppose icons of Christ but the precise point(s) of disagreement need to be noted and distinguished from areas where misunderstanding has taken place.

Again, the issue at stake in the Orthodox use of prayers to the saints needs to be identified and separated from ignorant misinformed opposition. The point is not that intercession is offered to saints; it is the belief that departed saints can hear our prayers and intercede on our behalf. The Bible does not encourage us to do this; indeed, it directs our hopes and prayers elsewhere.

On the matter of Scripture and tradition, we need to realize that both sides appeal to both sources. The Orthodox have a powerfully Biblical emphasis in both liturgy and theology, while the Reformers and the Reformed have a high view of the past teaching of the church. It is decidedly not a matter of the Bible alone versus the teaching of the church. The point at issue is where is the highest court of appeal, which has the decisive voice?

Areas where the Orthodox view of the Reformed needs to be adjusted
In turn, the Orthodox need to reconsider some of their opposition to Reformed teaching.

In opposing the Reformed doctrine of predestination, the Orthodox demonstrate a lack of familiarity with the classic Reformed statements, such as John Calvin's *Institute of the Christian Religion* and The Westminster Confession of Faith. In this, they confuse the Reformed doctrine with Islamic fatalism. Reformed theology teaches *both* the absolute sovereignty of God *and* the full responsibility of man. God's decrees contemplate the free actions of secondary causes. Thus, the reprobate will be condemned for their sins, not on the basis of a decree that left them without their own responsibility (WCF 3:7, 5:1-4). As such, the idea that the Reformed doctrine of predestination is monothelite, short-circuiting the involvement of the human will, is an accusation not borne out by the evidence.

Again, the Orthodox require a convert from the Reformed churches to renounce a doctrine of the eucharist that is effectively an anabaptist or Zwinglian one, rather than the one found in The Westminster Confession of Faith. The Zwinglian doctrine held that the bread and wine are merely symbolic; it is this teaching that the convert must abjure. Calvin and The Westminster Confession both teach that there is a real spiritual feeding on Christ, that more than symbolism is here. While stopping short of the Lutheran connection between the elements and the body of Christ, both Calvin and the Westminster Assembly taught that the faithful truly eat the body of Christ and drink his blood.[8]

On the question of the authority of Scripture, many Ortho-dox polemicists accuse Reformed Christians of ignoring the part played by the church. Unfortunately, they have here many ill-informed examples on which to draw. However, the classic Reformed creeds and confessions attest that the church is integral to the process of salvation, that the Christian faith is found in the Bible and taught by the church. Orthodoxy is confusing the Reformed churches with the free-wheeling individualists of a later era.

Critical concerns – areas of substantive disagreement
The East tends to downplay the preaching of the Word of God.
This is largely the result of historical events (the depredations of Islam) and is despite Orthodoxy's own heritage, which includes some of the greatest preachers the church has known (Chrysostom, Gregory Nazianzen). It is true that sermons are

---

[8] See R. Letham, *The Lord's Supper: Eternal Word in Broken Bread* (Philippsburg, New Jersey: Presbyterian & Reformed, 2001).

part of the liturgy in Orthodoxy. As Kallistos Ware comments, the priest preaches rather like a father advising and admonishing his family. Indeed, sermons have been an important part of the liturgy at the Oxford church for which Bishop Kallistos has been responsible.[9] However, the worship and liturgy are overwhelmingly visual. Not only are there a profusion of icons but the ritual movements of the clergy are, each one, fraught with symbolism. This is by no means to the exclusion of the verbal — we have already pointed to the powerful trinitarian emphasis — but the balance is quite a contrast to the Reformed. In chapter 6, we referred to Gregory of Nyssa and his stress on God's visible revelation in creation, together with his thoughts on the ambiguity and inadequacy of language. Lossky also comments that the Holy Spirit expresses the truth *both* in intelligible definitions *and* in sensible images and symbols.[10]

The problem here is that the East has never faced the great epistemological question resolved by Calvin. The medieval Western church also had a strong visual focus. The path of salvation led to the beatific vision, when the saint would be granted a vision of God. Knowledge of God was cast in a dominantly visual form. However, this beatific vision was not possible in this life. Therefore, the Christian could not have direct intuitive knowledge of God. This posed a huge problem for assurance of salvation. The way Calvin resolved this question was to understand the knowledge of God in auditive terms rather than visual ones. For Calvin, God reveals himself *in his Word* by the Holy Spirit. In the Word read and proclaimed, God addresses us personally. We cannot see him but we can hear him. Moreover, he is as he says he is — his self-revelation is true and reliable. The Holy Spirit, who is himself fully God and the whole God,

[9] A. Louth, 'Biographical Sketch,' *Abba: The Tradition of Orthodoxy in the West: Festschrift for Bishop Kallistos (Ware) of Diokleia* (J. Behr; Crestwood, New York: St. Vladimir's Seminary Press, 2003), 20.

[10] V. Lossky, 'Tradition and Traditions,' in Leonid Ouspensky and Vladimir Lossky, *The Meaning of Icons*, Trans., G.E.H. Palmer and E. Kadloubovsky (Crestwood, New York: St. Vladimir's Seminary Press, 1982), 16.

accompanies the preached Word and grants us, through faith, direct auditive intuitive knowledge of God. This resolves the problem of the knowledge of God and simultaneously enables us to have assurance of salvation through the direct work of God the Holy Spirit.[11] The East, through historical circumstance, has never dealt with this question. If, as, and when the Orthodox do face it, there should be a revival of preaching to empower the liturgy still further.

The relationship between Scripture and tradition.

Many similar concerns surface here as with Rome, except that the absence of a Pope, a magisterium, and a corresponding series of infallible dogmas, places fewer barriers between Orthodoxy and historic Protestantism at this point. For the East, the relationship between the Bible and tradition is a living one. The Bible exists within the tradition (in which the seven ecumenical councils are dominant), not apart from it. Here Orthodoxy occupies the position of the church of the first two centuries, as argued by A.N.S. Lane, in which the Bible and tradition (the teaching of the church) were effectively indistinguishable. Later developments in the West placed tradition over Scripture (as in medieval Rome), or pitted Scripture against tradition (the anabaptists and many contemporary evangelicals), or put Scripture over tradition without rejecting it (the Reformation).[12] With Orthodoxy, Scripture is a primary part of the organic nature of tradition.

We remarked earlier on the misunderstandings of both sides on this question. The two positions are not so far apart as is often supposed. There is a great area of common ground. However,

---

[11] See T. F. Torrance, 'Intuitive and Abstractive Knowledge: From Duns Scotus to John Calvin,' *De Doctrina Ioannis Duns Scoti: Acta Congressus Scotistici Internationalis Oxonii et Edimburgi 11–17 Sept. 1966 Celebrati* (Romae: Curae Commissionis Scotisticae, 1968) 4:291–305; T. Torrance, *The Hermeneutics of John Calvin* (Edinburgh: Scottish Academic Press, 1988).

[12] A. Lane, 'Scripture, Tradition and Church: An Historical Survey,' *VE* 9 (1975), 37–55.

at the same time there are definite disagreements. They focus on the question of what is the ultimate authority that determines what we are to believe and do. Protestants say this is the Bible, the Word of God, which must sit in judgment on all opinions of man. The Orthodox also believe in the authority of the Bible but place it in a context where it is one among a range of factors. These disagreements are significant on a strategic level. Like a traveller who arrives at the right airport but boards the wrong plane, and finds himself in Paris instead of Moscow, they open up the possibility of wider divergences flowing from them.

The Eastern doctrine of the trinity, following Palamas

While the doctrine of the trinity was forged in the Eastern church – and we have frequently remarked on its centrality in life and worship – the Eastern doctrine, as it has developed, has taken a turn that poses problems. Gregory Palamas' development of the distinction between the unknowable essence (being) of God and his energies has won widespread approval. However, this drives a wedge between the immanent and economic trinities, between God in himself and God as he has revealed himself. This threatens our knowledge of God with a profound agnosticism, since we have no way of knowing whether God is as he has revealed himself in Jesus Christ. It also defies rational discourse, since we cannot say anything about who God is. The acme of the Christian life becomes mystical contemplation rather than *fides quaerens intellectum* (faith seeking understanding). As Barth says, 'it goes beyond revelation to achieve a very different picture of God "antecedently in Himself."'[13]

The point here is that this is not merely a development from the Cappadocians, whose work led to the resolution of the trinitarian crisis. It is more than that – it is a distortion of the classic doctrine of the trinity. It introduces into God a division, not a distinction. As Dorothea Wendebourg comments, it results in the persons of the trinity having no soteriological

---

[13] Karl Barth, *CD*, I/1, 480.

functions. The classic doctrine affirmed that the three persons, each and together are the one God. By introducing a new level in God, the trinitarian settlement is undermined. It is the defeat of trinitarian theology.[14]

The veneration of Mary and the saints

It is important to remember that the East does not, in making intercession to the saints, see the saints as co-mediators with Christ. It corresponds to our own practice when we ask people to pray for us. We know full well that we can pray direct to the Father through the sole mediation of Christ the Son. Yet we have no hesitation in asking saints to intercede on our behalf with Christ. 'Please pray for me,' we say. The crucial difference is that we intercede with living saints while Orthodoxy considers it possible, legitimate and desirable to intercede with departed saints. So the issue concerns whether it is possible, legitimate and desirable to communicate with departed saints. The Bible indicates this is not possible. The parable of the rich man and Lazarus implies it, while neither Jesus nor Paul, when dealing with death and the intermediate state, ever suggest that it is possible for the departed to hear our prayers. Our encouragement in the face of death is the resurrection when Christ returns in glory. If such intercession is not possible it follows it is not desirable either. Is this heresy or error? I suggest the latter – it does not overthrow any crucial doctrine of the faith, although in practice it can divert faith's focus, which should be rooted firmly in Jesus Christ.

We discussed the question of icons at length in chapter 6. While, again, there is need for a more accurate appraisal of what occurs and there is also a surprising agreement on the reality of iconic and semiotic guides to the heavenly realm, there remain some crucial points of division. The Orthodox insist that the incarnation mandates icons of Christ, since God has chosen to reveal

---

[14] D. Wendebourg, 'From the Cappadocian Fathers to Gregory Palamas: The Defeat of Trinitarian Theology,' *StPatr* 17/1 (1982), 194–98.

himself in human form. The Reformed are equally emphatic that the second commandment prohibits the use of images in worship, and argue that this includes icons of Christ. The Orthodox accuse the Reformed, and Protestants in general, of Manichaeism, of a deficient view of matter. The Reformed argue that icons of Christ imply a Nestorian abstraction of his humanity.

Soteriological synergism

Dating back to the early church, at least to Chrysostom, the East has had a vigorous doctrine of free will. This puts Orthodoxy further away from the Reformed than is Rome. This is in many ways the most serious division of all. The Eastern view of salvation as deification, with the defeat of death central, contrasts to the more legal and forensic approach of the Western church, with its stress on law and grace, atonement for sin, and justification. However, these particular factors are all aspects of salvation. The question here is the balance between them. However, the issue of the weighting between grace and the human will is far reaching. It entails differing understandings of the extent of human sin, and thus the magnitude of the work of salvation Christ has brought about. The question, 'What is the gospel?' is an absolutely crucial one. How the Reformed, Rome, and Orthodoxy answer it differs in key respects.

Orthodoxy is very similar on soteriology to Arminianism. Having said that, the Reformed recognize that Arminians are Christian, although with a seriously defective theology. So too this does not negate the Christianity of the Orthodox but bespeaks, from the Reformed perspective, a less than thorough working out of the entailments of sin and the sovereign purposes of God.

Compared with Rome, how far away from Protestantism is Orthodoxy?

From our discussion it is clear that there are ways in which Orthodoxy is closer to classic Protestantism than is Rome. Both Orthodoxy and Protestantism have this in common, that they were forced into separation from the Roman church. Both agree in their opposition to the claims of the Papacy. The centralization of the church at Rome is foreign to the ecclesiology of both Orthodox and Reformed churches. Most important is their joint refusal to countenance the Roman church's belief that the Pope can make infallible pronouncements when speaking *ex cathedra*. In keeping with this, the structure of the Orthodox churches is much closer to the Reformed, especially to the Anglican. The Orthodox recognition of the parity of all believers, and the autonomy and autocephalous nature of local churches is far closer to Reformed polity than is the Roman hierarchy.

Following from this, there is in the East not the same conglomeration of authoritative and infallible dogmas as there is in Roman Catholicism. Orthodoxy has a relatively minimal basis of official doctrine. The seven ecumenical councils are as close to an authoritative body of dogma as can be. The Reformed agree with all these councils, except probably with Nicaea II's pronouncement on icons, although the two positions are closer than often supposed. Insofar as there is less dogmatic baggage in Orthodoxy than in Rome, there are correspondingly fewer obstacles between the Orthodox and the Reformed than there are between the Reformed and Rome.

Thirdly, the Orthodox stress on the Bible, albeit understood differently than in Reformed theology, opens up a large commonality of approach. Moreover, while there has never been a Calvinist Pope (yet), there has been a Calvinist Patriarch of Constantinople, although his Calvinism was soon repudiated.

There are, however, ways in which Orthodoxy is further removed from Reformed theology than is the Roman church. Protestantism and Roman Catholicism share an understanding of the trinity that has differed markedly from the East. The East's stance on the *filioque* controversy, and its distinction between the essence of God and the divine energies lends itself to a different form of piety. Reformed and evangelical faith is centred in Christ, and his death and resurrection; the East has more of a focus on the Holy Spirit. These differences over piety and the Christian life stem from the disagreements on the trinity.[15]

Again, in worship and liturgy, Orthodoxy gives a centrality to the visual in stark contrast to the Reformed church's insistence on the Word. Whereas in Reformed churches preaching has been the driving force, in the East icons and the comprehensive symbolism of the temple and altar has given the ritual and visual actions of the clergy prime place.

Recent dialogue and future prospects

In recent decades, the door has opened to genuine dialogue between East and West. While the Orthodox consider themselves to be the one holy catholic apostolic church, with the burden on all other churches to return to the Orthodox faith, they have nevertheless participated in ecumenical discussions with Rome and Protestant churches. The Eastern churches have taken part in the ecumenical movement of the past century, including the World Council of Churches. The Patriarch of Constantinople, Joachim III, issued an encyclical in 1902 stating that a rapprochement with the various Christian churches 'is highly desirable and necessary'. This process has been accelerated by the dispersion of many Orthodox to the West following the Bolshevik revolution. Discussions have taken place on two levels: firstly, there has been closer interaction in order to facilitate mutual awareness, while secondly there has also been substantive theological discussion. In 1965 the mutual anathemas of 1054 were withdrawn by Pope Paul VI and Patriarch Athenagoras I of Constantinople, although these anathemas were originally personal, not theological or ecclesiastical, and did not prevent joint participation in the councils of Lyons (1274) and Florence (1439). The International Theological Dialogue has issued a number of Agreed Statements between Eastern Orthodoxy and Roman Catholicism. Other Agreed Statements have been drawn up with Lutheran churches.[16] More success has been achieved

---

[15] See G. Bray, 'The Filioque Clause in History and Theology,' *TB* 34 (1983), 91–144.

[16] See S. N. Gundry, *Three Views on Eastern Orthodoxy and Evangelicalism* (Grand Rapids: Zondervan, 2004), 62–64.

in discussions with the Oriental Orthodox Churches – Copts, Syrians, Indians, Armenians – and it is now realized that the differences between these churches and the Eastern Orthodox are more verbal than substantive. In turn, the Anglicans have frequently had cordial relations with the Eastern Orthodox, due to contacts brought about by presence of the British Empire in the Mediterranean. However, the ordination of women by the Church of England places a barrier in the way.[17]

At this point we note the 1991 Agreement between Orthodox and Reformed Churches on the *filioque*.[18] This historic agreement is limited in its scope. The Western representatives were from the World Alliance of Reformed Churches, one particular strand of Reformed theology. There was no one from other Protestant bodies, nor any from Rome. Moreover, the documents indicate there was no adequate representation of Augustinian trinitarianism. The Reformed participants were already sympathetic – though not uncritically – to the East. The leading figure, T.F. Torrance, had already adopted the Athanasian soteriology, refracted through his reading of Calvin and Barth, and his interaction with modern physics. Its importance is underlined by the fact that the Greek Church had invited the fourteen other Orthodox communions to participate. Its weakness is that there were no representatives present committed to the Augustinian model. It is an agreement among those predisposed to agree. It is less than a major ecumenical breakthrough. To say, with Gary Deddo, that 'in principle the 1,000-year-old schism over the *filioque* has been resolved' is a trifle premature, since the schism was between Orthodoxy and *Rome*, not the World Alliance of Reformed Churches![19]

---

[17] K. Parry, *The Blackwell Dictionary of Eastern Christianity* (R. R. K. Ware; Oxford: Blackwell, 2001), 172–75.

[18] For the official text, see Thomas F. Torrance, *Theological Dialogue Between Orthodox and Reformed Churches, Volume 2* (Edinburgh: Scottish Academic Press, 1993), 219–32; or 'Agreed Statement on the Holy Trinity Between the Orthodox Church and the World Alliance of Refomed Churches,' *Touchstone* 5/1 (Winter 1992 1992), 22–23. For commentary on the agreement, T. F. Torrance, *Trinitarian Perspectives: Toward Doctrinal Agreement* (Edinburgh: T.&T. Clark, 1994), 110–43.

That said, the agreement does represent progress. Torrance's commentary indicates a thorough recognition of all the main theological parameters of classic trinitarian doctrine: the *homoousion* of all three persons; their full mutual indwelling, the *perichoresis*; the equal ultimacy of the one being of God and the three persons; the rejection of an impersonal divine essence and a concurrent recognition of the living, dynamic, personal being of God; the order and relationality of the persons. As a result, the monopatrism of Photios is undermined and, at the same time, any idea of subordinationism eliminated. The procession of the Holy Spirit is seen in the light of the full homoousial and perichoretic relations of the three persons in the one divine essence. So the Spirit proceeds from the being of God, inseparably from the Father and the Son.

The way ahead
The basic foundational agreements between the Reformed and the Orthodox on the trinity (albeit from differing paradigms), Christology, and the use of Scripture justify – indeed, require – discussion. In turn, it alerts the Reformed churches to root their preaching and teaching in the centre of the historic Christian faith rather than on ever more minute 'distinctives' that separate this or that branch of the Reformed from each other.

On the other hand, the existence of basic disagreements – synergism, the role of departed saints, and the authority of the church in particular – requires caution and forbids compromise. The great truths rediscovered at the Reformation cannot be bartered away. It is incumbent on the Reformed to demonstrate that these are entailments of the classic creeds and ecumenical councils.

The chances of lasting agreement with the East are not bright. Some of the Orthodox regard Augustine as effectively a heretic, with persistent and pervasive errors, estranged from the mind of the church, a speculator rather than a witness to the

---

[19] Gary W. Deddo, 'The Holy Spirit in T.F. Torrance's Theology,' in *The Promise of Trinitarian Theology: Theologians in Dialogue with T.F. Torrance*, Elmer M. Colyer (Lanham: Rowman & Littlefield Publishers, Inc., 2001), 107.

apostolic tradition, whose retractations were simply rejections of the errors of his youth and a mere *pro forma* literary device. Indeed, it has been claimed that his teachings were 'the wages of deception.'[20] In consequence, the Western church thereafter has been corrupted. This is quite a contrast to the Emperor Justinian's listing him, at the fifth ecumenical council, among the Fathers who the Eastern church followed! This points to sober realism concerning future possibilities. As Ware has said, 'the effects of an alienation which has lasted for more than nine centuries cannot be quickly undone.'[21] Whatever joint participation by individuals from East and West takes place, or increasingly eclectic approaches are introduced by theological textbooks, the real differences and disagreements between East and West cannot be diminished. They must be faced in all honesty and seriousness.

---

[20] Michael Azkoul, 'Saint Photios and the Filioque', in Photios, *On the Mystagogy of the Holy Spirit*, 25.

[21] T. Ware, *The Orthodox Church* (London: Penguin Books, 1969), 11.

12

The Long Term Perspective
(John 17)

In the face of the entrenched and seemingly intractable divisions of the Christian church, it is salutary to remind ourselves of Jesus' prayer that one day his church will demonstrate a visible unity in the truth. In his prayer in John 17, he gives us the closest access we can possibly have to the mind of God. Here the incarnate Son communes with the Father in the Holy Spirit. As the church recognizes, Jesus of Nazareth is the eternal Son of God in the flesh, in unbroken personal identity with the Logos who made all things, who was in the beginning with God and who is God. When we overhear his prayer to the Father we are eavesdropping on his relation to the Father that reaches into eternity.

Jesus prays for future believers

[20]I do not ask for these only, but also for those who will believe in me through their word.

Until this point, Jesus' prayer has been for the disciples present there and then, who had believed his word and followed him through thick and thin. He has prayed for them, particularly in view of the sorrow and turmoil they were about to undergo. He spoke of his departure and the persecution that would follow. He asked that they be sanctified in the truth, which is the word of God (v. 19). Now Jesus prays for future disciples, who were to believe through the preaching of the gospel by the apostles. He prays for the effectiveness of the apostolic witness. Jesus regards the church of the future as already present. His word, preached by the apostles and those who were to follow, is God's powerful means to call his church into existence. At the same time the apostles and the preachers are, as his disciples, part of the church themselves. Here, in embryo, is the mutually connected relationship between Scripture and the church. There may be a hint of a comparison between the Jewish character of the present church and the predominantly Gentile nature of the future church, if, as is sometimes supposed, the Fourth Gospel was written to a Jewish audience in and around Ephesus.

Jesus prays for his church's unity

> [21]...that they may all be one, just as you, Father, are in me, and I in you, that they also may be in us, so that the world may believe that you have sent me. [22]The glory that you have given me I have given to them, that they may be one even as we are one, [23]I in them and you in me, that they may become perfectly one, so that the world may know that you sent me and loved them even as you loved me.

Here Jesus focuses his prayer to the Father on the unity of his church. It is important to grasp precisely in what this unity consists.

The unity of the church is based on the revelation of the Father in the Son. The Father is in the Son, and the Son is in the Father. There is a mutual coinherence (indwelling) of the Father and the Son. The Father and the Son, together with the Holy Spirit, are in indivisible oneness. This union cannot be broken. The unity of the church, for which Jesus prays, is grounded on this union. It is infinitely greater than any other human union. It cannot be ended or destroyed.

This unity is observable: it should be seen: 'that the world may believe that you sent me.'

This is not identical to institutional unity, although that may be part of it if it is observable. Certainly the focus is not the institutional. Neither is it the same as the lowest common denominator theology that sweeps under the carpet any significant differences by a mere form of words. The trenchant warning of 2 John 10–11 precludes the toleration of heresy and so deters us from succumbing to ecumenical spin doctors and public relations gurus. Since the unity Jesus describes is grounded in the nature of the triune God, it follows that it is real and substantial. It is a unity that is present but it must be brought to perfection in the future (v. 23). Some might think that this is a unity only to be realized in heaven? This cannot be so, for Jesus prays for its effects here and now in the world; 'that the world may believe' (vv. 21b, 23b). The world can only believe if it sees the reality of the unity. It has an immensely powerful evangelistic force.

Is this unity a spiritual unity? Yes, it is spiritual since it comes from God, specifically from the Holy Spirit. Jesus prays for it; it is not the result of human effort by itself. It comes from the Father and the Son by the Holy Spirit. It is a gift of the Holy Spirit. It means we 'actually participate in the unity of God' (Newbigin). It is thus a living unity, for God is a living being, a dynamic communion of three persons in indivisible union. Consequently, the unity Jesus describes is more than simply being one in outlook or purpose; that could be said of a cricket team or an army. Here there is an interchange of the lifegiving energy of the life of God – leading to harmony in the church, a dynamic, living harmony.

However, is this unity **only** *a spiritual unity?* No, there is a visibility to it. It is a visible unity that is to exist here and now in this world. The world will be able to see it. There is an invisible source, the Holy Spirit, but a visible reality, which will lead to the world believing in Jesus.

Does this unity eliminate diversity? No, since it is grounded in the unity of God, the Father, the Son, and the Holy Spirit – the indivisible trinity – it is a unity-in-diversity and diversity-in-unity. God's unity exists in his diversity. The Father, the Son, and the Holy Spirit indwell one another in love. God is three irreducible persons, one indivisible being. Hence, the unity of the church is a personal and relational indivisible unity, from eternity.

Moreover, it is *a loving unity*, for the three trinitarian persons love perfectly in union. The Father loves the Son and has given all things into his hands, bringing his kingdom into effect with the Son in centre stage; the Son honours and glorifies the Father; the Holy Spirit does not speak of himself but brings glory to the Son. The Father is glorified in the exaltation and enthronement of his Son. As the three trinitarian persons delight in honouring the others in the unity of the indivisible trinity, so the church's unity described here is such as to promote and enhance the integrity of its parts.

It is *a personal unity*, reflecting the personal nature of God and of man made in his image. It is unity in truth, for God is truth, and his word by which we are sanctified is unbreakable truth.

It is *a differentiated unity* (the Father sent the Son, only the Son went to the cross – although the Father and the Holy Spirit were inseparably involved – the Father and the Son sent the Holy Spirit, but only the Spirit came at Pentecost). The works of the trinity are inseparable, while to one person a particular work is properly attributed.

This unity towards which the church is called is an imperative. The Son prays to the Father in the Holy Spirit for precisely this. It is not a matter peripheral or optional. To avoid it is idolatry; at best sectarian. The fragmentation of Protestantism is indefensible. This unity is grounded in truth and love (cf. Eph. 4:12). Doctrine matters, and so does the visible unity of the church. That too is doctrine.

This unity is certain to come

Jesus prays to the Father for it: how can it fail? His prayer is a request. When he prays it is not with the caveats that we must use – 'may such and such be, *if it is your will.*' The Son's will coincides with the Father's, for God has one indivisible will. The incarnate Christ's human will itself has not the slightest variance from his divine will, for the Son assumed into personal union the human nature and all that it entails. This is part of Jesus' continuing high priestly work. Moreover, Jesus' original disciples will share his glory (vv. 22-23) – the manifestation of God's character; the reality that gives rise to the Orthodox doctrine of deification. This sharing the glory of God in Jesus Christ is precisely in order to bring the church to complete unity.

Love, not evangelistic technique, will convince the world that the Father sent the Son. It is the unity that comes from this love that displays the relation of the Father, the Son and the Holy Spirit, and reflects the holy trinity in this world. Paul describes in Romans 11:25ff the future conversion of Israel as like life from the dead. The Jew-Gentile division, and the hostility that goes with it, will in Christ be broken down visibly just as it has already in reality by the cross. This argues that the return of Christ will be some way into the future.

Finally, in verses 24-26, Jesus prays for all the elect, that they may be where he is, and that they may see his glory which he had before creation. Here he encompasses by his prayer the church's progress into the fulness of the knowledge of God the holy trinity; the love of the Father for the Son in the Holy Spirit will be in his church and grow in it. God will dwell with and in his people – the fulfilment of his covenant promise.

What this mandates of us

Jesus' high priestly prayer requires of us prayer for the unity of the church, a firm commitment to the truth of the gospel, a readiness to remove misunderstandings, a need to recognize what are genuine disagreements, an onus to persuade, and patience.

Prayer. Jesus our high priest is our representative and example. He identified himself with us in his incarnation so as to be our head, one with us in our nature. In turn, we are united to him, conformed to his image. Our prayers are to be conformed to his. He prays for the unity of his disciples; so should we, as a matter of great urgency, with persistence and faith.

A firm commitment to the truth of the gospel. Since the unity of the church is grounded in the truth of God, who is truth, prayer for and movement towards such visibly exhibited unity must also be fully in conformity with the truth of the gospel of Christ. Therefore, this is a long and winding road. There are no short cuts: any agreements at the expense of real doctrinal substance are not merely to be avoided; they are counter-productive.

A readiness to remove misunderstandings. So many controversies involve two or more parties talking past each other, failing to place themselves in the position of the other. In this way, cheap and easy targets can be produced for attack. However, the net result is serious misunderstanding. When this happens, both sides are diminished in their appreciation of their own position, let alone that of the other.

A need to recognize genuine disagreements. When points of misunder-standing are identified and corrected, we are then in a better position to see precisely where the real areas of disagreement lie. Once these are seen, the true differences between the two communions – in this case, the Reformed Churches and Orthodoxy – can be appreciated.

An onus to persuade. If we are convinced we have been brought into an understanding of the truth of God, it is appropriate to seek to persuade other Christians. If, in the process, we have passed through the steps outlined above, we will be in a better position to effect positive change.

Patience. As we stated at the end of chapter 11, the road ahead is a difficult one. However, there will surely come a time when, in accordance with the prayer of Jesus Christ, our great high priest, his people on earth will visibly demonstrate the unity they have in him, and so – in conjunction with this – the world will believe that the Father sent him.

Glossary

ANHYPOSTASIA
The dogma that the human nature of Christ has no personal existence of its own, apart from the union into which it was assumed in the incarnation. This means the Son of God did not unite himself with a human being (which would entail two separate personal entities) but a human nature.

ANOMIANS
Prominent in the mid-fourth century, led by Aetius and Eunomius, the Anomians followed broadly in the path of Arius, holding that the Son was like the Father but not of the identical being, since he is inferior and not from eternity, created by the Father to be his minister in the creation of the world.

APOLLINARIS, APOLLINARIANISM
Apollinaris taught that the eternal Logos took the place of the human soul in the incarnate Christ. His teaching was condemned at Constantinople I (381 AD), since it entailed a less than fully

human Christ, threatening the gospel since if Christ had not
been fully human he would not have been able to save us.

APOPHATIC
The dominant idea in the Eastern church that we know God
primarily through mystical contemplation rather than through
positive propositions or intellectual activity. Indeed, we are to
empty our minds of logical and intellectual categories and in
ignorance engage in prayer.

APPROPRIATIONS
Since God is one, all three persons act together in all God's
works. Yet each work is particularly attributable (appropriated)
to one person. Only the Son became incarnate, only the Holy
Spirit came at Pentecost. This does not deny that the other two
persons were also involved in these acts.

ARIANS
Those who held the same or similar view to Arius (c.276–337), who
taught that the Son was a creature who came into being at some
point, and was the agent through whom the world was made, but
was not co-eternal with the Father, nor of the same being.

ATTRIBUTES
Particular characteristics of God, such as holiness, sovereignty,
justice, goodness, mercy and love.

AUTOCEPHALOUS
A term applied to a church that has full rights to determine
everything that happens within its jurisdiction, including the
appointment and enthronement of its chief bishop.

AUTONOMOUS
An autonomous church has full rights to determine everything
within its jurisdiction, except the appointment and enthronement
of its chief bishop.

BEING
Something that *is*, an existent.

CATAPHATIC
In Orthodox theology a cataphatic approach is contrasted to apophatic theology, which is based on negations. Instead, cataphatic theology consists of positive affirmations. According to Dionysius the Areopagite, it leads us to some knowledge of God, but is an imperfect way. The perfect way, the only way which is fitting in regard to God, who is of His very nature unknowable, is the apophatic method – which leads us finally to total ignorance.

CHRISTOLOGICAL
Teaching relating to the person of Christ.

CODEX VATICANUS
One of the main and earliest NT codices, containing the majority of the NT text. Its name derives from its location, in the Vatican Library.

CONSUBSTANTIALITY
The dogma that the Son and the Holy Spirit are of the same substance as the Father. This means all three persons are fully God, and the whole God.

DEIFICATION
According to the Eastern church, the goal of salvation is to be made God. This the Holy Spirit effects in us. It involves no blurring of the Creator-creature distinction but rather focuses on the union and communion we are given by God in which, as Peter says, we are made partakers of the divine nature (2 Peter 1:4).

DIPTYCHS
Ancient hinged, two-leaved writing tablets kept by each Patriarch, containing the names of those other Patriarchs he

regarded as orthodox. To exclude a name from the diptychs was
to declare that the one excluded was out of communion.

DOCETISM
The early heresy that Christ's humanity was apparent and not
real. The term is a derivative of the Greek verb *dokein*, to seem
or appear. This view is heretical since if Christ were not fully
man, we could not be saved since only a perfect, sinless man can
atone for the sins of man.

DOXOLOGY
An ascription of praise, normally to God.

DYOTHELETISM
The doctrine that there are two wills in the incarnate Christ.
This supposes that will is a property of the natures of Christ
(divine and human) rather than the person. It in no way entails
any idea that these wills are in conflict.

ECONOMIC TRINITY
The trinity as revealed in creation and salvation, acting in our
world, in human history.

ENERGIES
According to Gregory Palamas, the essence of God is
unknowable. We have to do with God's energies, his powers at
work in the creation.

ENHYPOSTASIA
The dogma promulgated at the Second Council of Constantinople
(553) that the eternal Son is the person of the incarnate Christ,
a human nature conceived by the Holy Spirit in the womb of
the Virgin Mary being taken into union. Behind this lies the
Biblical teaching than man is made in the image of God and
thus ontologically compatible with God on a creaturely level.

Thus the Son of God provides the personhood for the assumed human nature.

ESCHATOLOGICAL
Relating to the last things, from the Greek word *eschatos* (last).

ESSENCE OF GOD
What God *is*, his being (from *esse*, to be).

EUDOXIUS
A mid-fourth century heretic who held that the Son worships the Father.

EUNOMIUS
A fourth century heretic who, like Arius, believed that the Son was created and so was not of the same being as the Father.

EUTYCHIANISM
Eutyches so stressed the unity of Christ's person that his humanity was swamped by his deity. This threatened salvation for if Christ was not fully human we could not be saved. Eutyches was condemned as a heretic at the Council of Chalcedon (451 AD).

FILIOQUE
The Niceno-Constantinopolitan creed (381 AD) stated that the Holy Spirit proceeds 'from the Father'. Later the Western church added a phrase 'and the Son' (*filioque*), which has been the source of ongoing controversy and division ever since.

GENERATION (ETERNAL)
The unique property of the Son in relation to the Father. Since God is eternal, the relation between the Father and the Son is eternal. This is not to be understood on the basis of human generation or begetting, since God is spiritual. It is beyond our capacity to understand.

HERMENEUTIC
A principle of interpretation that governs how texts or realities are to be understood.

HYPOSTASIS
A Greek word meaning 'something with a concrete existence'. In terms of the trinity it came to mean 'person'. Thus, by the end of the fourth century controversy, it referred to what is distinct in God, the way he is three, while *ousia* was reserved for the one being of God.

HOMOOUSIOS
'Of the same being,' meaning that the Son, and the Spirit, are of the same identical being as the Father.

HOMOIOUSIOS
'Of similar or like being,' a term used by many who were afraid the Creed of Nicea identified the Father and the Son. Many of these *homoiousians* gave their support to the settlement of the trinitarian controversy in 381.

ICONOCLASTS
The iconoclasts were opposed to images of Christ or the saints, since they believed these to be in breach of the second commandment. They charged their opponents, the iconodules, with Nestorianism, since it appeared to them that an image of Christ represented an abstraction of his human nature and so threatened the unity of his person. As a result of the eighth century controversy, iconoclasm was declared heretical at Nicea II (787 AD).

ICONODULES
The iconodules defended images on the basis that the incarnation mandated them. While images were proscribed in the Old Testament, now that God had appeared *as man*, visual representations of Christ and the saints were required; to

oppose them was to fall into Manichaeism, whereby matter was conceived as inherently evil.

IMMANENT TRINITY (see ontological trinity)
The trinity in itself, or the three persons as they relate to one another without regard to creation.

LITURGY
The order of worship in a church service, usually in the form of written prayers, responses and ascriptions of praise to God.

MACEDONIANS
The putative followers of Macedonius, Bishop of Constantinople from 342 until his deposition in 360, who denied the deity of the Holy Spirit. Macedonius himself may not have shared these views.

MANICHAEISM
An extreme form of ontological dualism, holding that there are two co-equal realities, good and evil.

MARCELLIANS
Marcellus of Ancyra held that God is one *hypostasis* in one *ousia*. This appeared little different than modalism. The three are names only. The flesh of Christ will be discarded permanently at the end of his reign (1 Cor. 15:28). In rebuttal, the Niceno-Constantinopolitan creed, propounded at Constantinople I (381 AD) states that Christ's kingdom 'shall have no end'.

MODALISM
The blurring or erasing of the real, eternal and irreducible distinctions between the three persons of the trinity. This danger can arise when the unity of God, or the identity in being of the three, is overstressed at the expense of the personal distinctions. It can also surface where there is a pervasive stress on salvation history, so as to eliminate any reference to eternal

realities. When that is so, God's revelation in human history as the Father, the Son, and the Holy Spirit is no longer held to reveal who he is eternally in himself.

MONARCHY/ MONARCHIANISM
Sole rule, the rule of one. It refers to the unity of God, his oneness (cf. Deut 6:4). In the Eastern church it was common to base the monarchy in the Father. However, this could often lead to the subordination of the Son and the Spirit, or else to modalism by which the other persons were reduced to little more than attributes.

MONISTIC
Reduction of reality to one principle.

MONOENERGISM
The idea that the incarnate Christ has only one principle of action. This is an aspect of monotheletism (see below) and shares its failure to do justice to the human nature of Christ, thus threatening the gospel, for if Christ is not fully human we cannot be saved.

MONOPHYSITISM
The Monophysites stressed 'the one incarnate nature of God the Word' but in doing so they threatened the integrity of Christ's human nature.

MONOTHEISM
Belief in only one God.

MONOTHELETISM
The idea, rejected by the church, that in the incarnate Christ there was only one will. The reason for its rejection was that will was regarded as a predicate of the two natures. If there was only one will, the human nature of Christ would be eroded or worse.

NATURE OF GOD
What God is *like* (love, just, holy, omnipotent et. al.). These particular aspects of his nature are termed attributes. In the fourth century the nature of God was sometimes used as a synonym for God's essence or being.

NEOPLATONISM
A movement in the third and fourth centuries that built on and adapted certain aspects of Platonic philosophy together with elements from other sources, including Christianity. This influenced to varying degrees Clement of Alexandria, Origen and the pre-Christian Augustine. How far the latter extricated himself from the impact of neoPlatonism is a continued subject of debate.

NESTORIANISM
The followers of Nestorius, concerned to stress the reality of Christ's humanity, undermined the unity of his person. By focusing excessively on the two natures of Christ, it appeared that deity and humanity were separate, side-by-side, with no union between them, and so no incarnation. Nestorius was condemned as a heretic at the Council of Ephesus (431 AD).

ONTOLOGY
Relating to being, that which is.

ONTOLOGICAL TRINITY (see immanent trinity)
The trinity in itself, or the three persons as they relate to one another without regard to creation.

ORDER (*taxis*)
The relations between the three persons disclose an order, the Father begets the Son, and sends the Holy Spirit in or through the Son. These relations are never reversed.

ORDO SALUTIS
The order of salvation, or the way we are brought to salvation by the Holy Spirit and kept there. It encompasses effectual call-

ing, regeneration, faith and repentance, justification, adoption, sanctification, perseverance and glorification, all of which are received in union with Christ.

OUSIA

Being (that which is). Since there is only one God, he has only one *ousia*. The word refers to the one being of God. However, before the trinitarian crisis of the fourth century was resolved this word had a range of meanings and so there was much confusion. See chapter 5.

PELAGIANISM

The idea taught by Pelagius in the early fifth century that fallen man could of himself respond to the gospel, without the help of divine grace. This was rejected as heresy at the Council of Carthage in 418 AD.

PERICHORESIS

The mutual indwelling of the three persons of the trinity in the one being of God.

PERSONS

The Father, the Son and the Holy Spirit. There has been much debate about whether 'person' is an appropriate or adequate term for the three, in view of its modern usage which entails separate individuals. However, no proposed alternative has succeeded in establishing itself, for they invariably yield a less than personal view of God.

PHYSIS

A Greek word, meaning 'nature'.

PNEUMATOLOGICAL

Relating to the Holy Spirit.

PNEUMATOMACHII

The 'fighters against the Spirit' who, while accepting the deity of the Son did not hold that the Holy Spirit is God. Their rise to prominence in the fourth century occasioned the Council of Constantinople (381) which resolved the trinitarian crisis and declared this view heretical.

PROCESSIONS
The eternal begetting of the Son, the eternal procession of the Holy Spirit. These are matched by the *missions*, the historical sending of the Son and the Spirit. The Eastern church considers it an error to call the Father's begetting of the Son a procession. For the East, this is a typically Western confusion of the Father and the Son.

PROCESSION (eternal)
The eternal relation of the Holy Spirit to the Father (and to the Son, under Western eyes).

PROPERTIES
Paternity, filiation, active spiration, passive spiration, innascibility.

PROSŌPON
A Greek word meaning 'face', it was used in the ancient world as an attempt to describe human beings, with the connotation of a mask worn by an actor. As trinitarian and Christological doctrine developed, *hypostasis* came into use to refer to the human person and *prosōpon* fell by the wayside.

RELATIONS
The relation between the Father and the Son, the Son and the Father, the Father /the Son and the Holy Spirit, the Holy Spirit and the Father/Son. These are considered differently in the Eastern church than in the West. The relations between the three persons differ, in that the Father is first, the Son second, the Spirit third. The Father begets the Son and emits the Spirit, he neither is begotten nor proceeds: the Son is begotten and (according to the West) shares with the Father in the emission or

sending of the Spirit, and does not proceed: the Spirit proceeds from the Father and (or through) the Son, but does not beget nor is begotten. These relations are irreversible.

SABELLIANS
The followers of the third-century heretic, Sabellius, who taught that the Father, the Son, and the Holy Spirit were merely three ways in which the one God revealed himself.

SARX
A Greek word, meaning 'flesh'.

SOCIAL DOCTRINE OF THE TRINITY
An understanding of the trinity that sees the three persons as a community, interacting with one another. Its basic premise is the priority of the three persons over the one being (essence).

SOPHIA
Wisdom. This is a theme developed by Russian Orthodox theology in the last two centuries. It has had an appeal for feminist theologians, on the irrelevant basis that in Greek *sophia* is a feminine noun.

SOTERIOLOGY
The doctrine of salvation (from the Greek *sōtēr*, savior).

SPIRATION
The defining characteristic of the Holy Spirit, who proceeds (or is breathed out) by the Father. The West insists that the Spirit also proceeds from the Son (the *filioque* clause).

SUBORDINATIONISM
A teaching that the Son and the Holy Spirit are of lesser being or status than the Father.

SUBSTANCE

The 'stuff' which is God, the one identical substance in which the Father, the Son and the Spirit all participate fully and absolutely. The essence of God is what God *is* (from the Latin *esse*, to be).

TERTIUM QUID

Used in this book in reference to the Christological controversies, referring to the claim that the Nestorians so stressed the distinctiveness of the two natures of Christ, even to the point of apparent separation, that speech about the person of Christ could only mean 'a third thing'.

THEANDRIC

A term denoting that an entity is composed of both divine and human elements.

THEOTOKOS (God-bearer)

The term points to the fact that the Virgin Mary gave birth to the Son of God incarnate. It also entails his personal identity with the eternal Son. This term Nestorius and his followers rejected, preferring *Christotokos* (Christ-bearer). In so doing, they jeopardized the unity of Christ's person.

TRANSUBSTANTIATION

The claim that in the Lord's Supper, the bread and wine undergo a change of substance and become the actual physical body and blood of Christ. In the Roman Catholic Church this is explained by Aristotelian philosophical categories (the *substance* – what the thing is – is changed, while the *accidents* –what is adventitious to the thing, what the thing appears to be – remains the same). However, in the Eastern Church there has been no attempt to explain what happens, for it is regarded as a mystery.

TRITHEISM

The belief that there are three gods. An exaggerated stress on the three persons can, it is claimed, lead to a belief that there are three gods, not one.

UNBEGOTTEN / BEGOTTEN

The property of the Son is that he is begotten by the Father from eternity. The Father is unbegotten. Begetting is qualitatively different than creation, refers to the eternal relations of the Father and the Son, distinguishes the Son from the creatures, and is beyond our capacity to understand.

Bibliography

Abdullah Yusuf Ali. *The Meaning of the Holy Qur'an*. Beltsville, Maryland: Amana Publications, 1997.

Aquinas, Thomas. *Summa Theologica*.

Athanasius. *Letters to Serapion on the Holy Spirit*.

Athanasius. *On the Decrees of the Synod of Nicaea*.

Athanasius. *To the Antiochenes*.

Augustine. *De Trinitate*.

Augustine. *Letter 169*.

Ayres, Lewis. *Nicaea and its Legacy: An Approach to Fourth-Century Trinitarian Theology*. New York: Oxford University Press, 2004.

Barnes, Michel René. *The Power of God: Δύναμις in Gregory of Nyssa's Trinitarian Theology*. Washington, D.C.: The Catholic University of America Press, 2001.

Barraclough, Geoffrey. *The Medieval Papacy*. New York: W.W. Norton Company, 1979.

Barth, Karl. *Church Dogmatics*.

Bartos, Emil. *Deification in Eastern Orthodox Theology: An Evaluation and Critique of the Theology of Dumitru Staniloae*. Carlisle: Paternoster, 1999.

Basil of Caesarea. *Letters*.

Basil of Caesarea. *On the Holy Spirit*.

Bavinck, Herman. *The Doctrine of God*. Edinburgh: Banner of Truth, rpr, 1977.

Bavinck, Herman. *Reformed Dogmatics*. Translated by John Bolt, John Vriend. Grand Rapids: Baker, 2004.

Beckwith, Roger. *The Old Testament Canon of the New Testament Church: And Its Background in Early Judaism*. Grand Rapids: Eerdmans, 1985.

Benz, Ernst. *The Orthodox Church: Its Thought and Life*. Garden City, New York: Doubleday, 1963.

Bilz, J. *Die Trinitätslehre Des Johannes von Damaskus*. Paderborn, 1909.

Binns, John. *An Introduction to the Christian Orthodox Churches*. Cambridge: Cambridge University Press, 2002.

Blowers, Paul M. *On the Cosmic Mystery of Jesus Christ: Selected Writings of St. Maximus the Confessor*. Crestwood, New York: St. Vladimir's Seminary Press, 2003.

Bobrinskoy, Boris. *The Mystery of the Trinity: Trinitarian Experience and Vision in the Biblical and Patristic Tradition.* Anthony P. Gythiel. Crestwood, New York: St. Vladimir's Seminary Press, 1999.

Bonner, Gerald. *Augustine and Recent Research on Pelagius.* Villanova: Villanova University Press, 1972.

Bonner, Gerald. "How Pelagian Was Pelagius?" *Studia Patristica* 9 (1966): 350–58.

Bonner, Gerald. *St. Augustine of Hippo: Life and Controversies.* Norwich: Canterbury Press, 1986.

Bray, Gerald. "The Filioque Clause in History and Theology." *TB* 34 (1983): 91–144.

Brown, P. "Pelagius and His Supporters: Aims and Environment." *JTS* 21 (1970): 56–72.

Brown, P. *Augustine of Hippo: a Biography.* London: Faber and Faber, 1967.

Bruce. F.F. *The Spreading Flame: The Rise and Progress of Christianity from Its First Beginnings Until the Conversion of the English.* London: Paternoster Press, 1958.

Bulgakov, Sergei Nikolaevich. *Le Paraclet.* Constantin Andronikof. Paris: Aubier, 1946.

Cabasilas, Nicholas. *A Commentary on the Divine Liturgy.* J.M. Hussey. London: SPCK, 1960.

Cabasilas, Nicholas. *Life in Christ.* Margaret Lisney. London: Janus, 1995.

Calvin, John. *Commentaries on the First Book of Moses Called Genesis.*

Calvin, John. *Institute.*

Calvin, John. *Calvin: Theological Treatises.* J.K.S. Reid. Philadelphia: Westminster Press, 1954.

Catechism of the Catholic Church. London: Geoffrey Chapman, 1994.

Crouzel, H. *Origen.* Edinburgh: T. and T. Clark, 1989.

Chrysostom, John. *Homilies on 1 Corinthians.*

Chrysostom, John. *Homilies on 1 Thessalonians.*

Chrysostom, John. *Homilies on the Epistle to the Romans.*

Chrysostom, John. *Homilies on Hebrews.*

Chrysostom, John. *Homilies on Philippians.*

Chul Won Suh. *The Creation Mediatorship of Jesus Christ.* Amsterdam: Rodopi, 1982.

Clément, Olivier. *You Are Peter: An Orthodox Theologian's Reflection on the Exercise of Papal Primacy.* New York: New City Press, 2003.

Conticello, Vassa.S. "Pseudo-Cyril's De Sacrosancte Trinitate: a Compilation of Joseph the Philosopher." *OCP* 61 (1995): 117–29.

Craigie, Peter C. *The Book of Deuteronomy.* Grand Rapids: Eerdmans, 1976.

Cyprian. *On the Unity of the Church.*

Daley, B.E. "Leontius of Byzantium: a Critical Edition of His Works, with Prolegomena." D.Phil. dissertation. Oxford University, 1978.

Davis, Leo Donald. *The First Seven Ecumenical Councils (325–787)*. Collegeville, Minnesota: The Liturgical Press, 1990.

Deddo, Gary W. 'The Holy Spirit in T.F. Torrance's Theology' in Bruce M. Colyer (ed.), *The Promise of Trinitarian Theology: Theologians in Dialogue with T.F. Torrance*. Lanham: Rouman and Littlefield, 2001.

de Margerie S.J., Bertrand. *The Christian Trinity in History*. Edmund J. Fortman S.J. Petersham. Massachusetts: St. Bede's Publications, 1982.

Elert, Werner. *Eucharist and Church Fellowship in the first four Centuries*. St. Louis, Missouri: Concordia Publishing House, 2003.

Eusebius. *History of the Church*.

Every George. *The Byzantine Patriarchate, 451–1204*. London: SPCK, 1947.

Fairbairn, Donald. *Eastern Orthodoxy Through Western Eyes*. Louisville: Westminster John Knox Press, 2002.

Farrell, Joseph P. "Introduction." *Saint Photios: Mystagogy of the Holy Spirit*. Brookline, Massachusetts: Holy Cross Orthodox Press, 1987.

Fedotov, George P. *The Russian Religious Mind*. New York: Harper, 1946.

Ferguson, J. *Pelagius: a Historical and Theological Study*. Cambridge: Cambridge University Press, 1956.

Finney, Paul Corby. *The Invisible God: The Earliest Christians on Art*. New York: Oxford University Press, 1994.

Frend, W.H.C. *The Rise of the Monophysite Movement*. Cambridge: Cambridge University Press, 1972.

Geanakoplos, Deno John. *Byzantium: Church, Society, and Civilzation Seen Through Contemporary Eyes*. Chicago: University of Chicago Press, 1984.

Grant, Robert M. *From Augustus to Constantine: The Rise and Triumph of Christianity in the Roman World*. San Francisco: Harper and Row, 1970.

Green, Michael. *Evangelism in the Early Church*. Grand Rapids: Eerdmans, 1970.

Gregg, Robert C. *Early Arianism – a Way of Salvation*. Philadelphia: Fortress Press, 1981.

Gregory Nazianzen. *Oration on Holy Baptism 40*.

Gregory of Nyssa. *Against Eunomius*.

Gregory Palamas. *The Triads*.

Grillmeier S.J., Aloys. *Christ in Christian Tradition: Volume One: From the Apostolic Age to Chalcedon (451)*. Second, revised. John Bowden. Atlanta: John Knox Press, 1975.

Grillmeier S.J., Aloys. *Christ in Christian Tradition: Volume Two: From the Council of Chalcedon (451) to Gregory the Great (590–604): Part Two: The*

Church of Constantinople in the Sixth Century. Translated by Theresia Hainthaler, John Cawte. London: Mowbray, 1995.

Robert Grosseteste: On the Six Days of Creation: a Translation of the Hexaëmeron by C.F.J. Martin. Auctores Britannici Medii Aevi. Oxford University Press for the British Academy, 1996.

Gundry, S.N. *Three Views on Eastern Orthodoxy and Evangelicalism.* Grand Rapids: Zondervan, 2004.

Gunton, Colin. "Augustine, the Trinity, and the Theological Crisis of the West." *SJT* 43 (1990): 33–58.

Hadjiantoniou, George A. *Protestant Patriarch: The Life of Cyril Lukaris (1572–1638) Patriarch of Constantinople.* Richmond, Virginia: John Knox Press, 1961.

Hanson, R.P.C. *The Search for the Christian Doctrine of God: The Arian Controversy 318–381.* Edinburgh: T.&T. Clark, 1988.

Hapgood, Isabel Florence, comp. and trans. *Service Book of the Holy Orthodox-Catholic Apostolic Church.* 3rd. ed. Brooklyn, New York: Syrian Antiochene Orthodox Archdiocese of New York and All North America, 1956.

Hardy, Edward Roche. *Christology of the Later Fathers.* The Library of Christian Classics. Philadelphia: Westminster Press, 1954.

Harrison, F. "The Nottinghamshire Baptists: Polity." *BQ* 25 (1974): 212–31.

Harrison, R.K. *Leviticus: An Introduction and Commentary.* Leicester: Inter-Varsity Press, 1980.

Harrison, Verna. "Perichoresis in the Greek Fathers." *StVladThQ* 35 (1991): 53–65.

Haugh, R.M. *Photius and the Carolingians: The Trinitarian Controversy.* Belmont, Massachussetts: Norland, 1975.

Hughes, Christopher. *On a Complex Theory of a Simple God: An Investigation in Aquinas' Philosophical Theology.* Ithaca: Cornell University Press, 1989.

Hughes, Philip Edgcumbe. *The True Image: The Origin and Destiny of Man in Christ.* Grand Rapids, Michigan: Eerdmans, 1989.

John of Damascus. *On the Orthodox Faith.*

Kallis, Anastasios. "Orthodox Church." *The Encyclopedia of Christianity.* Ed., E. Fallbusch et. al. Trans. Geoffrey W. Bromiley. Grand Rapids: Eerdmans, 2003. 3:866–68.

Kaspar, Walter, ed. *Lexicon Für Theologie und Kirche.* Freiburg: Herder, 1999.

Kelly, J.N.D. *Early Christian Creeds.* London: Longman, 1972.

Kelly, J.N.D. *Early Christian Doctrines.* London: Adam & Charles Black, 1968.

Kelly, J.N.D. *Golden Mouth: The Story of John Chrysostom - Ascetic, Preacher, Bishop.* Grand Rapids: Baker, 1995.

Kitzinger, E. "The Cult of Images in the Age Before Iconoclasm." *Dumbarton Oaks Papers* 7 (1954): 83–150.

Kotter, Bonifatius, OSB, ed. *Die Schriften Des Johannes von Damaskos: 5 Vols.* Patristische Texte und Studien. Berlin and New York: Walter de Gruyter, 1975.

Laats, Alar. *Doctrines of the Trinity in Eastern and Western Theologies: a Study with Special Reference to K. Barth and V. Lossky.* Frankfurt am Main: Peter Lang, 1999.

Lampe, G.W.H., ed. *A Patristic Greek Lexicon.* Oxford: Clarendon Press, 1961.

Lancel, Serge. *Saint Augustine.* Antonia Nevill. London: SCM Press, 2002.

Lane, Anthony N.S. *John Calvin: Student of the Church Fathers.* Grand Rapids: Baker, 1999.

Lane, Anthony N.S. "Scripture, Tradition and Church: An Historical Survey." *Vox Evangelica* 9 (1975): 37–55.

Letham, Robert. *The Work of Christ.* Leicester: Inter-Varsity Press, 1993.

Letham, Robert. *The Holy Trinity: In Scripture, History, Theology, and Worship.* Phillipsburg, New Jersey: Presbyterian & Reformed, 2004.

Loder, James E. *The Knight's Move: The Relational Logic of the Spirit in Theology and Science.* Colorado Springs: Helmers & Howard, 1992.

Lossky, Vladimir. *The Mystical Theology of the Eastern Church.* London: James Clarke & Co. Ltd, 1957.

Louth, Andrew. *Maximus the Confessor.* London: Routledge, 1996.

Louth, Andrew. *John Damascene: Tradition and Originality in Byzantine Theology.* Oxford: Oxford University Press, 2002.

Louth, Andrew. "Biographical Sketch." In *Abba: The Tradition of Orthodoxy in the West: Festschrift for Bishop Kallistos (Ware) of Diokleia*, John Behr. Crestwood, New York: St. Vladimir's Seminary Press, 2003.

Lyman, R. *Christology and Cosmology: Models of Divine Activity in Origen, Eusebius and Athanasius.* Oxford: Claredon, 1993.

McGuckin, John A. *St. Gregory of Nazianzus: An Intellectual Biography.* Crestwood, New York: St Vladimir's Seminary Press, 2001.

McGuckin, John A. *St. Cyril of Alexandria and the Christological Controversy: Its History, Theology, and Texts.* Crestwood, New York: St. Vladimir's Seminary Press, 2004.

Maximus the Confessor. *On the Cosmic Mystery of Jesus Christ: Selected Writings from St. Maximus the Confessor.* Paul M. Blowers. Crestwood, New York: St. Vladimir's University Press, 2003.

Meredith, Anthony. *The Cappadocians.* Crestwood, New York: St. Vladimir's Seminary Press, 1995.

Meyendorff, John. *Byzantine Theology: Historical Trends and Doctrinal Themes.* New York: Fordham University Press, 1979.

Meyendorff, John. *Christ in Eastern Christian Thought.* Crestwood, New York: St. Vladimir's Seminary Press, 1975.

Meyendorff, John, ed., trans.. *Gregory Palamas: The Triads*. New York: Paulist Press.

Meyendorff, John. "Orthodox Christianity." *The Encyclopedia of Christianity*. Ed., E. Fallbusch, et. al. Trans., Geoffrey W. Bromiley. Grand Rapids: Eerdmans, 2003. 3:861–66.

Moltmann, Jürgen. "Theological Proposals Towards the Resolution of the Filioque Controversy." In *Spirit of God, Spirit of Christ: Ecumenical Reflections on the Filioque Controversy*, edited by Lukas Vischer. London: SPCK, 1981, 164–73.

Moltmann, Jürgen. *The Trinity and the Kingdom: The Doctrine of God*. London: SCM, 1991.

Mosser, Carl. "The Greatest Possible Blessing: Calvin and Deification." *SJT* 55 (2002): 36–57.

Mother Mary and Archimandrite Kallistos Ware, trans. *The Festal Menaion*, South Canaan, Pennsylvania: St. Tikhon's Seminary Press, 1998.

Mother Mary and Archimandrite Kallistos Ware, trans. *The Lenten Triodion*, South Canaan, Pennsylvania: St. Tikhon's Seminary Press, 2002.

Muller, Richard A. *Post-Reformation Reformed Dogmatics: The Rise and Development of Reformed Orthodoxy, ca. 1520 to ca. 1725: Volume 4: The Triunity of God*. Grand Rapids: Baker, 2003.

Murray, Mary Charles. "Art and the Early Church." *JTS* 28 (1977): 304–45.

Needham, Nick. "The Filioque Clause: East or West?" *SBET* 15 (1997): 142–62.

Neill, Stephen. *Christian Missions*. London: Penguin, 1964.

Nellas, Panayiotis. *Deification in Christ: Orthodox Perspectives on the Nature of the Human Person*. Norman Russell. Crestwood, New York: St Vladimir's Seminary Press, 1987.

Norris Jr., Richard A. *The Christological Controversy*. Philadelphia: Fortress Press, 1980.

Oberdorfer, Bernd. *Filioque: Geschichte und Theologie Eines Ökumenischen Problems*. Göttingen: Vandenhoeck & Ruprecht, 2001.

O'Carroll, Michael C.S.Sp. *Trinitas: a Theological Encyclopedia of the Holy Trinity*. Collegeville, Minnesota: The Liturgical Press, 1987.

Oden, Thomas C. *The Justification Reader*. Grand Rapids: Eerdmans, 2002.

Ouspensky, Leonid and Lossky, Vladimir. *The Meaning of Icons*. Trans., G.E.H. Palmer and E. Kadloubovsky. Crestwood, New York: St. Vladimir's Seminary Press, 1982.

Packer, J.I. *'Fundamentalism' and the Word of God: Some Evangelical Principles*. London: Inter-Varsity Fellowship, 1958.

Pannenberg, Wolfhart. *Systematic Theology*. Geoffrey W. Bromiley. Grand Rapids: Eerdmans, 1991.

Papadakis, Aristeides. *Crisis in Byzantium: The Filioque Controversy in the Patriarchate of Gregory II of Cyprus (1283-1289)*. Crestwood, New York: St. Vladimir's Seminary Press, 1997.

Parry, K. *The Blackwell Dictionary of Eastern Christianity*. R.R.K. Ware. Oxford: Blackwell, 2001.

Pelikan, Jaroslav. *The Christian Tradition 1: The Emergence of the Catholic Tradition (100–600)*. Chicago: University of Chicago Press, 1971.

Pelikan, Jaroslav. *The Christian Tradition 2: The Spirit of Eastern Christendom*. Chicago: University of Chicago Press, 1974.

Percival, Henry R. *The Seven Ecumenical Councils of the Undivided Church: Their Canons and Dogmatic Decrees*. A Select Library of Nicene and Post-Nicene Fathers of the Christian Church: Second Series. Edinburgh: T.&T. Clark, 1997 reprint.

Person, R.E. *The Mode of Decision Making at the Early Ecumenical Councils: An Inquiry Into the Function of Scripture and Tradition at the Councils of Nicea and Ephesus*. Basel: Friedrich Reinhardt Kommissionsverlag, 1978.

Petterson, Alvyn. *Athanasius*. London: Geoffrey Chapman, 1995.

The Philokalia. G.E.H. Palmer. London: Faber and Faber, 1983.

Photios. *On the Mystagogy of the Holy Spirit*.

Prestige, G.L. *Fathers and Heretics*. London: SPCK, 1940.

Prestige, G.L. *God in Patristic Thought*. London: SPCK, 1952.

Quasten, Johannes. *Volume III: The Golden Age of Greek Patristic Literature from the Council of Nicea to the Council of Chalcedon*. In *Patrology*. Westminster, Maryland: Christian Classics, Inc, 1992.

Ratzinger, Joseph Cardinal. *The Spirit of the Liturgy*. San Francisco: Ignatius Press, 2000.

Refoulé, F. "Julien d'Éclane: Théologien et Philosophe." *Recherches de Science Religieuse* 52 (1964): 42–84, 233–47.

Relton, Herbert M. *A Study in Christology: The Problem of the Relation of the Two Natures in the Person of Christ*. London: SPCK, 1917.

Reymond, Robert L. *A New Systematic Theology of the Christian Faith*. New York: Nelson, 1998.

Riddell, Peter G. *Islam in Context: Past, Present, and Future*. Grand Rapids: Baker, 2003.

Ritschl, Dietrich. "Historical Development and the Implications of the Filioque Controversy." In *Spirit of God, Spirit of Christ*, Lukas Vischer. London and Geneva, 1981.

Russell, Norman. *Cyril of Alexandria*. London: Routledge, 2000.

St. Cyril of Alexandria. *On the Unity of Christ*. John Anthony McGuckin. Crestwood, New York: St. Vladimir's Seminary Press, 1995.

St. Nikodimos of the Holy Mountain. *The Philokalia*. G.E.H. Palmer. London: Faber and Faber, 1983.

Samuel, V.C. "The Christology of Severus of Antioch." *Abba Salama* 4 (1973): 126–90.

Samuel, V.C. "Further Studies in the Christology of Severus of Antioch." *Ekklesiastikos Pharos* 58 (1976): 270–301.

Schaff, Philip. *Select Orations of Saint Gregory Nazianzen.* Vol. 7 of *A Select Library of the Nicene and Post-Nicene Fathers of the Christian Church: Second Series.* Edinburgh: T.&T. Clark, 1989.

Schaff, Philip. *The Creeds of Christendom.* Grand Rapids: Baker, 1966.

Schimmelpfennig, Bernhard. *The Papacy,* Trans., James Sievert. New York: Columbia University Press, 1992.

Schmemann, Alexander. *Introduction to Liturgical Theology.* Asheleigh E. Moorhouse. Leighton Buzzard: Faith Press, 1996.

Schmemann, Alexander. *For the Life of the World: Sacraments and Orthodoxy.* Crestwood, New York: St. Vladimir's Seminary Press, 1997.

Sellers, R.V. *The Council of Chalcedon: a Historical and Doctrinal Survey.* London: SPCK, 1953.

Service Book of the Holy Orthodox-Catholic Apostolic Church. Third ed. Isabel Florence Hapgood. Brooklyn, New York: Syrian Antiochene Orthodox Archdiocese of New York and all North America, 1956.

Staniloae, Dumitru. *The Experience of God: Orthodox Dogmatic Theology Vol 1: Revelation and Knowledge of the Triune God.* Iona Ionita. Brookline, Massachusetts: Holy Cross Orthodox Press, 1994.

Stead, Christopher. *Divine Substance.* Oxford: Clarendon, 1977.

Studer, Basil. *Trinity and Incarnation: The Faith of the Early Church.* Edited by Matthias Westerhoff. Andrew Louth. Collegeville, Minnesota: Liturgical Press, 1993.

Stylianopoulos, Theodore and Heim, S. Mark, eds. *Spirit of Truth: Ecumenical Perspectives on the Holy Spirit. Communion on Faith and Order, NCCCUSA October 24–25, 1985 - Brookline, Massachusetts.* Brookline, Massachusetts: Holy Cross Orthodox Press, 1986.

Stylianopoulos, Theodore. "The Biblical Background of the Article on the Holy Spirit in the Constantinopolitan Creed." In *Études Theologiques: Le Ile Concile Oecuménique Chambésy-Genève: Centre Orthodoxe Du Patriarcat Oecuménique,* 1982.

Stylianopoulos, Theodore, eds. *The New Testament: An Orthodox Perspective: Volume One: Scripture, Tradition, Hermeneutics.* Brookline, Massachusetts: Holy Cross Orthodox Press, 1997.

Thompson, J.A. *Deuteronomy: An Introduction and Commentary.* Leicester: Inter-Varsity Press, 1974.

Torrance, Iain R. *Christology After Chalcedon: Severus of Antioch and Sergius the Monophysite.* Norwich: Canterbury Press, 1988.

Torrance, T.F. *The Hermeneutics of John Calvin*. Edinburgh: Scottish Academic Press, 1988.

Torrance, T.F. "Intuitive and Abstractive Knowledge: From Duns Scotus to John Calvin." In *De Doctrina Ioannis Duns Scoti: Acta Congressus Scotistici Internationalis Oxonii et Edimburgi 11–17 Sept. 1966 Celebrati*. Romae: Curae Commissionis Scotisticae, 1968, 4:291–305.

Torrance, T.F. *The Christian Doctrine of God: One Being, Three Persons*. Edinburgh: T.&T. Clark, 1996.

Torrance, T.F. *Theological Dialogue between Orthodox and Reformed Churches*. Volume 2. Edinburgh: Scottish Academic Press, Ltd., 1993.

Torrance, T.F. *Trinitarian Perspectives: Toward Doctrinal Agreement*. Edinburgh: T.&T. Clark, 1994, 110-143.

Ullmann, Walter. *The Growth of Papal Government in the Middle Ages: a Study in the Ideological Relation of Clerical to Lay Power*. London: Methuen, 1970.

Vischer, Lukas, ed. *Spirit of God, Spirit of Christ: Ecumenical Reflections on the Filioque Controversy*. London: SPCK, 1981.

Wallace-Hadrill, D.S. *Christian Antioch: a Study of Early Christian Thought in the East*. Cambridge: Cambridge University Press, 1982.

Ware, Timothy. *The Orthodox Church*. London: Penguin Books, 1969.

Warfield, Benjamin Breckinridge. *The Inspiration and Authority of the Bible*. Philadelphia: Presbyterian and Reformed, 1970.

Weinandy, Thomas G. *The Theology of St. Cyril of Alexandria*. London: T.&T. Clark, 2003.

Wendebourg, Dorothea. "From the Cappadocian Fathers to Gregory Palamas: The Defeat of Trinitarian Theology." *StPatr* 17 (1982): 194–98.

Wesche, Kenneth Paul. *On the Person of Christ: The Christology of Emperor Justinian*. Crestwood, New York: St. Vladimir's Seminary Press, 1991.

Westminster Assembly. *The Confession of Faith, the Larger and Shorter Catechisms with the Scripture Proofs at large together with The Sum of Saving Knowledge*. Applecross, Ross-shire: The Publications Committee of the Free Presbyterian Church of Scotland, 1970.

Widdicombe, P. *The Fatherhood of God from Origen to Athanasius*. Oxford: Clarendon, 1994.

Williams, A.N. *The Ground of Union: Deification in Aquinas and Palamas*. New York: Oxford University Press, 1999.

Young, Frances. *From Nicea to Chalcedon: a Guide to the Literature and Its Background*. London: SCM, 1983.

Zabolotsky, N.A. "The Christology of Severus of Antioch." *Ekklesiastikos Pharos* 58 (1976): 357–86.

Zizioulas, John. *Eucharist, Bishop, Church: The Unity of the Church in the Divine Eucharist and the Bishop during the first three Centuries*. Brookline, Massachusetts: Holy Cross Orthodox Press, 2001 .

Christian Focus Publications

publishes books for all ages

Our mission statement –

STAYING FAITHFUL

In dependence upon God we seek to help make His infallible Word, the Bible, relevant. Our aim is to ensure that the Lord Jesus Christ is presented as the only hope to obtain forgiveness of sin, live a useful life and look forward to heaven with Him.

REACHING OUT

Christ's last command requires us to reach out to our world with His gospel. We seek to help fulfil that by publishing books that point people towards Jesus and help them develop a Christ-like maturity. We aim to equip all levels of readers for life, work, ministry and mission.

Books in our adult range are published in three imprints.

Christian Focus contains popular works including biographies, commentaries, basic doctrine and Christian living. Our children's books are also published in this imprint.

Mentor focuses on books written at a level suitable for Bible College and seminary students, pastors, and other serious readers. The imprint includes commentaries, doctrinal studies, examination of current issues and church history.

Christian Heritage contains classic writings from the past.

Christian Focus Publications, Ltd
Geanies House, Fearn,
Ross-shire, IV20 1TW, Scotland, United Kingdom
info@christianfocus.com

Our titles are available from quality bookstores and
www.christianfocus.com